STUDY GUIDE
FOR

MARKETING
SECOND EDITION

Joel R. Evans/Barry Berman
HOFSTRA UNIVERSITY / HOFSTRA UNIVERSITY

Prepared by

Barbara Jane Feinberg

Joel R. Evans and Barry Berman

Macmillan Publishing Company
NEW YORK

Collier Macmillan Publishers
LONDON

Macmillan Publishing Company
866 Third Avenue, New York, New York 10022

Collier Macmillan Canada, Inc.

printing number
2 3 4 5 6 7 8 9 10

ISBN   0-02-334680-9

Preface

This study guide accompanies *Marketing*, Second Edition by Joel R. Evans and Barry Berman. It is a comprehensive involvement and self-instruction guide. The format of the study guide parallels that of the text. It contains twenty-five chapters divided into eight parts.

Each chapter contains:

1. Objectives
2. Overview
3. Key terms and concepts
4. True/false questions
5. Completion questions
6. Matching definitions
7. Multiple-choice questions
8. Discussion questions
9. Exercises

Chapter 20, "Applications of Pricing Techniques," also contains ten pricing problems.

At the end of each part, there is a review quiz, which tests knowledge for all the chapters in the part. Definitions, sequences, and sentence questions are used. In total, there are about 2,000 questions and problems in this study guide.

There are a variety of learning aids for students in the study guide. The completion questions have answers listed alongside every question to make it easy to check one's knowledge. The other short-answer questions are answered at the end of each chapter. All of the questions (except exercises) have text page references for the answers at the end of each chapter. These references offer starting points for thought-provoking questions. Throughout the study guide, questions vary in length and difficulty. This helps students test the full extent of their knowledge without becoming discouraged.

J.R.E.
B.B.
B.J.F.

Contents

Part

One

An Introduction to Marketing

1

An Overview of Marketing

CHAPTER OBJECTIVES

1. To illustrate the dynamic, exciting, changing nature of marketing
2. To define marketing and delineate its importance, scope, and functions in modern society
3. To trace the evolution of marketing from a production to a sales to a marketing department to a marketing company orientation
4. To examine the marketing concept
5. To present and contrast successful and unsuccessful approaches to marketing

CHAPTER OVERVIEW

Marketing is an exciting and dynamic contemporary field that involves a wide variety of activities. The classical definition of marketing emphasizes the flow of goods and services from producer to consumer to user. In modern terms, marketing is defined as the anticipation, management, and satisfaction of demand through the exchange process.

The evolution of marketing can be traced to people's earliest use of the exchange process. Marketing has really developed since the Industrial Revolution, as mass production and improved transportation enabled more transactions to occur. For companies such as Pillsbury, marketing has evolved through four eras: production, sales, marketing department, and marketing company. The marketing concept requires a company to be consumer-oriented, have an integrated marketing program, and be goal-oriented.

When contrasting a marketing approach with a sales approach, marketing is found to be more involved with profit planning, analysis of trends, opportunities, and threats, assessments of customer types and differences, and coordinated decision making.

The field of marketing is important for several reasons: stimulation and regulation of demand, marketing costs, the number of people employed in marketing, its support of entire industries such as advertising agencies and marketing research firms, the recognition that all

3

people are consumers in some situations, the necessity of the efficient use of scarce resources, its impact on people's beliefs and life-styles, and its input into the quality of life. The scope of marketing is quite broad and diversified.

The major classifications of marketing functions are environmental analysis and marketing research, consumer analysis, product (service) planning, distribution planning, promotion planning, price planning, social responsibility, and marketing management. The responsibility for performing these functions can be shifted and shared in several ways among manufacturers and service providers, wholesalers, retailers, marketing specialists, and consumers. One party usually does not perform all the functions. This is due to costs, assortment requirements, specialized abilities, company size, established methods of distribution, and consumer interests.

The IBM PC has done so well because IBM has done an outstanding marketing job. The Texas Instruments 99/4A computer had to be removed from the market as a result of poor marketing performance.

KEY TERMS AND CONCEPTS

Marketing	The anticipation, management, and satisfaction of demand through the exchange process.
Consumer demand	Refers to the characteristics and needs of employees, unions, stockholders, consumer groups, the general public, government agencies, and other internal and external forces that affect company operations.
Publics' demand	Refers to the characteristics and needs of employees, unions, stockholders, consumer groups, the general public, government agencies, and other internal and external forces that affect company operations.
Exchange	The process by which consumers and publics give money, a promise to pay, or support for the offering of a firm, institution, person, place, or idea.
Production era	Devotion to the physical distribution of goods and services due to high demand and low competition. Consumer research, product modifications, and adapting to consumer needs are unnecessary.
Sales era	Involves hiring a sales force and conducting advertising to sell merchandise, after production is maximized. The goal is to fit consumer desires to the attributes of the products being manufactured.
Marketing department era	Stage during which the marketing department participates in company decisions but remains in a subordinate or conflicting position to the production, engineering, and sales departments.

Marketing company era	Recognition of the central role of marketing. The marketing department becomes the equal of others in the company. Company efforts are integrated and frequently re-evaluated.
Marketing concept	A consumer-oriented, integrated, goal-oriented philosophy for a firm, institution, or person.
Marketing functions	Include environmental analysis and marketing research, consumer analysis, product (service) planning, price planning, social responsibility, and marketing management.
Marketing performers	Include manufacturers and service providers, wholesalers, retailers, marketing specialists, and organizational and final consumers.

TRUE/FALSE

Circle the appropriate letter.

T   F   1. Classical definitions of marketing are broader than modern ones.

T   F   2. Classical definitions of marketing undervalue the role of physical distribution and marketing channels.

T   F   3. Nonprofit as well as profit-making institutions are involved in marketing.

T   F   4. Central to a modern definition of marketing is a consumer orientation.

T   F   5. Anticipation of demand requires a firm to arouse consumers to want a firm's offering through attractive product design and intensive promotion.

T   F   6. According to critics, a broad definition of marketing may lead to inefficiency.

T   F   7. The modern concept of marketing arose during the Industrial Revolution.

T   F   8. During the production era of marketing, the goal was to increase supply to keep up with demand.

T   F   9. During the sales era of marketing, consumer tastes were determined before a product was manufactured.

T   F   10. During the marketing company era of marketing, the marketing department participated in company decisions but remained subordinate to the production, engineering, and sales departments.

T   F   11. The marketing concept is a product-oriented, sales-pitched, profit-centered philosophy.

T   F   12. From a marketing viewpoint, customer dissatisfaction leads to a stronger or different sales pitch, not to changes in policy.

T **F** 13. The existence of a large marketing department and elaborate marketing plans ensures that an organization is properly applying the marketing concept.

T **F** 14. The elimination of marketing activities would lower prices.

T **F** 15. Between one fourth and one third of the civilian labor force is engaged in marketing activities.

T **F** 16. Marketing has a strong impact on people's beliefs and life-styles.

T **F** 17. The basic marketing functions must be performed by one party or another; they cannot be eliminated in most situations.

T **F** 18. Usually one party is able to perform all necessary marketing functions by itself.

T **F** 19. High-volume sales almost always necessitate intensive, shared distribution.

T **F** 20. Texas Instruments' price-cutting and mass production strategies were examples of successful marketing.

COMPLETION

Fill in the missing word or words in the blanks provided.

[distribution, channels, nonprofit, government, exchange, p. 9]

1. Classical definitions of marketing overvalue the role of physical _____ and marketing _____ , while they frequently omit _____ institutions and _____ . They overlook the importance of _____ between buyers and sellers.

[demand, regulate, supply, p. 10]

2. Marketing is not just concerned with enlarging _____ ; it also attempts to _____ demand to match _____ .

[consumer orientation, anticipation, stimulation, facilitation, regulation, satisfaction, p. 10]

3. Central to any modern definition of marketing must be a _____ _____ , and it should cover the _____ , _____ , _____ , _____ , and _____ of demand.

[Consumer demand, publics' demand, pp. 11-12]

4. _____ _____ refers to the characteristics and needs of channel members, government institutions, and international markets, for example, whereas _____ _____ refers to the characteristics and needs of unions, government agencies, and stockholders, for example.

[exchange, p. 12]

5. The marketing process is not complete until consumers _____ their money for the offering they have selected.

[barter, Industrial Revolution, p. 12]

6. The origins of marketing can be traced to _____ , trading one resource for another, but the modern concept of marketing arose during the _____ _____ .

[production, sales, p. 13]   7. During the _____ era of marketing, the goal was to increase supply to keep up with demand, and during the _____ era of marketing, business manufactured and sold goods without first determining consumer needs.

[marketing department, marketing company, p. 13]   8. In the _____ _____ era of marketing, production, engineering, or sales was dominant, whereas in the _____ _____ era of the past twenty years, the central role of marketing has been recognized.

[marketing concept, products, services, p. 13]   9. The _____ _____ is a consumer-oriented, integrated, goal-oriented philosophy for a firm, institution, or person that does not view _____ or _____ as ends in themselves.

[integrated marketing focus, p. 16]   10. Under an _____ _____ _____ , all activities related to products and services are coordinated.

[marketing, selling, pp. 16-17]   11. Whereas a _____ philosophy views customer needs broadly, a_____ philosophy regards them narrowly.

[industries, p. 18]   12. Marketing activities support entire _____ , such as advertising and marketing research.

[life-styles, beliefs, p. 19]   13. Marketing has a large impact on people's _____ and _____ and has been criticized as developing materialistic attitudes.

[analysis, marketing, consumer, product, planning, responsibility, management, pp. 19-20]   14. The basic marketing functions are environmental _____ and _____ research; _____ analysis; _____ (service) planning; distribution, promotion, and price _____ ; social _____ ; and marketing _____ .

[IBM, Texas Instruments, pp. 22-26]   15. Two different approaches to marketing were taken by _____ which had been thoroughly involved with marketing planning and adaptation and _____ _____ which made a number of marketing errors.

DEFINITIONS

Match the terms and concepts with the appropriate definitions. Each term or concept may only be used once; there are more terms and concepts than definitions.

Column A

a. consumer demand

b. exchange

c. marketing

d. marketing company era

e. marketing concept

Column B

___ 1. Refers to the characteristics and needs of employees, unions, stockholders, consumer groups, the general public, government agencies, and other internal and external forces that affect company operations.

___ 2. A consumer-oriented, integrated, goal-oriented philosophy for a firm, institution, or person.

f. marketing department era

g. marketing functions

h. marketing performers

i. production era

j. publics' demand

k. sales era

_____ 3. Devotion to the physical distribution of goods and services due to high demand and low competition.

_____ 4. Recognition of the central role of marketing. The marketing department becomes the equal of others in the company.

_____ 5. Involves hiring a sales force and conducting advertising to sell merchandise, after production is maximized.

_____ 6. Refers to the characteristics and needs of final consumers, industrial consumers, channel members, government institutions, international markets, and nonprofit institutions.

_____ 7. Stage during which the marketing department participates in company decisions but remains in a subordinate or conflicting position to the production, engineering, and sales departments.

_____ 8. The process by which consumers and publics give money, a promise to pay, or support for the offering of a firm, institution, person, place, or idea.

_____ 9. Include manufacturers and service providers, wholesalers, retailers, marketing specialists, and organizational and final consumers.

_____ 10. The anticipation, management, and satisfaction of demand through the exchange process.

MULTIPLE CHOICE

Place the letter of the answer you think best in the blank provided.

_____ 1. Radio Shack has recently benefited from
 a. new distribution methods.
 b. product strategy.
 c. environmental analysis.
 d. an integrated marketing-management structure.

_____ 2. MCI Communications competes in the long-distance telephone service industry by
 a. constant advertising.
 b. aggressive pricing.
 c. marketing research.
 d. abandoning markets.

_____ 3. Which of the following is most likely to be covered by a classical definition of marketing?
 a. Ideas
 b. People
 c. Services
 d. Places

_____ 4. Among the weaknesses of the classical definitions of marketing is
   a. overvaluing the role of marketing in pricing and promotion.
   b. stressing the role of government in marketing.
   c. overlooking the importance of exchange between buyers and sellers.
   d. neglecting physical distribution and marketing channels.

_____ 5. Central to any definition of marketing must be
   a. enlarging demand.
   b. consumer orientation.
   c. goods and services.
   d. distribution.

_____ 6. Anticipation of demand requires a firm to
   a. arouse consumers to want the firm's offering.
   b. make it easy to buy the firm's offering.
   c. do consumer research to provide attractive offerings.
   d. provide offerings with options and after-sales service.

_____ 7. Demarketing involves
   a. reducing overall demand.
   b. stimulating demand.
   c. facilitating overall demand.
   d. satisfying overall demand.

_____ 8. Publics' demand refers to the characteristics and needs of
   a. international markets.
   b. industrial consumers.
   c. nonprofit institutions.
   d. stockholders.

9. The modern concept of marketing began
   a. with the rise of the barter system.
   b. twenty years ago.
   (c.) during the Industrial Revolution.
   d. when currency was devised.

_____ 10. During the production era of marketing,
   a. business manufactured and sold products without first determining consumer desires.
   b. research became necessary to determine consumer desires and needs.
   c. consumer research and analysis were integrated into all company efforts.
   d. businesses increased supply to keep up with demand.

_____ 11. The role of advertising and the sales force was to make the desires of consumers fit the attributes of the products being manufactured during the
   a. production era of marketing.
   b. sales era of marketing.
   c. marketing department era of marketing.
   d. marketing company era of marketing.

_____ 12. Which of the following is not stressed in the marketing concept?
   a. Customer orientation
   b. Distribution
   c. Integrated focus
   d. Goal orientation

_____ 13. A customer orientation does *not* usually focus on
   a. market needs.
   b. planning.
   c. production capability.
   d. goals.

_____ 14. In comparison with a marketing orientation, a selling orientation emphasizes
   a. consumer satisfaction.
   b. a narrow view of customer needs.
   c. sales as a way of understanding customers.
   d. the long-run view.

_____ 15. Which of the following corporations has failed to understand and practice sophisticated marketing?
   a. Texas Instruments
   b. McDonald's
   c. Eastman Kodak
   d. Xerox

_____ 16. Which of the following statements about the importance and scope of marketing is *false*?
   a. Some estimates place the costs of marketing at about 50 per cent or more of sales.
   b. Between one half to three fourths of the civilian labor force is engaged in marketing activities.
   c. Marketing activities support entire industries.
   d. Marketing has a large impact on people's beliefs and life-styles.

_____ 17. Basic marketing functions
   a. can be eliminated in most situations.
   b. are usually performed by one party.
   c. can only be organized in a limited number of ways.
   d. can be shifted and shared.

_____ 18. Direct marketing would require a company to
   a. make or sell complementary products.
   b. seek a marketing specialist.
   c. share distribution of high-volume sales items.
   d. eliminate many marketing functions.

_____ 19. Packaged bakery products, beer, and soda
   a. are sold directly to widely dispersed consumers.
   b. are usually bought in bulk by individual consumers.
   c. are usually sold through established distribution methods.
   d. do not require the services of advertising agencies to increase sales.

_____ 20. In comparison with IBM, Texas Instruments
   a. exercised limited control over product distribution.
   b. correctly analyzed the environment and consumer needs.
   c. refused to let itself be drawn into a price war.
   d. withdrew from the market in a socially responsible way.

DISCUSSION QUESTIONS

1. Comment on this statement: "Some aspect of marketing influences every part of our daily lives, yet the role of marketing changes in each new situation."

2. What are some of the criticisms of a broadened definition of marketing and how valid do you think they are?

3. How did the expansion of supply affect the evolution of marketing?

4. How would the elimination of marketing affect the American economy?

5. In what ways is a knowledge of marketing useful to doctors, college presidents, and local fire departments?

6. Describe some of the ways in which responsibility for marketing functions can be shifted and shared.

7. What marketing lessons can be learned from Texas Instruments' failure with its 99/4A home computer?

EXERCISES

1-1.   The Buick division of General Motors has developed a new-vehicle inspection/ delivery checklist for car buyers to review and sign prior to accepting their new Buick. The salesperson must also review and sign this document.

      Among the tasks of the salesperson prior to the final sale are verifying whether the predelivery inspection procedure has been performed, inspecting the vehicle, and completing the warranty folder.

      Together, the salesperson and customer must go over the owner's manual (including such information as how to start and operate the automobile, emergency procedures, service and maintenance, and auto specifications), and the optional extended-warranty plan. In addition, the customer is to be given a tour of the dealer's facilities (service department, parts department, and body shop), have dealer policies explained (with respect to days and hours open, acceptance of credit cards), and taken on an orientation ride. Customers are also assured of being able to examine their new car prior to accepting delivery.

      According to Buick advertising, "...this checklist is just one of the many checkpoints your Buick passes through on its way from us to you. It's part of an entire program dedicated to keeping you, a Buick customer, a satisfied Buick owner."

Questions

1.   Why would Buick develop its new-vehicle inspection/delivery procedure checklist?

2.   How is the checklist consistent with a broadened definition of marketing?

3.   Does the use of the checklist mean that Buick dealers are following the marketing concept? Explain your answer.

4.   Is Buick following a marketing or selling philosophy? Why?

Student's Name ________________ **Class/Section** __________ **Instructor** ________________

1-2. Figure 1 contains a short, eight-item questionnaire designed to measure whether a firm has adopted the marketing concept. Five concepts are covered: consumer need evaluation, integrated marketing effort, consumer satisfaction, feedback/adaptation, and achievement of organizational goals.

Figure 1
Marketing Questionnaire

Would you please take a few minutes to answer these questions regarding your organization's marketing practices.

1. Are key decisions affecting overall strategy made on the basis of marketing research?
2. Are trends such as sales, market share, population characteristics, and competitive dynamics tracked? If yes, how?
2. Is a marketing executive involved in a decision-making capacity in decision areas such as new-product evaluation, required inventory levels, pricing, and entry into new geographic markets?
4. Is consumer satisfaction studied? If yes, how?
5. How are customer complaints handled?
6. Is marketing strategy reviewed and revised on a regular basis? If yes, how?
7. Is marketing planning conducted on an integrated (as opposed to an informal) basis? Please explain.
8. What are the two most important objectives of your organization? How well are they being achieved?

Questions

1. Add two of your own questions to this questionnaire in order to better measure an organization's use of the marketing concept. Explain your choices.

2.   Interview two marketing executives using the questionnaire in this exercise, one from a small company (less than $20 million in annual sales) and one from a larger firm. What aspects of the marketing concept are these firms following? Not following? Explain your answer.

3.   Should the responses of a smaller firm be different from a larger firm? Why or why not?

4.   Assess the strengths and weaknesses of the two firms you examine.

1-3.   What marketing functions are performed by professionals (such as attorneys and CPAs) and nonprofit organizations (such as hospitals and libraries)? Contrast a production orientation with a marketing orientation for professionals and nonprofit organizations.

1-4.   Examine a successful retailer near your college with which most students are familiar. What marketing practices have made this retailer a success? Compare these practices to those of a less successful retailer.

ANSWERS

True/False

1. F, p. 9
2. F, p. 9
3. T, pp. 10-11
4. T, p. 10
5. F, p. 11
6. T, p. 12
7. T, p. 12
8. T, p. 13
9. F, p. 13
10. F, p. 13

11. F, p. 13
12. F, p. 16
13. F, p. 17
14. F, p. 18
15. T, p. 18
16. T. p. 19
17. T, p. 21
18. F, p. 21
19. T, p. 22
20. F, pp. 25-26

Multiple Choice

1. c, p. 5
2. b, pp. 7-8
3. c, p. 9
4. c, p. 9
5. b, p. 10
6. c, p. 11
7. a, p. 11
8. d, p. 12
9. c, p. 12
10. d. p. 13

11. b, p. 13
12. b, p. 13
13. c, p. 16
14. b, pp. 16-17
15. a, p. 17
16. b, pp. 17-19
17. d, p. 21
18. a, p. 22
19. c, p. 22
20. a, pp. 25-26

Definitions

1. j
2. e
3. i
4. d
5. k

6. a
7. f
8. b
9. h
10. c

Discussion Questions

1. pp. 7-8
2. p. 12
3. pp. 12-13
4. pp. 10-13, 17-19
5. pp. 16-17
6. pp. 19-22
7. pp. 22-26

2

The Environment of Marketing

CHAPTER OBJECTIVES

1. To examine the environment of marketing and show why it is necessary for marketers to understand the total environment in which they operate
2. To view the environment in a systematic and integrated manner
3. To enumerate the controllable elements of a marketing plan and to differentiate between those elements controlled by top management and those controlled by marketers
4. To enumerate the uncontrollable elements that affect a marketing plan and how marketers may respond to them
5. To explain why feedback and adaptation to change are essential for marketers

CHAPTER OVERVIEW

The environment of marketing encompasses all of the controllable factors that are utilized by a firm and its marketers to achieve established objectives as well as the uncontrollable factors that influence the ability of a firm and its marketers to achieve these objectives.

Controllable variables are the elements of a strategy that are determined by the firm and its marketers. Top management decides on the line of business, overall objectives, the role of marketing, and the role of other business functions. Marketing directs the selection of a target market, the marketing mix (product or service, distribution, promotion, and price), and the control function. In addition, it is the responsibility of marketing to create a differential advantage, the set of unique factors in a company's marketing program that causes consumers to patronize the company and not its competitors.

Uncontrollable variables are the elements affecting an overall strategy that cannot be directed by the firm and its marketers. Among the most important uncontrollable variables are consumers, competition, government, the economy, technology, and the independent media.

An organization's level of success or failure is based on the interaction of controllable and uncontrollable factors. When implementing a marketing strategy, a marketer obtains feedback from the environment and adjusts the strategy to correct any deficiencies. Marketing myopia must be avoided.

KEY TERMS AND CONCEPTS

Marketing environment	Consists of controllable and uncontrollable factors, the organization's level of success or failure in reaching objectives, feedback, and adaptation.
Controllable factors	Decision elements that are directed by the organization and its marketers. Some of these are under the direction of top management; others by marketers.
Target market	The defined customer group to which a firm appeals.
Marketing objectives	More customer-oriented than the overall goals set by top management.
Differential advantage	The set of unique features in a company's marketing program that causes consumers to patronize the company and not its competitors.
Marketing organization	The structural arrangement for directing marketing functions. The organization outlines authority, responsibility, and the tasks to be performed.
Marketing mix	Describes the specific combination of marketing elements used to achieve objectives and satisfy the target market. The marketing mix consists of four major factors: product or service, distribution, promotion, and price.
Control	The monitoring and reviewing of overall and specific performance.
Uncontrollable factors	Those elements affecting an organization's performance that cannot be directed by the organization and its marketers. These include consumers, competition, government, the economy, technology, and independent media.
Monopoly	A situation in which only one firm sells a particular product or service.
Oligopoly	A situation in which there are few firms, generally large, that comprise most of an industry's sales.
Monopolistic competition	A situation in which there are several competing firms, each trying to offer a unique marketing mix.
Pure competition	A situation with many firms selling identical products or services.
Federal Trade Commission (FTC)	The major federal agency that monitors restraint of trade and enforces rules against unfair methods of competition.
Gross National Product (GNP)	The total value of goods and services produced in a country each year.

Real income	Income adjusted for inflation.
Technology	Refers to the development and use of machinery, products, and processes.
Independent media	Those not controlled by the firm; they can influence the government's, consumers', and public's perceptions of a company's products and overall image.
Feedback	Information about the uncontrollable environment, the organization's performance, and how well the marketing plan is received.
Adaptation	Responses to the surrounding environment, including both opportunities and threats.
Marketing myopia	A short-sighted, narrow-minded view of marketing and its environment.

TRUE/FALSE

Circle the appropriate letter.

T   F   1. In business organizations, marketing plans should be stated first and then broad policy should be formulated to adjust to the plans.

T   F   2. The importance of marketing to a firm is evident when marketing is given staff status within the company.

T   F   3. The larger the role of marketing, the greater the likelihood of a firm having an integrated marketing organization.

T   F   4. An example of an uncontrollable factor that a firm must consider is the selection of a target market.

T   F   5. Marketing objectives are more customer-oriented than objectives set by top management.

T   F   6. An organization is considered functional if there are product managers for each product category and brand managers for each individual brand.

T   F   7. Distribution decisions involve determining what to sell, the level of quality, and the number of items to be sold.

T   F   8. A well-conceived marketing plan makes continuous monitoring of the external environment unnecessary.

T   F   9. When a firm has an exclusive patent on a particular product or service or is allowed to become a public utility, it usually acts as a monopolist.

T   F   10. Private-sector monopolists are able to control their marketing plans totally.

T   F   11. In an oligopolistic market, the demand for one firm's offering will drop sharply if its prices are increased; demand will only increase slightly if prices are decreased.

T   F   12. In an oligopoly firms tend to offer widely different prices for similar products.

T   F   13. In monopolistic competition it is difficult for new firms to enter the market.

T   F   14. In pure competition, no differential advantage is possible because the prices and the products are the same.

T   F   15. When a firm defines its competition in generic terms, it defines competition as narrowly as possible.

T   F   16. Since the 1960s legislation has been geared toward protecting small businesses from large businesses.

T   F   17. State and local laws regulate where a firm may locate, the hours it may be open, and if unit pricing is required.

T   F   18. Marketers have found that low unemployment leads to increased sales of large ticket items.

T   F   19. Marketers should note that the activities of independent media are uncontrollable.

T   F   20. Feedback helps firms avoid marketing myopia.

COMPLETION

Fill in the missing word or words in the blanks provided.

[top management, marketers, p. 34]

1. Some controllable factors are directed by _____ _____ ; these become uncontrollable by _____ , who must develop plans to satisfy organizational goals within established broad policy guidelines.

[line of business, overall objectives, role of marketing, business functions, p. 34]

2. Four basic decisions of extreme importance to marketers are _____ _____ _____ , referring to general product or service category and geographical coverage, for example; _____ _____ , measurable goals set by top management; the _____ _____ _____ , for example in research, advertising and promotion; and the role of other _____ _____ , delineating relationships to avoid overlaps, jealousy, and conflicts.

[target market, marketing objectives, marketing organization, marketing plan, mix, control, p. 36]

3. Factors controllable by marketing include the selection of a _____ _____ , defined customer group; _____ _____ , customer-oriented goals; a _____ _____ , the structural arrangement for directing marketing functions; the _____ _____ or _____ , which describes the specific combination of marketing elements; and _____ , monitoring and reviewing overall and specific performance.

[differential advantage, p. 37]

4. Marketers seek to create a _____ _____ , a set of unique features that attract consumers and cause them to patronize a company rather than its competitors.

[functional, product oriented, market oriented, pp. 37-38]

5. A marketing organization can be described as _____ , with responsibility assigned on the basis of buying and selling, promotion, and distribution; as _____ _____ , with managers for each category or brand; or as _____ _____ , with managers assigned on the basis of geographical markets or customer types.

[product, service, distribution, promotion, price, p. 37]

6. Four elements in the marketing mix or plan are _____ or _____ , _____ , _____ . and _____ .

[Uncontrollable factors, p. 39]

7. _____ _____ are those elements affecting an organization's performance that cannot be directed by the organization or its marketers.

[consumer, p. 42]

8. Recently _____ groups and organizations have spoken out at public hearings and stockholders' meetings to require marketers to communicate with them to avoid negative consequences.

[monopoly, oligopoly, p. 43]

9. In a _____ there is only one firm selling a particular product or service, whereas in an _____ there are a few firms, generally large, that comprise most of an industry's sales.

[elasticity of demand, inelastic, p. 44]

10. Consumer sensitivity to price changes is called _____ _____ _____ , and for public utilities, where people will tend to use the service no matter how high prices go, demand is usually relatively _____ .

[Monopolistic competition, pure competition, p. 44]

11. _____ _____ occurs when there are several firms, each of which is trying to offer a unique marketing mix; in _____ _____ many firms sell identical products or services.

[federal legislation, deregulation, p. 45]

12. In the 1960s and 1970s, _____ _____ was oriented toward protecting small businesses from large businesses, but today it is geared more toward _____ .

[inflation, real income, unemployment, pp. 48-49]

13. Economic factors of importance to marketers include the rate of _____ that occurs when widespread cost increases drive prices up, _____ _____ which is adjusted for inflation, and the rate of _____ that will affect the sales of large-ticket items.

[Patents, p. 49]

14. _____ are the exclusive rights to sell new products or services for seventeen years.

[marketing myopia, feedback, adapt, p. 50]

15. To improve the marketing plan and ensure long-run attainment of objectives, as well as to avoid _____ _____ (a short-sighted, narrow-minded view of marketing and its environment), the organization needs to acquire _____ and to _____ its marketing plans to environmental changes.

DEFINITIONS

Match the terms and concepts with the appropriate definitions. Each term or concept may only be used once; there are more terms and concepts than definitions.

Column A

a. adaptation

b. control

c. controllable factors

d. differential advantage

e. Federal Trade Commission

f. feedback

g. Gross National Product

h. independent media

i. marketing environment

j. marketing mix

k. marketing myopia

l. marketing objectives

m. marketing organization

n. monopolistic competition

o. monopoly

p. oligopoly

q. pure competition

r. real income

s. target market

t. technology

u. uncontrollable factors

Column B

_____ 1. The structural arrangement for directing marketing functions outlining authority, responsibility, and the tasks to be performed.

_____ 2. The defined customer group to which a firm appeals.

_____ 3. The monitoring and reviewing of overall and specific performance.

_____ 4. Describes the specific combination of marketing elements used to achieve objectives and satisfy the target market, consisting of product or service, distribution, promotion, and price.

_____ 5. A situation with many firms selling identical products or services.

_____ 6. Information about the uncontrollable environment, the organization's performance, and how well a marketing plan is received.

_____ 7. Income adjusted for inflation.

_____ 8. A situation in which only one firm sells a particular product or service.

_____ 9. A situation in which there are several competing firms, each trying to offer a unique marketing mix.

_____ 10. A set of unique features in a company's marketing program that causes consumers to patronize the company and not its competitors.

_____ 11. Refers to the development and use of machinery, products, and processes.

_____ 12. A short-sighted, narrow-minded view of marketing and its environment.

_____ 13. A situation in which there are few firms, generally large, that comprise most of an industry's sales.

_____ 14. The total value of goods and services produced in a country each year.

_____ 15. Responses to the surrounding environment, including both opportunities and threats.

MULTIPLE CHOICE

Place the letter of the answer you think best in the blank provided.

_____ 1. Which of the following is *not* a factor primarily controlled by top management?
   a. Line of business
   b. Marketing mix
   c. Role of marketing
   d. Overall objectives

_____ 2. When it is considered important by a firm, marketing is
   a. equated with sales.
   b. given staff status.
   c. the recipient of line authority.
   d. controlled by a production vice-president.

_a_ 3. Even when marketing functions are limited or restricted, they still include
   a. selling.
   b. research.
   c. planning.
   d. pricing.

_d_ 4. In selecting a target market, marketers usually
   a. create a differential advantage.
   b. determine the marketing mix.
   c. control the marketing plan.
   d. engage in market segmentation or mass marketing.

_b_ 5. Which of the following is *not* a form of marketing organization?
   a. Functional
   b. Coordinated
   c. Product-oriented
   d. Market-oriented

_____ 6. Product, price, promotion, and distribution are components of the
   a. target market.
   b. marketing organization.
   c. marketing mix.
   d. marketing objectives.

_____ 7. Level of quality, type of packaging, and features are examples of decisions marketers must make about
   a. promotion.
   b. product.
   c. distribution.
   d. price.

_____ 8. Distribution decisions typically involve questions about
   a. channel members.
   b. publicity.
   c. billing terms.
   d. company innovativeness.

9. The most effective approach to the uncontrollable factors in the marketing environment is
   a. continuous monitoring of their effects.
   b. the practice of marketing myopia.
   c. insulating the marketing plan from them.
   d. constantly reorganizing the marketing organization.

10. Firms can control
    a. population characteristics.
    b. cultural and social influences on buyers.
    c. the consumer decision process.
    d. selection of the target market.

11. In a monopoly, the firm
    a. seeks to avoid price wars.
    b. has total control of the marketing plan.
    c. has no control over price because merchandise is standardized.
    d. finds that consumer elasticity of demand is kinked.

12. Where a few large firms comprise most of an industry's sales, the competitive structure is *best* described as
    a. pure competition.
    b. monopolistic competition.
    c. oligopoly.
    d. monopoly.

13. In monopolistic competition,
    a. there is only one firm selling a particular product or service.
    b. a few firms comprise most of the industry's sales.
    c. there are several firms individually trying to offer a unique marketing mix.
    d. many firms sell identical products or services.

14. Demand is perfectly elastic in
    a. pure competition.
    b. monopolistic competition.
    c. oligopoly.
    d. monopoly.

15. A differential advantage is *not* possible in
    a. pure competition.
    b. monopolistic competition.
    c. oligopoly.
    d. monopoly.

16. When a firm defines its competition in generic terms, it
    a. examines its existing channel relationships.
    b. analyzes the competitive structure within a specific industry.
    c. focuses on patent expiration dates.
    d. looks at competition as broadly as possible.

17. Which of the following was a main concern of federal legislation during the early part of the twentieth century?
    a. Helping the consumer deal with deceptive and unsafe practices
    b. Protecting small businesses from large businesses
    c. Regulating business hours
    d. Determining where businesses could be located

18. Real income is income adjusted for the
    a. relative value of other currencies.
    b. growth of the Gross National Product.
    c. level of unemployment.
    d. rate of inflation.

19. Which of the following statements about technology is true?
    a. Major technological advances are often beyond the reach of small firms.
    b. Patents provide exclusive rights to sell new products or services for virtually unlimited time periods.
    c. Technology cannot eliminate the impact of resource shortages.
    d. Loss of patent protection decreases competition.

20. To attain its objectives, a firm is well advised to
    a. maintain its existing strategies at all costs.
    b. acquire feedback from the environment.
    c. ignore uncontrollable factors.
    d. bypass the independent media entirely.

DISCUSSION QUESTIONS

1. How can you determine when the role of marketing is considered important to a firm? Unimportant?

2. Compare and contrast marketing objectives and a firm's overall objectives.

3. "While a marketer has control of a target market, he or she cannot control the characteristics of the population." Discuss.

4. Why is a differential advantage attainable in oligopoly and in monopolistic competition situations and not in pure competition situations?

5. What types of legislation has the federal government enacted to control and limit business? How does this regulation differ from state laws?

6. How might feedback overcome marketing myopia?

7. Compare the adaptation approaches of General Foods and Greyhound. Can you think of other firms that have taken similar steps?

EXERCISES

2-1.   Jim Jenkins, the founder and owner of a four-branch tire store chain—Tires for You—located in a Boston suburb, is perplexed. His daughter Julie, after completing an Introduction to Marketing course, believes her father's business is not employing a good marketing plan or reacting well to its marketing environment.

Several things about Tires for You concern Julie:

- Her father supervises all the stores himself, driving an average of one and a half hours each day. There are no long-run plans or goals.
- The stores have a poor atmosphere. They are situated in highway strip locations on former service station/garage sites. The waiting rooms are small, with limited seating space. The tire-changing areas are dingy and cluttered with worn tires. Julie feels that the stores are unappealing to females.
- The chain is very passive. There is no active mailing list of past customers; therefore, it cannot conduct special promotions aimed at satisfied customers or remind customers to inspect their tires for tread wear. The firm also does not know where its customers come from. Julie believes it is essential to have customer information.
- Competition from gasoline service stations (which cater to the full-service needs of their customers) and department store service stations (which are open long hours and draw their own credit customers) is growing.
- Sales are greatly affected by the economy, since Tires for You sells only tires.
- The technology of manufacturer-installed tires is improving, causing motorists to wait longer before repurchasing tires.

In reply, Jim points to these Tires for You advantages: twenty years of business, a loyal clientele, low-rent locations, a large tire assortment, very low prices, easy credit for customers, contacts with area used-car dealerships, and knowledgeable employees.

Questions

1.   Are Julie's concerns valid? Why or why not?

2.   Compare the differential advantage(s) of Tires for You with those for a neighbor-
     hood gasoline service station and a department store service station.

3.   Is Jim Jenkins practicing marketing myopia? Explain your answer.

4.   Offer at least five specific marketing recommendations for Tires for You to follow
     over the next two years.

2-2.   Table 2-2 in the text outlines three forms of key federal legislation affecting marketers. The first relates to antitrust, discriminatory pricing, and unfair trade practices; the second relates to consumer protection; and the third to industry deregulation.

The antitrust, discriminatory pricing, and unfair trade practice laws prohibit such practices as tie-in sales (a wholesaler/retailer being required to buy one product to obtain another), price discrimination to competing channel members acquiring the same merchandise, mergers and acquisitions if they would lessen competition, and price fixing. Consumer protection legislation relates to labeling and disclosure requirements, the setting of safety and inspection standards, specifying recall procedures, fair-credit practices, and consumer goods pricing. Industry deregulation laws seek to increase competition on both a price and a service basis by making it easier for new firms to enter business, for existing firms to enter new geographic markets, and for firms to have control over their marketing strategies.

Questions

1.   Find a major recent case relating to either tie-in sales, price discrimination, or price fixing. Describe the circumstances surrounding the case and the legal outcome.

2.   The Consumer Product Safety Act created the Consumer Product Safety Commission and set safety standards. Briefly describe the conditions of this act.

3.   Deregulation can have both positive and negative influences on consumers. Outline these influences using the airline industry as an example.

4.   "In a regulated environment marketers must focus on legislation; in a deregulated environment they must carefully analyze and respond to consumer satisfaction." How does this change in focus affect the role of marketing in a company?

2-3.   In the late 1970s, the U.S. Bureau of the Mint issued Susan B. Anthony dollar coins. Consumer resistance to the coins was high. The coins resembled quarters and consumers were used to dollar bills. To overcome resistance, bank giveaways featured the coins. Vending and pinball machines were equipped to handle the coins. Other ideas were considered. However, by the middle of 1980, it was clear that these tactics were ineffective. Consumer resistance was too high to be overcome. The Susan B. Anthony dollar coins were a major failure.

Conduct an informal survey of ten of your fellow students (not taking this course) about their attitudes toward the Susan B. Anthony dollar. Evaluate these answers. What else could have been tried to get people to use the coin?

2-4.   Since the late 1970s, there has been a trend toward deregulation of airlines, trucks, railroads, natural gas, intercity bus transportation, and banking. Interview a marketing executive in one of these industries and determine the effect of deregulation on his/her firm's marketing strategy. Has deregulation increased price competition? Has deregulation encouraged new entrants to the industry? What are the differential advantages (or disadvantages) of these new entrants? What has been the effect of deregulation on firm and industry profitability? Has deregulation affected service to small market areas? Explain each of these answers.

ANSWERS

True/False

1. F, p. 34	11. T, p. 43
2. F, p. 34	12. F, p. 44
3. T, p. 35	13. F, p. 44
4. F, p. 36	14. T, p. 44
5. T, p. 37	15. F, p. 45
6. F, pp. 37-38	16. F, p. 45
7. F, p. 37	17. T, p. 45
8. F, p. 39	18. T, p. 49
9. T, p. 43	19. T, p. 49
10. T, p. 43	20. T, p. 50

Multiple Choice

1. b, p. 34	11. b, p. 43
2. c, p. 35	12. c, p. 43
3. a, p. 35	13. c, p. 44
4. d, p. 37	14. a, p. 44
5. b, pp. 37-38	15. a, p. 44
6. c, p. 37	16. d, p. 45
7. b, p. 37	17. b, p. 45
8. a, p. 37	18. d, p. 48
9. a, p. 39	19. a, p. 49
10. d, pp. 37, 39	20. b, p. 50

Definitions

1. m	9. n
2. s	10. d
3. b	11. t
4. j	12. k
5. q	13. p
6. f	14. g
7. r	15. a
8. o	

Discussion Questions

1. p. 35
2. p. 37
3. pp. 37, 39-49
4. pp. 37, 43-44
5. pp. 45-46
6. p. 50
7. pp. 50-52

3

Strategic Planning in Marketing

CHAPTER OBJECTIVES

1. To define strategic planning and consider its importance in marketing
2. To study the different types of marketing plans
3. To examine the relationships between marketing and the other functional areas in the organization
4. To thoroughly describe the steps in the strategic planning process: defining organizational mission, establishing strategic business units, setting marketing objectives, situation analysis, developing marketing strategy, implementing tactics, and monitoring results
5. To present examples of strategic marketing plans in diverse companies

CHAPTER OVERVIEW

Strategic planning in marketing enables an organization to coordinate the factors directed by top management with those directed by marketing. Strategic marketing plans provide guidance, clarify objectives, encourage coordination among departments, focus on strengths and weaknesses, examine alternatives, help allocate resources, and point up the value of monitoring results.

Marketing plans may be short-run, moderate in length, or long-run. They may be developed for each major product or service, presented as one organizational marketing plan, or considered part of an overall business plan. A bottom-up or top-down management approach may be used.

The interests of marketing and the other key functional areas in an organization need to be accommodated in a strategic plan. Departmental conflict can be reduced by improving communications, employing personnel with broad backgrounds, establishing interdepartmental development programs, and blending departmental objectives.

The strategic planning process in marketing consists of seven interrelated steps. One, organizational mission, the long-term commitment to a type of business and a place in the market, is defined. Two, an organization divides itself into strategic business units (SBUs), which are distinct parts of the overall organization with specific markets and separate managers. Three, quantitative and qualitative marketing objectives are set. Four, through situation analysis, an organization identifies the marketing opportunities and potential problems it faces.

Five, a marketing strategy outlines the manner in which marketing is used to accomplish an organization's objectives. Four approaches to strategy planning are the product/market opportunity matrix, the Boston Consulting Group matrix, PIMS (Profit Impact of Market Strategy), and the Porter generic strategy model. All of these approaches involve portfolio analysis, by which each of an organization's opportunities, products, and/or businesses are individually assessed and positioned. Then company resources are allocated and appropriate strategies developed. These approaches should be viewed as one element in planning, not as the entire process.

Six, tactics (specific actions) are undertaken to implement the organization's marketing strategy. Of particular concern are the level of marketing investment and the timing of marketing actions. Seven, monitoring results compares planned performance against actual performance.

KEY TERMS AND CONCEPTS

Strategic plan
Outlines what marketing actions a firm should undertake, why these actions are necessary, who is responsible for carrying them out, where they will be accomplished, and how they will be completed.

Strategic planning process
Consists of seven interrelated steps: defining organizational mission, establishing strategic business units, setting marketing objectives, situation analysis, developing marketing strategy, implementing tactics, and monitoring results.

Organizational mission
A firm's long-term commitment to a type of business and a place in the market. Mission can be defined in terms of customer groups served, customer functions, and technologies utilized.

Strategic business unit (SBU)
A distinct part of the overall organization with a specific market focus and a manager with complete responsibility for integrating all functions into a strategy. SBUs are the basic building blocks of a strategic marketing plan.

Situation analysis
The identification of marketing opportunities and potential problems facing the company. Situation analysis seeks answers to two general questions: Where is the firm now? In what direction is the firm headed?

Marketing strategy
Outlines the manner in which marketing is used to accomplish an organization's objectives.

Portfolio analysis
A technique by which an organization individually assesses and positions each of its opportunities, products, and/or businesses. Company efforts and resources are allocated and appropriate strategies are developed on the basis of these assessments.

Product/market opportunity matrix — A broad method for strategy planning that suggests four alternative strategies for maintaining and/or increasing sales: market penetration, market development product development, and diversification.

Market penetration — A product/market opportunity matrix strategy in which a firm seeks to expand sales of its present products through more intensive distribution, aggressive promotion efforts, and highly competitive prices.

Market development — A product/market opportunity matrix strategy in which a firm seeks greater sales of present products from new markets or new product uses.

Product development — A product/market opportunity matrix strategy in which a firm develops new or modified products to appeal to present markets.

Diversification — A product/market opportunity matrix strategy in which a firm markets new products aimed at new markets.

Boston Consulting Group matrix — A framework which enables a company to classify each of its strategic business units (SBUs) in terms of its market share relative to major competitors and the annual growth rate of the industry. The matrix identifies four types of products: star, cash cow, problem child (question mark), and dog, and suggests appropriate strategies for each.

Star — A category in the Boston Consulting Group matrix that describes a high market-share product in a high-growth industry. A star generates substantial profits but requires large amounts of resources to finance continued growth.

Cash cow — A category in the Boston Consulting Group matrix which describes a leading SBU (high market share) in a relatively mature or declining industry (low growth). Cash cows generate more cash than is required to retain their market share.

Problem child or question mark — A category in the Boston Consulting Group matrix which describes a low market-share SBU in a high-growth industry. A problem child requires substantial cash to maintain or increase market share in the face of strong competition.

Dog — A category in the Boston Consulting Group matrix which describes a low market-share SBU in a mature or declining industry. A dog usually has cost disadvantages and few growth opportunities.

Profit Impact of Market Strategy (PIMS) — A program which gathers data from a number of corporations in order to establish relationships between a variety of business factors and two measures of organizational performance: return on investment and cash flow.

Porter generic strategy model — A model that examines two major marketing planning concepts and the alternatives available with each: selection of a target market (industrywide or segmented) and strategic advantage (uniqueness or price).

These basic strategies are identified: overall cost leadership, differentiation, and focus.

Tactics   Specific actions undertaken to implement a given strategy.

Order-processing costs   Costs associated with filling out and handling order forms, computer time, and merchandise handling. Order-processing costs per unit usually drop as order size increases.

Order-generating costs   Costs that are revenue producing, such as advertising and personal selling.

Monitoring results   Involves the comparison of planned performance against actual performance for a specified period of time.

TRUE/FALSE

Circle the appropriate letter.

T   F   1. A strategic marketing plan uses product lines or company divisions as the basis for planning efforts.

T   F   2. Separate marketing plans for each product line are most often used by service firms.

T   F   3. Top-down plans can diminish lower-level morale.

T   F   4. Departmental conflict can be reduced by discouraging open discussion of differences and interfunctional contact.

T   F   5. The concept of an organizational mission is less comprehensive than the line-of-business concept.

T   F   6. Strategic business units are the basic building blocks of a strategic marketing plan.

T   F   7. Situation analysis can reveal whether a firm should leave the market.

T   F   8. Each strategic business unit in an organization should have a separate marketing strategy.

T   F   9. A product modification strategy is more flexible than a price strategy.

T   F   10. A market penetration strategy is effective for saturated markets.

T   F   11. A product development strategy is effective when a company has a core of strong brands and a sizable consumer following.

T   F   12. The primary assumption of the Boston Consulting Group matrix is that the higher a strategic business unit's market share, the higher its per unit costs, and the higher its profitability.

T   F   13. Stars generate substantial profits but require large amounts of resources to finance continued growth.

T   F   14. Cash cows generate less cash than is required to retain their market share.

T F 15. According to PIMS findings, growing markets drain company cash.

T F 16. The Porter model suggests that a small firm can profit by concentrating on one competitive niche, even though its market share may be low.

T F 17. Reducing order-gathering costs can have a detrimental effect on a firm's sales and profits.

T F 18. Procter & Gamble has abandoned its long standing marketing objective of doubling unit sales volume every ten years.

T F 19. Westinghouse is placing more emphasis on mature businesses and less effort on faster-growing businesses.

T F 20. On the basis of situation analysis, Holiday Inns has recognized that its traditional middle market for hotel facilities and services is saturated. Now it is developing upscale hotel chains.

COMPLETION

Fill in the missing word or words in the blanks provided.

[strategic plan, p. 59] 1. A _____ utilizes competitive analysis, productivity analysis, and planning models to apportion resources. It considers both short-term and long-term implications of decisions.

[top-down, bottom-up, p. 61] 2. Marketing plans can be developed through either _____ or _____ approaches.

[functional, pp. 62-63] 3. Planners need to accommodate the distinct needs of marketing as well as other _____ areas in an organization that have different orientations.

[mission, p. 66] 4. Organizations that diversify too much may lack a clear sense of _____, defined in terms of customers served, customer functions, and technologies utilized.

[strategic business unit, pp. 66-67] 5. Each _____ has a specific orientation, precise target market, senior marketing executive in charge, control over its resources, its own strategy, clear-cut competitors, and a distinctive differential advantage.

[quantitative, qualitative, p. 68] 6. Marketing objectives are described in _____ terms (dollar sales, percentage profit growth) and _____ terms (image, level of innovativeness).

[situation analysis, p. 68] 7. In _____, an organization identifies the marketing opportunities and potential problems it faces.

[strategy, p. 70] 8. A separate marketing _____ to accomplish objectives is necessary for each strategic business unit in an organization.

[portfolio, p. 70]

9. The approaches used by the product/market opportunity matrix, the Boston Consulting Group matrix, the Profit Impact on Market Strategy, and the Porter generic strategy model all rely on _____ analysis.

[penetration, development, product, diversification, pp. 71-72]

10. The product/market opportunity matrix is a method of strategy planning involving four alternative ways to maintain or increase sales: market _____ , market _____ , _____ development, and _____ .

[star, cash cow, problem child or question mark, dog, pp. 72-73]

11. Four types of strategic business units identified by the Boston Consulting Group matrix are _____ , _____ , _____ , and _____ .

[return on investment, cash flow, pp. 74-75]

12. Profit Impact of Market Strategy (PIMS) gathers data to establish relationships between a variety of business factors and two measures of organizational performance: _____ _____ _____ and _____ _____ .

[Porter generic strategy, p. 75]

13. The basic strategies of overall cost, leadership, differentiation, and focus are examined by the _____ _____ _____ model.

[order-processing, order-generating, p. 78]

14. Two important tactical decisions relating to the level of investment in marketing activities are _____ _____ costs and _____ _____ costs.

[Monitoring results, pp. 79-80]

15. _____ _____ tells companies if actual performance lags behind plans.

DEFINITIONS

Match the terms and concepts with the appropriate definitions. Each term or concept may only be used once; there are more terms and concepts than definitions.

Column A	*Column B*
a. Boston Consulting Group matrix	____ 1. A category in the Boston Consulting Group matrix that describes a leading SBU in a relatively mature or declining industry which generates more money than is required to retain its market share.
b. cash cow	
c. diversification	____ 2. A distinct part of an overall organization with a specific market focus and a manager with complete responsibility for integrating all functions into a strategy.
d. dog	
e. market development	
f. market penetration	____ 3. Associated with filling out and handling forms, computer time, and merchandise handling.
g. marketing strategy	
h. monitoring results	____ 4. A product/market opportunity matrix strategy in which a firm seeks greater sales of present products or new product uses.
i. order-generating costs	
j. order-processing costs	

k. organizational mission

l. Porter generic strategy model

m. portfolio analysis

n. problem child

o. product development

p. product market opportunity matrix

q. Profit Impact of Market Strategy

r. situation analysis

s. star

t. strategic business unit

u. strategic plan

v. strategic planning process

w. tactics

_____ 5. A product/market opportunity matrix strategy in which a firm seeks to expand sales of its present products through more intensive distribution, aggressive promotion efforts, and highly competitive prices.

_____ 6. Specific actions undertaken to implement a given strategy.

_____ 7. A category in the Boston Consulting Group matrix that describes a high market-share product in a high-growth industry that generates substantial profits but requires large amounts of resources to finance continued growth.

_____ 8. A technique by which an organization individually assesses and positions each of its opportunities, products, and/or businesses.

_____ 9. Outlines what marketing actions a firm should undertake, why these actions are necessary, who is responsible for carrying them out, where they will be accomplished, and how they will be completed.

_____ 10. A category in the Boston Consulting Group matrix which describes a low-market-share SBU in a mature or declining industry that has cost disadvantages and few growth opportunities.

_____ 11. Involves the comparison of planned performance against actual performance for a specified period of time.

_____ 12. Expenses that are revenue-producing, such as advertising and personal selling.

_____ 13. A category in the Boston Consulting Group matrix which describes a low market-share SBU in a high-growth industry that requires substantial cash to maintain or increase market share in the face of strong competition.

_____ 14. A firm's long-term commitment to a type of business and a place in the market which can be defined in terms of customer functions, customer groups served, and technologies utilized.

_____ 15. A product/market opportunity matrix strategy in which a firm markets new products aimed at new markets.

MULTIPLE CHOICE

Place the letter of the answer you think best in the blank provided.

_____   1. A firm's current position, future orientation, and allocation of resources are usually determined by its
   a. tactics.
   b. diversification.
   c. strategic business units.
   d. strategic plan.

_____   2. In contrast to long-run plans, short-run and moderate-length plans tend to
   a. be developed top-down.
   b. integrate all products and services.
   c. describe details.
   d. provide uniform direction.

_____   3. An advantage of bottom-up plans is that they
   a. are realistic.
   b. ease integration.
   c. provide uniform direction.
   d. utilize complex assumptions.

_____   4. In contrast with other functional areas, marketers seek
   a. well-balanced budgets.
   b. routinized transactions.
   c. a variety of product versions.
   d. infrequent orders.

_____   5. Departmental conflict can be reduced by
   a. encouraging bottom-up plan development.
   b. developing interfunctional task forces.
   c. limiting discussion of differences.
   d. hiring employees with distinct fields of expertise.

_____   6. The first step in the strategic planning process is
   a. establishing strategic business units.
   b. setting marketing objectives.
   c. defining the organizational mission.
   d. developing marketing strategy.

_____   7. Yamaha, a leading motorcycle manufacturer, redefines its organizational mission by
   a. diversifying its products and services.
   b. liquidating part of the business.
   c. deleting an old product.
   d. abandoning an existing customer group.

_____   8. Which of the following companies was criticized for having "too cluttered a plate?"
   a. Yamaha
   b. Campbell Soups
   c. Worth Sports Co.
   d. Greyhound

———— 9. The basic building block of a strategic marketing plan is
a. a star.
b. a strategic business unit.
c. cash flow.
d. focus.

———— 10. Which of the following is the *least* important marketing objective for consumer products manufacturers?
a. Profit margins
b. New-product development
c. Sales promotion
d. Customer service

———— 11. Which one of the following questions does situation analysis seek to answer?
a. In what direction is the firm headed?
b. Who shall carry out the firm's marketing actions?
c. Where will marketing actions be accomplished?
d. How will resources be allocated?

———— 12. Market penetration, market development, product development, and diversification are alternatives found in the
a. Boston Consulting Group matrix.
b. Profit Impact of Market Strategy.
c. product/market opportunity matrix.
d. Porter generic strategy model.

———— 13. Market penetration involves
a. expansion in present markets.
b. greater sales in new markets.
c. new products to appeal to present markets.
d. new products and new markets.

———— 14. A problem child or question mark is a strategic business unit that has a
a. high market share and high growth.
b. high market share and low growth.
c. low market share and low growth.
d. low market share and high growth.

———— 15. Par reports, analysis reports, optimum strategy reports, and look-alike reports give participating firms information from the
a. Boston Consulting Group matrix.
b. Profit Impact of Market Strategy.
c. product/market opportunity matrix.
d. Porter generic strategy model.

———— 16. Absent from the Porter generic strategy model is the basic strategy of
a. overall cost leadership.
b. cash flow.
c. focus.
d. differentiation.

_____ 17. With a focus strategy, a company
   a. aims at a large market by offering a distinctive product.
   b. appeals to a mass market and manufactures products in large quantities.
   c. seeks a specific market segment through low prices or uniqueness.
   d. tries to expand in present markets with new products.

_____ 18. A major strength of the strategic approaches using portfolio analysis is that they
   a. are easy to implement.
   b. are extremely sensitive to changes in SBU definitions.
   c. adequately account for environmental conditions.
   d. compare performance against designated goals.

_____ 19. The level of investment in marketing activities and the timing of marketing actions are decisions relating to
   a. implementing tactics.
   b. establishing SBUs.
   c. developing marketing strategy.
   d. monitoring results.

_____ 20. The shortage of Coleco's Cabbage Patch Kids dolls illustrates the problem of
   a. timing marketing actions.
   b. losing sight of the organizational mission.
   c. insufficient order-generating costs.
   d. departmental conflict.

DISCUSSION QUESTIONS

1. Describe the distinctive characteristics of a strategic marketing plan.

2. Compare and contrast top-down and bottom-up approaches to developing a marketing plan. Which method might be preferred by a middle-level employee? Why?

3. Evaluate Campbell Soup Company's redefinition of its organizational mission.

4. Create a product development strategy and a diversification strategy for a jeans manufacturer.

5. Explain which portfolio analysis approach a small business that specialized in customizing cars (e.g., installing sun roofs) might select and why.

6. What order-generating costs might mail-order houses like L.L. Bean and Sears be expected to incur?

7. In what ways can candidates for public office monitor the results of their marketing strategies?

EXERCISES

3-1.   The highlights of a situation analysis conducted by a local real estate broker are as follows:

1. The mortgage market continues to be uncertain. Interest rates on constant-rate mortgages have increased markedly in recent years, precluding many potential buyers from purchasing homes.

2. An increasing proportion of the apartment housing market in the area is being renovated and converted into cooperative ownership (whereby a consumer purchases the apartment in which he/she resides or will reside; common areas property are jointly owned). Cooperative apartment ownership has become more popular due to tax advantages, centralized maintenance, and lower costs.

3. A shortage of apartments in the area (created by increased cooperative conversion and improved neighborhood image) is developing. This has increased the importance of the broker in obtaining rental housing.

4. Many new brokerage offices have opened in the area in response to rising property values and increased investor and consumer interest.

5. Strengths relative to competitors include high name awareness in the community, being established in the neighborhood for over ten years, an excellent location with good visibility, and an excellent relationship with property owners.

6. Weaknesses relative to competitors include an image that is known to favor landlords (at the expense of tenants), high staff turnover (many of whom have established their own competing offices), the use of many part-time employees, and being open daily 9 A.M. to 6 P.M. and from 9 A.M. to 3 P.M. on Saturday (competitors are often open from 9 A.M. to 9 P.M. daily and 9 A.M. to 5 P.M. on Saturdays and Sundays).

7. An examination of commission income yields these data:

	Income Five Years Ago	Current Income	Projected Income Five Years from Now
Apartment rentals	$30,000	$ 70,000	$ 50,000
Cooperative apartment sales	40,000	180,000	300,000
House sales	140,000	30,000	30,000
	$210,000	$280,000	$380,000

Questions

1. Describe an organizational mission for the real estate broker described in this exercise.

2. Evaluate the information gathered by the real estate broker in its situation analysis.

3. Apply the product/market opportunity matrix to this real estate broker.

4. Distinguish between order-generating and order-processing costs for this broker.

3-2.   In the Boston Consulting Group (BCG) matrix, it is common to use 1x as the cutoff point between low and high relative market share and a 10 per cent industry growth rate as the cutoff point between low and high industry growth. The size of each SBU (strategic business unit) is shown by making its circle diameter proportional to sales volume. Thus, an SBU accounting for 30 per cent of a firm's total share would have a circle with a diameter twice that of an SBU with 15 per cent of total sales.

By evaluating the size and location of each SBU, the degree of balance in a firm's portfolio can be determined (by examining what per cent of a firm's SBU's fit into star, cash cow, problem child, and dog classifications). A firm's future portfolio can also be forecast by anticipating long-run relative market share and industry growth.

Figure 1 shows one firm's current SBU positions using the BCG matrix. Figure 2 indicates its forecast for future SBU positions based on a five-year projection. During the next five years, most industry analysts expect annual industry growth to decline from 20 to 7 per cent and the firm's relative market share to remain stable.

Figure 1	**Figure 2**
Current BCG Portfolio	**Projected BCG Portfolio**

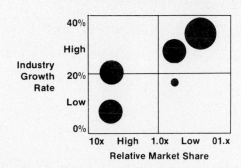

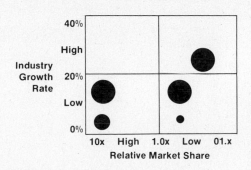

Questions

1.   Is the firm's portfolio (Figure 1) currently well balanced? Explain your answer.

2. Is the firm's projected portfolio (Figure 2) well balanced? Explain your answer.

3. How would you improve the firm's projected BCG portfolio?

4. Why should the firm include the Porter generic strategy model in its planning, and not rely only on the BCG matrix?

3-3.　　A major conglomerate plans to acquire an office equipment manufacturer with a regional focus that specialized in file cabinets and metal typewriter tables. The conglomerate plans to broaden the focus of the firm to take advantage of its reputation and to allow salespeople to do related-item selling.

Questions

1.　Develop a new broadened organizational mission for the office equipment manufacturer using the characteristics of potential customer groups, potential customer functions, and potential technologies served.

2.　What are the benefits of a broadened organizational mission?

3.　What are the disadvantages of a broadened organizational mission?

4.　Are there limits to the degree to which a firm can broaden its mission? Explain.

3-4.   Executives from a small luggage manufacturer recently attended an all-day seminar on strategic planning in marketing. While they learned many interesting points during the seminar, they are unsure how to apply strategic planning to a firm with twenty employees (five at the executive level), annual sales of $2,000,000, and a product line consisting of four sizes of men's and women's luggage. What suggestions would you make to these executives?

ANSWERS

True/False

1. F, p. 59	11. T, p. 71
2. F, p. 60	12. F, p. 72
3. T, p. 61	13. T, p. 72
4. F, p. 63	14. F, p. 72
5. F, p. 64	15. T, p. 75
6. T, p. 67	16. T, p. 76
7. T, p. 68	17. T, p. 78
8. T, p. 70	18. F, p. 80
9. F, p. 70	19. F, p. 80
10. F, p. 71	20. T, pp. 82-83

Multiple Choice

1. d, p. 59	11. a, p. 68
2. c, p. 60	12. c, p. 71
3. a, p. 61	13. a, p. 71
4. c, p. 62	14. d, p. 71
5. b, p. 63	15. b, p. 75
6. c, pp. 64-65	16. b, pp. 75-76
7. a, pp. 64-65	17. c, p. 76
8. d, p. 66	18. d, pp. 76-77
9. b, p. 67	19. a, p. 78
10. d, p. 68	20. a, p. 79

Definitions

1. b	9. u
2. t	10. d
3. j	11. h
4. e	12. i
5. f	13. n
6. w	14. k
7. s	15. c
8. m	

Discussion Questions

1. pp. 59-60
2. pp. 61-62
3. pp. 64, 66
4. pp. 71, 73
5. pp. 71-76
6. p. 78
7. pp. 79-80

4

Information for Marketing Decisions

CHAPTER OBJECTIVES

1. To explain why marketing information is needed
2. To define marketing research and its components
3. To examine the scope of marketing research
4. To describe the marketing research process: problem definition, examination of secondary data, generation of primary data (when necessary), analysis of data, recommendations, and implementation of findings
5. To explain the role and importance of the marketing information system

CHAPTER OVERVIEW

Marketing information is necessary to reduce risk, obtain consumer attitudes, assess the uncontrollable environment, integrate the marketing strategy, and evaluate success or failure. It also helps to enhance credibility and meet legal requirements, gain support or defend a decision, and validate intuition.

Marketing research is the systematic gathering, recording, and analyzing of data about problems related to marketing. The scientific method requires objectivity, accuracy, and thoroughness. The use of marketing research varies by company and type of information required. Larger firms and consumer goods companies are most likely to engage in marketing research.

The marketing research process involves a series of actions: problem definition, examination of secondary data, generation of primary data (when necessary), analysis of data, recommendations, and implementation of findings. Many considerations and decisions are needed in each stage of the process.

Exploratory research is used to develop a clear problem definition. Conclusive research is structured data collection and analysis for the solution of a specific problem or objective. Secondary data, those previously gathered for purposes other than the solution of the current problem, are available from internal and external (government, nongovernment, commercial) sources. Primary data, those collected to solve a specific problem under investigation, are available through surveys, observation, experiments, or simulation. Primary data collection requires a research design: the specified framework for controlling data. Primary data are gathered only if secondary data are insufficient. Costs must be weighed against the benefits of research.

The concluding stages of marketing research are data analysis (including coding, tabulation, and analysis), recommendations, and the implementation of findings by management.

The marketing information system is an organized, interacting, continuous structure that directs the flow and uses of information for marketing decision making. The marketing intelligence phase of an MIS consists of marketing research, continuous monitoring, and data storage. An MIS can be used by both small and large firms, and the applications of marketing information systems are spreading rapidly. Today, many marketing executives are likely to have computer terminals in their offices.

KEY TERMS AND CONCEPTS

Marketing research	The systematic gathering, recording, and analyzing of data about problems relating to the marketing of goods and services. It is used to obtain precise information to solve research problems.
Scientific method	A philosophy of marketing research based on objectivity, accuracy, and thoroughness.
Marketing research process	Consists of a series of activities: definition of the problem or issue to be resolved, examination of secondary data, generation of primary data (if necessary), analysis of information, recommendations, and implementation of findings.
Problem definition	A statement of the topic to be investigated in marketing research. It directs the research process toward the collection and analysis of specific information for the purpose of decision making.
Exploratory research	Used when the researcher is uncertain about the precise topic to be investigated. This technique develops a clear definition of the research problem by utilizing informal analysis.
Conclusive research	Structured data collection and analysis for the solution of a specific problem or objective.
Secondary data	Those data that have been previously gathered for purposes other than solving the current problem under investigation. The two types of secondary data are internal and external.
Primary data	Collected to solve the specific problem or issue under investigation.
Research design	The framework for a study used as a guide in collecting and analyzing data. A research design includes decisions relating to the person collecting the data,

data to be collected, group of people or objects studied, data-collection techniques employed, study costs, method of data collection, length of study period and time, and location of data collection.

Sampling — Requires the analysis of selected people or objects in the specified population, rather than all of them.

Survey — The systematic gathering of information from respondents by communicating with them in person, over the telephone, or by mail.

Semantic differential — A survey technique that uses rating scales of bipolar (opposite) adjectives. An overall company or product profile is then developed.

Multidimensional scaling — A survey research tool in which respondents' attitudes are ascertained for many product and company attributes. Then computer analysis enables the firm to develop a single product or company rating, rather than a profile of several individual characteristics.

Observation — A research technique by which present behavior or the results of past behavior are observed and recorded. People are not questioned, and their cooperation is not necessary.

Experiment — A type of research whereby one or more factors are manipulated under controlled conditions. Experiments are able to show cause and effect.

Simulation — A computer-based marketing research tool that recreates the use of various marketing factors on paper rather than in a real setting.

Data analysis — The coding, tabulation, and analysis of marketing research data.

Marketing information system (MIS) — A set of procedures and methods designed to generate, store, analyze, and disseminate anticipated marketing decision information on a regular, continuous basis.

Marketing intelligence network — The part of a marketing information system that consists of marketing research, continuous monitoring, and data storage.

Continuous monitoring — The stage in a marketing information system during which a changing environment is regularly viewed.

Data storage — The stage in a marketing information system involving the retention of all types of relevant company records (such as sales, costs, personnel performance) as well as the information collected through marketing research and continuous monitoring.

TRUE/FALSE

Circle the appropriate letter.

T   F   1. An advertisement or sales presentation that emphasizes factual information has a higher level of acceptance by customers than one that is merely entertaining.

T   F   2. Advertisements that make claims must be substantiated by research findings.

T   F   3. Marketing research is usually a one-step activity.

T   F   4. A company's decision to use marketing research means it must undertake extensive, expensive studies, such as test marketing and national consumer attitude surveys.

T   F   5. Although there are many similarities in the types of research they conduct, industrial companies spend more on marketing research than consumer goods companies do.

T   F   6. Firms are often able to solve their marketing research problems without having to gather new data.

T   F   7. A company's budget and performance in the attainment of budgetary goals are good sources for secondary data.

T   F   8. Secrecy is more easily maintained with primary data than with secondary data.

T   F   9. Exploratory research requires less data collection than conclusive research does.

T   F   10. Nonprobability samples are more costly, difficult, and accurate than probability samples.

T   F   11. In disguised surveys, respondents tend to answer what they think the researcher wants to hear or read.

T   F   12. The semantic differential is a survey technique that uses random digit-dialing services.

T   F   13. Multidimensional scaling surveys respondents' attitudes toward many product and company attributes.

T   F   14. Observation is a research technique in which interviewer and question bias are minimized.

T   F   15. A major advantage of the experiment as a type of research is that it is able to show cause and effect.

T   F   16. Simulation requires consumer cooperation, and it is unable to handle many of the interrelated factors that affect the marketing plan.

T   F   17. Administered questionnaires offer more privacy and less control than self-administered questionnaires.

T   F   18. Observation and experiments usually require longer time frames than do personal and telephone surveys.

T   F 19. Coding is the process whereby summary data for each response category are computed.

T   F 20. A marketing information system offers broad perspectives, coordination of the marketing plan, and cost-benefit analysis on a continuous basis.

COMPLETION

Fill in the missing word or words in the blanks provided.

[risk, consumer, environment, marketing, sell, decision, intuition, pp. 90-91]

1. In order to operate properly in the marketing environment, it is necessary to have adequate information to make decisions in order to reduce _____ , determine _____ attitudes, monitor the uncontrollable _____ , coordinate or integrate _____ strategy, _____ a product, support or defend a _____ already made, and verify _____ .

[marketing research, scientific method, objectivity, accuracy, thoroughness, pp. 90-91]

2. The systematic gathering, recording, and analyzing of data about problems relating to the marketing of goods and services is called _____ _____ and should be based on the _____ _____ , which involves _____ , _____ , and _____ . As a result, studies will be unbiased, will utilize carefully constructed tools, and will be comprehensive.

[problem, secondary data, primary data, analysis, recommendations, implementation, pp. 93-94]

3. Six steps in the marketing research process are the definition of the _____ , examination of the _____ _____ , generation of _____ _____ (when necessary), _____ of information, _____ , and the _____ of findings.

[exploratory research, conclusive research, p. 94]

4. When a researcher is uncertain about the precise topic to be investigated, _____ _____ should be used; _____ _____ should be used after problem definition has been clarified.

[Internal secondary data, external secondary data, primary data, pp. 96-97, 99]

5. _____ _____ _____ are information accumulated within the company for purposes other than solving the current problem under investigation, whereas _____ _____ _____ are available from sources outside the firm. Both can be contrasted with _____ _____ collected to solve the specific problem under investigation.

[research design, p. 100]

6. A _____ _____ is the specified framework for controlling data collection.

[population, probability, nonprobability, p. 101]

7. The people or objects to be studied are known as a _____ , and if they have an equal chance of being chosen for analysis, the sampling method being used to study them is called a _____ sample; if they are chosen by the researcher or interviewer on the basis of convenience or judgment, the sampling method being used is called _____ .

[survey, observation, experiment, simulation, p. 101]

8. Four basic methods for primary data collection are _____ , _____ , _____ , and _____ .

[nondisguised, disguised, p. 102]

9. In a _____ survey, respondents are told the real purpose of the study, whereas that information is withheld from them in a _____ survey.

[semantic differential, multidimensional scaling, p. 103]

10. The _____ _____ is a list of bipolar (opposite) adjective scales; _____ _____ is another popular survey research tool that uses computer analysis to enable a firm to develop an overall product or company rating.

[experiment, simulation, p. 104]

11. In an _____ one or more factors are manipulated under controlled conditions; _____ involves creating a complex model and is a computer-based research technique.

[administered, self-administered, pp. 104-105]

12. Data collection can be _____ where interviewers ask questions or _____ where respondents read questions and write their own answers.

[coded, tabulated, analyzed, recommendations, p. 107]

13. Completed data forms are _____ , _____ , and _____ before _____ or suggestions for future company actions can be made.

[marketing information system, p. 107]

14. The term _____ _____ _____ describes an ongoing, integrated information process.

[marketing research, continuous monitoring, data storage, pp. 109-110]

15. A marketing intelligence network consists of _____ _____ , _____ _____ , and _____ _____ .

DEFINITIONS

Match the terms and concepts with the appropriate definitions. Each term or concept may only be used once; there are more terms and concepts than definitions.

Column A	Column B
a. conclusive research	___ 1. A statement of the topic to be investigated in marketing research which directs the research process toward the collection and analysis of specific information for the purpose of decision making.
b. continuous monitoring	
c. data analysis	
d. data storage	___ 2. A philosophy of marketing research based on objectivity, accuracy, and thoroughness.
e. experiment	
f. exploratory research	___ 3. A type of research whereby one or more factors are manipulated under controlled conditions to show cause and effect.
g. marketing information system	
h. marketing intelligence network	___ 4. Requires analysis of selected people or objects in the specified population, rather than all of them.

i. marketing research

j. marketing research process

k. multidimensional scaling

l. observation

m. primary data

n. problem definition

o. research design

p. sampling

q. scientific method

r. secondary data

s. semantic differential

t. simulation

u. survey

___ 5. The stage in a marketing information system during which a changing environment is regularly viewed.

___ 6. The part of a marketing information system that consists of marketing research, continuous monitoring, and data storage.

___ 7. Collected to solve the specific problem or issue under investigation.

___ 8. The coding, tabulation, and analysis of marketing research data.

___ 9. A survey technique that uses rating scales of bipolar (opposite) adjectives from which to develop an overall company or product profile.

___ 10. The systematic gathering, recording, and analyzing of data about problems relating to the marketing of goods and services.

___ 11. Structured data collection and analysis for the solution of a specific problem or objective.

___ 12. A computer-based marketing research tool that recreates the use of various marketing factors on paper rather than in a real setting.

___ 13. The stage in a marketing information system involving the retention of all types of relevant company records as well as information collected through marketing research and continuous monitoring.

___ 14. The systematic gathering of information from respondents by communicating with them in person, over the telephone, or by mail.

___ 15. A survey research tool in which respondents' attitudes are ascertained for many product and company attributes, and then computer analysis enables the firm to develop a single product or company rating, rather than a profile of several individual characteristics.

MULTIPLE CHOICE

Place the letter of the answer you think best in the blank provided.

_____ 1. Companies that gather marketing information are less likely to
a. rely on the past.
b. enhance their credibility.
c. verify intuition.
d. substantiate their claims.

_____ 2. To be effective, marketing research should
   a. avoid informal meetings and discussions.
   b. include test marketing and national consumer attitude surveys.
   c. be undertaken by an outside agency.
   d. involve a systematic process.

_____ 3. As applied to marketing research, the scientific method requires that
   a. conclusions be reached as the data are being gathered.
   b. research tools be pretested and checked.
   c. extensive and expensive studies be undertaken.
   d. studies skim the field under investigation.

_____ 4. Firms most likely to use marketing research
   a. have sales of $25 million or less.
   b. are small in size.
   c. are industrial companies.
   d. sell consumer goods.

_____ 5. The first step in the marketing research process is
   a. conclusive research.
   b. definition of the problem.
   c. examination of secondary data.
   d. generation of primary data.

_____ 6. Among the advantages of secondary data are
   a. currency of statistics.
   b. guaranteed suitability.
   c. speed.
   d. secrecy.

_____ 7. Which of the following is _not_ an example of internal secondary data?
   a. Sales figures
   b. Customer billings
   c. Inventory records
   d. Subscriptions to marketing journals

_____ 8. Among the disadvantages of using primary data are the
   a. time spent in collecting materials.
   b. lack of secrecy.
   c. conflicting results from different sources.
   d. difficulties in determining reliability.

_____ 9. A research design is constructed when a company undertakes
   a. exploratory research.
   b. primary data research.
   c. external secondary data research.
   d. internal secondary data research.

_____ 10. Which of the following is _not_ typically included in population studies involving people?
   a. Company personnel
   b. Channel members
   c. Customers
   d. Company performance

_____ 11. In comparison with nonprobability samples, probability samples are
   a. less accurate.
   b. more costly.
   c. focused on objects.
   d. dependent on populations chosen by researchers.

_____ 12. In a survey,
   a. interviewer and question bias are minimized.
   b. factors under investigation are manipulated.
   c. many interrelationships among variables are analyzed.
   d. semantic differentials and multidimensional scaling may be used.

_____ 13. To overcome the problem of unlisted phone numbers, telephone surveys rely on
   a. wide area telephone service.
   b. follow-up mail surveys.
   c. random digit-dialing devices.
   d. follow-up personal interviews.

_____ 14. A major disadvantage of observation as a research technique is that
   a. question bias may occur.
   b. people's cooperation is necessary.
   c. attitudes cannot be determined.
   d. it is rarely used in actual settings.

_____ 15. In experiments,
   a. cause and effect can be demonstrated.
   b. no factors in or affecting the marketing plan can be controlled.
   c. actual situations are used more often than contrived settings.
   d. costs are usually quite low.

_____ 16. A phase of marketing research that is too often improperly planned is
   a. training data-collection personnel.
   b. selecting the population to be studied.
   c. the costs of the study.
   d. the research techniques to be used.

_____ 17. Which of the following research methods generally takes the shortest time to complete?
   a. Observation
   b. Mail surveys
   c. Experiments
   d. Personal surveys

_____ 18. The process of calculating summary data for each response category is called
   a. coding.
   b. analysis.
   c. tabulation.
   d. continuous monitoring.

_____ 19. Which of the following is *not* a component of the marketing information system?
    a. Data storage
    b. Simulation
    c. Marketing research
    d. Continuous monitoring

_____ 20. According to a major study on the use of marketing information systems,
    a. data storage is unimportant.
    b. half of marketing executives have a computer terminal in their office.
    c. only 1 per cent of firms use an MIS.
    d. government data are rarely collected.

DISCUSSION QUESTIONS

1. What are the advantages and disadvantages of using primary data? Secondary data?

2. Describe the range of information the government makes available to companies as sources of external data. Choose three sources and suggest ways in which they might be used.

3. Evaluate the advantages and disadvantages of personal, telephone, and mail surveys for a company eager to start marketing a new product.

4. Can you think of any ethical problems posed by disguised surveys and observations? Would you recommend their continued use? Why? Why not?

5. Which research techniques would be most suitable for a small company with limited resources to use when engaging in marketing research? Which techniques should the company avoid? Why?

6. Enumerate some of the difficulties of data collection. How might these affect the nature of the recommendations to be presented?

7. In what respect is marketing research but one aspect of the marketing information system?

EXERCISES

4-1.   Often important data for marketing can be found in external secondary sources. Some important secondary sources are the *Statistical Abstract of the U.S., Standard Rate & Data Service, Fortune,* and *Advertising Age.*

        The *Statistical Abstract of the U.S.* is published yearly and is a basic directory of important governmental data. *Standard Rate & Data Service* lists important information relating to media. *Fortune,* in May and June of each year, lists the characteristics of the 500 largest U.S. industrial and nonindustrial corporations. *Advertising Age*, in September of each year, lists the 100 largest U.S. advertisers and their advertising expenditures.

Questions

1.   A firm plans to conduct a special promotional mailing to physicians in the U.S. How many physicians are there? How many physicians are there per 100,000 people? (Refer to the most recent *Statistical Abstract.*)

2.   Determine media costs (for one insertion of a four-color full-page ad) and circulation for *People, Reader's Digest, Rolling Stone,* and *Sports Illustrated.* (Refer to *Standard Rate & Data Service's Consumer Magazine Agri-Media Rates and Data*, latest issue.)

3.   You have been asked by a marketing executive to obtain important financial data on competitive oil companies. The competitive firms are Exxon, Mobil, Texaco, Standard Oil of California, and Gulf Oil. Provide data on sales, net income, and the number of employees. (Refer to the latest *Fortune* 500 issue.)

4.   As a new employee in an advertising agency, you have been asked to determine the ten largest advertisers in the U.S. and their advertising expenditures as a per cent of their sales. (Refer to *Advertising Age*'s latest report.)

4-2.   A consumer foods manufacturer is contemplating developing a low-salt margarine aimed at people who must restrict their salt intake—mainly individuals with high blood pressure and other ailments. The margarine is to be sold alongside traditional margarine products in supermarkets and health-food stores.

      A brand manager has developed the questionnaire shown in Figure 1. It is addressed at final consumers in order to determine the potential market size for this product. As a product manager in the marketing research department, you have been asked to evaluate the questionnaire and make appropriate revisions. The director of your department would also like a list of reasons for your revisions.

Figure 1
Food Research Associates
100 Madison Ave.
New York, N.Y. 10010

Dear Sir:

     We would appreciate it if you could complete the enclosed questionnaire, which is designed to determine whether our client should market a salt-free margarine. We understand that you currently are on either a low-sodium or a salt-free diet.

1. What brand of butter or margarine do you use?

2. What factors influence your brand of margarine or butter?
   - _____ a. Low salt content
   - _____ b. Price
   - _____ c. Taste
   - _____ d. Spreadability
   - _____ e. Use in recipes

3. What form is your brand of butter or margarine?
   - _____ a. 1/4 lb. bars
   - _____ b. Whipped 1/6 lb. bars
   - _____ c. 8-oz. whipped, in plastic containers

4. If a salt-free margarine was available at a reasonable price, would you buy it?
   - _____ Yes   _____ No   _____ Don't Know

5. What type of store is the most convenient place for you to purchase this product?
   - _____ a. Supermarket
   - _____ b. Health-food store

6. Your age _____ .
   Number of persons in household _____ .
   Other members of family who must restrict salt usage _____

     Thank you for your cooperation.

Sincerely,

Fred Holmes

Fred Holmes
Research Analyst

P.S. Please mail this questionnaire back in the enclosed self-addressed stamped envelope.

Questions

1. What revisions would you make in the questionnaire?

2. Why?

4-3.   You have been hired as a consultant by a local soda distributor to develop an exploratory research study aimed at explaining the firm's recent decline in sales. Generate a list of areas to be investigated. Explain what you would do next.

4-4.　　What research questions should Hertz consider prior to approving a proposed car-rental location? Which questions can be answered through secondary data? Which require the collection of primary data? Explain your answer.

ANSWERS

True/False

1. T, p. 91
2. T, p. 91
3. F, p. 91
4. F, p. 92
5. F, p. 92
6. T, p. 93
7. T, p. 96
8. T, p. 100
9. T, p. 94
10. F, p. 101

11. F, p. 102
12. F, p. 103
13. T, pp. 103, 105
14. T, p. 103
15. T, pp. 104-105
16. F, p. 105
17. F, p. 107
18. T, p. 107
19. F, p. 107
20. T, pp. 109-111

Multiple Choice

1. a, pp. 91-92
2. d, p. 91
3. b, p. 92
4. d, p. 92
5. b, pp. 93-94
6. c, pp. 94-95
7. d, p. 96
8. a, p. 100
9. b, p. 100
10. d, p. 101

11. b, p. 101
12. d, pp. 101-103
13. c, p. 102
14. c, p. 103
15. a, p. 103
16. a, pp. 104-105
17. d, pp. 106-107
18. c, p. 107
19. b, p. 107
20. b, p. 110

Definitions

1. n
2. q
3. e
4. p
5. b
6. h
7. m
8. c

9. s
10. i
11. a
12. t
13. d
14. u
15. k

Discussion Questions

1. pp. 95-96, 99-100
2. pp. 96-97
3. pp. 101-102
4. pp. 102-103
5. pp. 101-106
6. pp. 101-105
7. pp. 109-111

Part One Review Quiz

DEFINITIONS

Define the following terms and concepts in your own words and then check your answers with the Key Terms and Concepts sections of the Study Guide, Chapters 1-4.

marketing functions
controllable factors
differential advantage
organizational mission
product/market opportunity matrix
exploratory research
observation

SEQUENCES

For each of the following questions, arrange the events in chronological order by writing the numbers in the blanks provided, indicating the first in each series by 1.

1. The Evolution of Marketing
   _____ marketing department era
   _____ production era
   _____ marketing company era
   _____ sales era

2. Stages in the Evolution of Federal Legislation About Business
   _____ helping consumers deal with deceptive and unsafe practices
   _____ deregulating business
   _____ protecting small businesses from large businesses

3. Steps in the Strategic Planning Process
_____ implementing tactics
_____ establishing strategic business units
_____ situation analysis
_____ defining organizational mission
_____ developing marketing strategy
_____ monitoring results
_____ setting marketing objectives

4. Steps Taken in the Marketing Research Process
_____ examination of secondary data
_____ analysis of information
_____ implementation of findings
_____ definition of the problem
_____ generation of primary data
_____ recommendations

SENTENCES

In each sentence, circle the word or phrase that is most appropriate.

1. Describing marketing as "the performance of business activities that direct the flow of goods and services from producer to consumer to user" is an example of a [classical/ modern] and [narrow/broad] definition.

2. During the marketing department era of marketing, competition [grew/declined] and supply was [greater/less] than demand.

3. [Selling/Marketing] philosophies are oriented toward the long run.

4. A [large/small] amount of each sales dollar goes to cover marketing costs.

5. [High/Low] volume sales almost always necessitate intensive, shared distribution of goods.

6. Decisions concerning the company's line of business are usually determined by [top management/marketers].

7. Marketers consider the external environment as a/an [controllable/uncontrollable] factor.

8. There is [monopolistic/pure] competition when each of several firms tries to offer a unique marketing mix.

9. Laws regulating business hours, locations, unit pricing, and labeling are usually enacted by [federal/state] government.

10.   When costs are stable, marketers have [more/fewer] opportunities to differentiate their offerings and expand sales.

11.   Long-run marketing plans tend to be [more/less] detailed and operational in nature than short-run ones.

12.   In comparison with top-down planning, bottom-up planning tends to be [more/less] realistic and [better/worse] for morale.

13.   If an organization has too [many/few] strategic business units, it may be unable to recognize important differences in the planning requirements or strategy and tactics of each unit.

14.   The Boston Consulting Group matrix, Profit Impact on Market Strategy (PIMS), Porter generic strategy model, and product/market opportunity matrix all involve [situation/portfolio] analysis that enables a company to assess and position its products.

15.   Advertising and personal selling are considered examples of order- [processing/generating] costs.

16.   Consumer goods companies have [higher/lower] expenditures for marketing research than industrial firms.

17.   *Business Week* provides companies with [external/internal] [primary/secondary] data.

18.   A probability sample is [more/less] accurate and [more/less] expensive than a non-probability sample.

19.   Personal surveys take [more/less] time to complete than observations.

20.   Developing a marketing information system can be [difficult/easy] because the time required and the manpower costs are [high/low].

ANSWERS

Sequences

1. 3,1,4,2, pp. 12-13
2. 2,3,1, p. 45
3. 6,2,4,1,5,7,3, pp. 64-65
4. 2,4,6,1,3,5, pp. 93-94

Sentences

1. classical, narrow, p. 9
2. grew, greater, p. 13
3. Marketing, p. 16
4. large, p. 18
5. high, p. 22
6. top management, pp. 34-35
7. uncontrollable, p. 39
8. monopolistic, p. 43
9. state, p. 45
10. greater, p. 47
11. less, p. 60
12. more, better, p. 61
13. few, p. 67
14. portfolio, pp. 70-71
15. generating, p. 78
16. greater, p. 92
17. external, secondary, pp. 94-95, 96-97
18. more, more, p. 101
19. less, p. 107
20. difficult, high, p. 111

Part
Two

**Understanding
Consumers**

5 Consumer Demographics

CHAPTER OBJECTIVES

1. To show the importance and scope of consumer analysis
2. To define and enumerate important demographics in the United States: population size, gender, and age; location, housing, and mobility of the population; income and expenditures of the population; occupations and education of the population; and marital status of the population
3. To examine trends and projections of important demographics and study their marketing implications
4. To describe several applications of consumer demographics and consider the limitations of demographics

CHAPTER OVERVIEW

By understanding consumers, a firm is able to determine the most appropriate audience to which to appeal and the combination of marketing factors that will satisfy this audience. The scope of consumer analysis includes who, what, why, how, when, where, and how often. This chapter examined consumer demographics. Chapters 6 to 8 focus on social and psychological factors affecting behavior, the consumer's decision process, organizational consumers, the development of a target market, and sales forecasting.

Demographics are the easily identifiable and measurable statistics that are used to describe the population. The U.S. population numbers about 235 million people, increasing less than 1 per cent each year. A large proportion of births is contributed by firstborns. There are slightly more women (who live longer) than men, with both having life expectancies into the seventies.

The Bureau of the Census recently redefined the urban areas that contain 75 per cent of the U.S. population into Metropolitan Statistical Areas (MSAs), Primary Metropolitan Statistical Areas (PMSAs), and Consolidated Metropolitan Statistical Areas (CMSAs). About two thirds of the population reside in homes they own, with the number occupying multiple-unit dwellings going up. About 12 to 17 per cent of the population moves every year. Major growth is occurring in the South Atlantic, West South Central, and Mountain regions.

Average annual real family income is over $21,000, up slightly since the early 1970s. Almost 40 per cent of families have incomes of $25,000 and higher. Total annual consumption exceeds $2 billion, and can be categorized in terms of disposable income and discretionary income expenditures. The rate of inflation and cost of living are measured through the Consumer Price Index (CPI).

The U.S. labor force of well over 100 million people continues its movement towards white-collar and service occupations. Women comprise a significant and rising portion of the labor force. In 1981 and 1982, U.S. unemployment reached a post-depression high of 11 per cent. Educational attainment has been maintained, with more Americans graduating high school and attending college than ever before.

The percentage of adults 18 and older who are married has remained stable, while men and women are waiting until they are older for marriage. A family consists of relatives residing together. A household consists of a person or persons occupying a housing unit, related or not. Both family and household size have declined, as single-person households have grown rapidly.

These limitations of demographics are noted: obsolete data, hidden trends or implications, limited use of single demographic statistics, and lack of explanation of the factors affecting behavior, consumer decision making, and motivation.

KEY TERMS AND CONCEPTS

Final consumers — Purchase products and/or services for personal, family, or household use.

Organizational consumers — Purchase products and services for further production, usage in operating the organization, or resale to other consumers.

Consumer demographics — Easily identifiable and measurable statistics that are used to describe the population.

Metropolitan Statistical Area (MSA) — A Bureau of Census designation which contains either a city of at least 50,000 population or an urbanized area of 50,000 population (with a total population of at least 100,000).

Primary Metropolitan Statistical Area (PMSA) — A Bureau of Census designation which consists of at least 1 million people and includes a large urbanized county or a cluster of counties that have strong economic and social links as well as ties to neighboring communities.

Consolidated Metroppolitan Statistical Area (CMSA) — A Bureau of Census designation which contains several overlapping and interlocking PMSAs.

Disposable income — Aftertax income to be used for spending and/or savings.

Discretionary income — Earnings remaining for luxuries after necessities are bought.

Consumer Price Index (CPI)	A federal government measure of the cost of living. Measures the monthly and yearly changes in the prices of selected consumer items in different product categories, expressing the changes in terms of a base year.
Family	A group of two or more persons residing together who are related by blood, marriage, or adoption.
Household	A person or group of persons occupying a housing unit, whether related or unrelated.

TRUE/FALSE

Circle the appropriate letter.

T   F   1. Final consumers purchase products and services for personal, family, or household use.

T   F   2. The *Survey of Buying Power* contains many statistics not available from the *Census of Population*.

T   F   3. Unlike in earlier decades, a large proportion of babies born in the 1980s and 1990s will be firstborns.

T   F   4. Female life expectancy is longer than that for males.

T   F   5. The high annual rate of population growth offers substantial marketing opportunities for all types of products and services.

T   F   6. The term "Standard Metropolitan Statistical Area" is used by the current Bureau of the Census to replace an earlier category, the "Metropolitan Statistical Area."

T   F   7. In the United States since 1960, ownership of dwellings has been increasing, while the percentage of single-unit housing has been declining.

T   F   8. In terms of population mobility, the New England and East South Central regions are stable.

T   F   9. The density of the U.S. population makes marketing programs less cost efficient.

T   F   10. Marketing efforts directed at consumers in states such as Texas, Florida, Georgia, and California have declined dramatically.

T   F   11. Although incomes will rise between 1980 and 1990, the growth rate will be lower than it was in the 1960s and the 1970s.

T   F   12. The percentage of income spent on food, beverages, tobacco, clothing, accessories, and jewelry has been increasing substantially.

T   F   13. Since 1967 the greatest price increases have occurred in apparel, upkeep, and entertainment.

T   F   14. Affluent consumers have been drawn to generic brands and do-it-yourself products in increasing numbers.

T   F   15. The American labor force is continuing its steady movement toward white-collar and service occupations and away from blue-collar and farm occupations.

T   F   16. For the 1980s the U.S. Bureau of Labor Statistics predicts strong gains in the occupational categories of education, office-machine operators, and the printing trades.

T   F   17. The life-styles of working women have increased sales of microwave ovens and prepared foods.

T   F   18. Home and home furnishing industries can benefit from the growth of single-person households in the United States.

T   F   19. In comparison to two-earner families, single-earner families spend substantially more on transportation, dry cleaning, and appliances.

T   F   20. Aggregate data and trends may hide opportunities and risks in small markets and specialized product categories.

COMPLETION

Fill in the missing word or words in the blanks provided.

[consumer, consumer analysis, final consumers, organizational consumers, p. 126]

1. Because the central focus of marketing is the _____ , firms engage in _____ _____ to determine appropriate audiences to which to appeal. Firms study the characteristics of decision processes used by _____ _____ , who purchase products and services for personal, family, or household use, and _____ _____ , who purchase products and services for further production, use, or resale.

[Consumer demographics, consumer profiles, p. 127]

2. _____ _____ are easily identifiable and measurable statistics that are used to describe the population and that can be used in combination to establish _____ _____ , which may pinpoint attractive and declining market opportunities.

[*Census of Population,* Citywide, p. 128]

3. A federal government publication that presents a wide range of demographic data is the _____ _____ _____ . _____ statistics are annually reported in the *Editor & Publisher Market Guide.*

[slowed, firstborns, females, p. 129]

4. The rate of population growth has _____ and the largest portion of births in the 1980s and the early 1990s will be _____ ; _____ have a longer life expectancy.

[Metropolitan Statistical Areas, Primary Metropolitan Statistical Areas, Consolidated Metropolitan Statistical Areas, p. 131]

5. To replace SMSAs, the Bureau of Census has developed three new categories of urban areas: _____ _____ _____ , _____ _____ _____ , and _____ _____ _____ _____ .

[declined, condominiums, cooperatives, p. 132]

6. More and more American households reside in homes they own, while the percentage of single-unit dwellings has _____ ; this paradox can be explained by the growth of _____ and _____ .

[mobility, region, abroad, p. 132]

7. The _____ of the U.S. population is quite high, with the greatest amount of people moving within the same _____ and the least amount of people moving from _____ .

[cost efficient, transportation, delivery, p. 132]

8. The density of the U.S. population makes marketing programs more _____ _____ and available to bigger groups of consumers. Suburban shopping is growing leading to improved _____ and _____ services.

[North, competition, pp. 132-133]

9. Marketers should reappraise regions that are being abandoned by some firms because of geographic decline, such as the _____ , by comparing population trends with the level of _____ .

[Disposable, discretionary, p. 135]

10. _____ income is after-tax income used for spending and/or savings; _____ income is the earnings remaining for luxuries after the necessities have been bought.

[Consumer Price Index, transportation, entertainment, pp. 135-136]

11. Changes in the prices of selected consumer items monitored by the federal government through the _____ _____ _____ suggest that the cost of living has increased; particularly great price increases have occurred in medical services, food, housing, and _____ with the smallest increase occurring in apparel, upkeep, and _____ .

[generic, p. 136]

12. Marketers are responding to the needs of lower- and middle-income consumers by developing _____ brands, do-it-yourself products, and smaller homes.

[blue-collar, farm, women, educational, p. 137]

13. Among the changes in the composition of the labor force are a steady movement away from _____ _____ and _____ occupations, an increase in the number and percentage of _____ in the labor force, and a rise in the _____ attainment of Americans.

[working women, p. 139]

14. The market for time-saving appliances, prepared foods, and mail-order purchases reveals great opportunities because of the number of _____ _____ in the American population.

[family, household, divorce, p. 140]

15. A _____ is a group of two or more persons residing together who are related by blood, marriage, or adoption; a _____ is a housing unit with one or more people, of which the number of single-person units is increasing because of rising _____ rates.

[dated, hidden, psychological, social, p. 144]

16. Demographic data have limitations: information may be _____ , opportunities and risks in small markets or for specialized product categories may be _____ , single demographic statistics may not be useful, and the _____ and _____ factors explaining the decision process consumers utilize are not explained.

DEFINITIONS

Match the terms and concepts with the appropriate definitions. Each term or concept may only be used once; there are more terms and concepts than definitions.

Column A

a. Consolidated Metropolitan Statistical Area

b. consumer demographics

c. Consumer Price Index

d. discretionary income

e. disposable income

f. family

g. final consumers

h. household

i. Metropolitan Statistical Area

j. organizational consumers

k. Primary Metropolitan Statistical Area

Column B

_____ 1. Purchase products and services for further production, usage in operating the organization, or resale to other consumers.

_____ 2. After-tax income to be used for spending and/or savings.

_____ 3. A federal government measure of the cost of living.

_____ 4. Purchase products and/or services for personal, family, or household use.

_____ 5. A Bureau of Census designation which contains either a city of at least 50,000 population or an urbanized area of 50,000 population (with a total population of at least 100,000).

_____ 6. A person or group of persons occupying a housing unit, whether related or unrelated.

_____ 7. A Bureau of Census designation which consists of at least one million people and includes a large urbanized county or a cluster of counties that have strong economic and social links as well as ties to neighboring communities.

_____ 8. Easily identifiable and measurable statistics that are used to describe the population.

_____ 9. Earnings remaining for luxuries after necessities are bought.

_____ 10. A group of two or more persons residing together who are related by blood, marriage, or adoption.

MULTIPLE CHOICE

Place the letter of the answer you think best in the blank provided.

_____ 1. By using consumer demographics, firms are likely to
   a. appeal to the traditional family of four.
   b. focus on organizational consumers to the exclusion of final consumers.
   c. pinpoint attractive and declining market opportunities.
   d. understand consumer decision making.

_____ 2. _The Survey of Buying Power_ is a collection of statistics
   a. published annually.
   b. duplicating the _Census_.
   c. gathered every ten years.
   d. limited to cities.

_____ 3. Projections of the size of the U.S. population reveal that
   a. the number of people is decreasing.
   b. the rate of population growth is slow.
   c. the Northeast is expanding rapidly.
   d. population growth is increasing at a rapid rate.

_____ 4. Which statement about American population characteristics is _false_?
   a. There are more females than males in the U.S. population.
   b. The largest portion of 1980s births will be firstborns.
   c. The median age of the population is expected to decline by the year 2000.
   d. The rate of growth of the U.S. population is less than 1 per cent a year.

_____ 5. Companies should be expected to focus somewhat more on the specific marketing opportunities presented by
   a. males.
   b. females.
   c. teens.
   d. stable age groups.

_____ 6. In the 1980s and 1990s, the over-65 age group market is expected to
   a. be declining.
   b. be strong.
   c. face major difficulties.
   d. least need a marketing orientation.

_____ 7. As of July 1, 1983, the Bureau of the Census classification system eliminated the category of
   a. MSA.
   b. PMSA.
   c. CMSA.
   d. SMSA.

_____ 8. Syracuse, New York, Fargo, North Dakota, and Sheboygan, Wisconsin are examples of
   a. MSAs.
   b. PMSAs.
   c. CMSAs.
   d. SMSAs.

_____ 9. In terms of housing characteristics, the prevailing trend is for
  a. the percentage accounted for by single-unit housing to decline.
  b. all units constructed to be occupied immediately.
  c. the portion of households residing in multiple-unit structures to decline.
  d. the rate of ownership to remain low.

_____ 10. The greatest amount of mobility occurs for people moving
  a. from abroad.
  b. within the same state.
  c. within the same region.
  d. within the same county.

_____ 11. Among the geographic regions showing a relative population decline is the
  a. South Atlantic.
  b. Pacific region.
  c. West North Central region.
  d. New England region.

_____ 12. The density of the U.S. population is likely to
  a. make marketing programs less cost efficient.
  b. improve opportunities for mass distribution.
  c. lead to a decline in suburban shopping.
  d. reduce the size of consumer groups available to marketing programs.

_____ 13. As a result of population shifts, marketing efforts are less likely to be directed toward
  a. Texas.
  b. California.
  c. Florida.
  d. Connecticut.

_____ 14. The number of families with annual incomes of $25,000 or more in 1980 was
  a. 10 per cent of the U.S. population.
  b. 20 per cent of the U.S. population.
  c. 30 per cent of the U.S. population.
  d. 40 per cent of the U.S. population.

_____ 15. Changing consumption patterns suggest that people are tending to spend less of their income on
  a. housing.
  b. medical care.
  c. recreation.
  d. food.

_____ 16. Since 1967, the Consumer Price Index has shown that the smallest price increases have occurred in
  a. entertainment.
  b. housing.
  c. medical care.
  d. food.

_____ 17. Affluent consumers are more likely to
a. want electronic features on their major appliances.
b. purchase generic brands.
c. buy more do-it-yourself products.
d. hold on to durable products for longer periods.

_____ 18. Which of the following occupations has shown the greatest percentage increase since 1960?
a. Sales workers
b. Professionals
c. Operatives
d. Craftsmen

_____ 19. For the 1980s, the U.S. Bureau of Labor Statistics predicts limited growth or decline for those employed in
a. engineering.
b. science.
c. medicine.
d. education.

_____ 20. Mail-order and take-out food retailers are finding increased marketing opportunities because
a. the American population is better educated.
b. more women are working.
c. more Americans are marrying.
d. there are more adults in the overall population.

_____ 21. As the educational level of the U.S. population rises, there is greater need for
a. additional hotel security.
b. longer retail business hours.
c. better products and services.
d. small homes.

_____ 22. Which of the following is an important change in the marital and family status of the American population?
a. Adults are marrying earlier.
b. The size of the average household is increasing.
c. The number of divorced adults has declined.
d. The number of single-person households is increasing.

_____ 23. A family is defined as
a. two or more related people residing together.
b. one or more people residing together.
c. a husband, wife, and children, regardless of whether they reside together.
d. all relatives, including cousins, regardless of whether they reside together.

_____ 24. According to B. Dalton's demographic studies, heavy readers tend to be
a. male.
b. middle-income.
c. over fifty years of age.
d. employed in management positions.

_____ 25. Which of the following is *not* a limitation of demographic data?
  a. It may be dated.
  b. It may hide opportunities for specialized product categories.
  c. It is difficult to analyze.
  d. It does not explain the decision process consumers use when making purchases.

DISCUSSION QUESTIONS

1. If you were starting a nationwide chain of health spas, what sources might you consult to obtain demographic statistics?

2. Describe the impact of demographic statistics regarding women's longevity and participation in the labor force on marketers.

3. How do recent trends in urbanization affect marketers?

4. By 1990, families with incomes over $50,000 will more than double. How might this affect marketers?

5. Why is it important for marketers to understand the Consumer Price Index?

6. How will shifts in the marital status of the American population influence marketing?

7. Evaluate the strengths and weaknesses of demographic data from a marketing point of view.

EXERCISES

5-1. *Sales & Marketing Management's Survey of Buying Power* annually measures each U.S. metropolitan area's sales potential through a buying power index (BPI).

Two of the *Survey*'s terms need to be defined. Effective buying income is similar to disposable personal income. (It equals personal income less income taxes and nontax payments such as social security.) The BPI is a single weighted measure combining each metropolitan area's effective buying income, retail sales, and population size into an indicator of an area's sales potentials, expressed as a percentage of total U.S. sales.

The BPI formula is:

Buying power index = 0.5 (the area's percentage of U.S. effective buying income)
+ 0.3 (the area's percentage of U.S. retail sales)
+ 0.2 (the area's percentage of U.S. population)

A Texas air conditioner manufacturer is interested in using the *Survey of Buying Power* to allocate marketing effort (e.g., number of salespeople, advertising expenditures, and sales promotions) among four markets: Austin, Dallas, Houston, and San Antonio. Table 1 contains relevant *Survey of Buying Power* data for all of these areas.

Table 1
Selected Survey of Buying Power Data for Four Texas Markets

A. Actual Data

	Austin	Dallas	Houston	San Antonio
Population—12/31/82	588,900	2,090,800	3,028,000	1,130,100
Households—12/31/82	223,100	783,800	1,114,800	380,700
Total retail sales, 1982 (millions)	$3,263.231	$12,849.943	$19,664.925	$5,485.801
Furniture/furnishings/ appliance sales, 1982 (millions)	$ 134,421	$ 663,447	$ 776,745	$ 215,158
Average household Effective Buying Income, 1982	$ 26,092	$ 26,269	$ 31,188	$ 25,031
1982 Buying Power Index	.2737	1.0582	1.5966	.4659

B. Projections

	Austin	Dallas	Houston	San Antonio
Population—12/31/87	701,000	2,383,300	3,638,000	1,229,600
Households—12/31/87	271,300	910,200	1,375,700	424,600
Total retail sales, 1987 (millions)	$6,498.427	$24,238.002	$38,851.138	$10,046.463
Average household Effective Buying Income, 1987	$ 41,754	$ 45,117	$ 47,965	$ 40,454
1987 Buying Power Index	.3133	1.1341	1.8052	.4919

Source: Adapted from *Survey of Buying Power*, Sales & Marketing Management (July 25, 1983), pp. C185, C186, C188, C189; and *Survey of Buying Power: Part II*, Sales & Marketing Management (October 31, 1983), pp. 84, 85. Reprinted by permission.

Questions

1. Evaluate the tables using both 1982 and 1987 data.

2. What additional information would be helpful in better preparing an analysis of each of these markets?

3. Using the data in Table 1, how would you allocate marketing effort among Austin, Dallas, Houston, and San Antonio?

4. Examine the latest *Survey of Buying Power* available in your library. Comment on and explain the differences with Table 1.

5-2.   The *1980 Census of Population* offers a wide variety of demographic data
that can be used by marketers. The data offer both current information and estimates well into the future, as illustrated in Tables 1 and 2. Table 1 shows selected
data for the ten largest cities in the U.S. (as of 1980). Table 2 shows several projections for the year 2050.

Table 1
Selected Demographic Data on the Ten Largest
U.S. Cities, as of 1980

City	% Pop. Change 1970-1980	% Whites (1980)	% Blacks (1980)	% Hispanics (1980)	Median Household Income (1979)	% Aged 65+ (1980)	Families with Children as % of Total Households (1980)
New York	-10.4	60.7	25.2	19.9	$13,855	13.5	18.6
Chicago	-10.8	49.6	39.8	14.0	15,301	11.4	20.3
Los Angeles	+ 5.5	61.2	17.0	27.5	15,746	10.6	21.1
Philadelphia	-13.4	58.2	37.8	3.7	13,169	14.0	19.5
Houston	+29.2	61.3	27.6	17.6	18,474	6.9	26.1
Detroit	-20.5	34.3	63.0	0.2	13,981	11.7	18.7
Dallas	+ 7.1	61.4	29.4	12.3	16,227	9.5	21.9
San Diego	+25.5	75.4	8.9	14.8	16,409	9.7	23.1
Baltimore	-13.1	43.9	54.8	1.0	12,811	12.8	17.8
San Antonio	+20.1	78.6	7.3	53.6	13,775	9.6	32.0

Source: U.S. Bureau of the Census, *1980 Census of Population.*

Table 2
Selected U.S. Demographic Projections, to the Year 2050

	1980	2050
Total population size	227 million	309 million
% of population under age 35	58	42
Life expectancy at birth (in years)	74	80
Ratio of workers to retirees	5.5	2.5
Annual number of births	3.6 million	3.6 million
Annual number of deaths	2 million	4 million

Questions

1.   Evaluate the data in Table 1 from a marketing perspective.

2.　　Evaluate the data in Table 2 from a marketing perspective.

3.　　What are the values and limitations of the data shown in Tables 1 and 2?

4.　　How could each of the following use the information in Tables 1 and 2?
　　　a. A magazine publisher
　　　b. A clothing manufacturer
　　　c. A supermarket

5-3.   Using government data, determine the current overall Consumer Price Index (CPI) for your area. Also detail the CPI for food, apparel, housing, personal care, and entertainment. How do these figures compare with the national average? What are the implications of these data for marketers?

5-4.   You have been hired by an ice cream parlor chain to prepare a demographic profile of the city closest to your university. The firm is seeking to determine how many franchises the city can sustain. Important references to be considered include *Editor & Publisher Market Guide, Sales & Marketing Management's Survey of Buying Power*, and the *Census of Population*.

ANSWERS

True/False

1. T, p. 126
2. T, p. 128
3. T, p. 129
4. T, p. 129
5. F, p. 129
6. F, p. 131
7. T, pp. 131-132
8. T, p. 132
9. F, p. 132
10. F, pp. 132-133
11. T, pp. 133-134
12. F, p. 135
13. F, p. 136
14. F, p. 137
15. T, p. 137
16. F, pp. 139-140
17. T, p. 141
18. T, p. 141
19. F, p. 143
20. T, p. 144

Multiple Choice

1. c, p. 127
2. a, p. 128
3. b, p. 129
4. c, p. 129
5. b, pp. 130-131
6. b, p. 131
7. d, p. 131
8. a, p. 131
9. a, pp. 131-132
10. c, p. 132
11. c, p. 132
12. b, p. 132
13. d, p. 132
14. d, p. 134
15. d, p. 135
16. a, pp. 135-136
17. a, pp. 136-137
18. b, p. 137
19. d, p. 137
20. b, pp. 138-139
21. c, p. 140
22. d, p. 140
23. a, p. 140
24. d, p. 144
25. c, p. 144

Definitions

1. j
2. e
3. c
4. g
5. i
6. h
7. k
8. b
9. d
10. f

Discussion Questions

1. pp. 127-128
2. pp. 129, 137
3. pp. 131-132
4. pp. 133-137
5. p. 135
6. pp. 140-142
7. pp. 142-144

6

Consumer Life-Styles and Decision Making

CHAPTER OBJECTIVES

1. To define and describe consumer life-styles and decision making
2. To demonstrate the importance of consumer life-styles and decision making for marketers and present appropriate marketing applications
3. To explain the interaction of consumer demographics, social concepts, psychological factors, and decision making
4. To point out the limitations of social, psychological, and decision-making analysis of consumers

CHAPTER OVERVIEW

Because demographic data alone are often inadequate for making marketing decisions, many firms analyze consumer social, psychological, and decision-making information in conjunction with demographics and then develop descriptive consumer profiles.

Social and psychological factors comprise a consumer's life-style, the pattern in which a person lives and spends time and money. Psychographics is the technique by which life-styles are measured. A consumer's social profile is made up of several elements, including culture, social class, performance, reference groups, family life cycle, and time expenditures. A psychological profile is based on a combination of these attributes: personality, attitudes, level of class consciousness, motivation, perceived risk, innovativeness, opinion leadership, and importance of purchase.

Even though social and psychological concepts have many marketing applications, they can be difficult to measure, somewhat subjective, based on self-reports by consumers, and sometimes hidden from view. There are disputes over terms, misuse of data, and reliability.

The consumer's decision process is composed of the process itself and the factors affecting it (demographics, social factors, and psychological factors). It can be delayed or terminated by the consumer at any point. The process consists of six steps: stimulus, problem awareness, information search, evaluation of alternatives, purchase, and postpurchase behavior. There are three types of consumer decision making: extended, limited, and routine. Brand loyalty, the consistent repurchase of and preference for a brand, is the consumer's attempt to minimize risk, time, and thought.

The limitations of the decision process for marketers lie in the unexpressed nature of many parts of the process, the subconscious nature of many actions by consumers, and the impact of demographic, social, and psychological factors.

KEY TERMS AND CONCEPTS

Life-style	The pattern in which a person lives and spends time and money. The combination of personality and social values that has been internalized by an individual.
Psychographics	A technique with which life-styles can be measured. An AIO (activities, interests, and opinions) inventory is used in psychographic research to determine consumer life-styles.
Culture	A group of people sharing a distinctive heritage.
Social class	The ranking of people within a culture. Social classes are based on income, occupation, education, and type of dwelling.
Social performance	How a person carries out his or her roles as a worker, family member, citizen, and friend.
Reference group	A group that influences a person's thoughts and actions.
Family life cycle	Describes how a typical family evolves from bachelorhood to marriage to children to solitary retirement. At each stage in the cycle, needs, experience, income, and family composition change.
Joint decision making	The process by which two or more consumers have input into purchases.
Time expenditures	Involve the types of activities in which a person participates and the amount of time allocated to them.
Personality	The sum total of an individual's traits that make the individual unique.
Attitude (Opinion)	A person's positive, neutral, or negative feelings about products, services, companies, issues, and institutions.
Class consciousness	The extent to which social status is desired and pursued by a person.
Inner-directed person	One who is interested in pleasing him- or herself.
Outer-directed person	One who is interested in pleasing the people around him or her.
Motivation	The driving force within individuals that impels them to act.

Motive	A reason for behavior.
Perceived risk	The level of risk a consumer believes exists regarding the outcome of a purchase decision; this belief may or may not be correct. Perceived risk can be divided into five major types: functional, physical, financial, social, and psychological.
Innovativeness	The willingness to try a new product or service that others perceive as having a high degree of risk.
Opinion leader	Person who influences the purchase behavior of other consumers through face-to-face interaction. An opinion leader normally has an impact over a narrow range of products.
Importance of purchase	Related to the degree of decision making, level of perceived risk, and amount of money to be spent/invested. The level of importance of a purchase has a major impact on the time and effort a consumer will spend shopping for a product or service and on the amount of money allocated.
Consumer's decision process	Involves the steps a consumer goes through in purchasing a product or service: stimulus, problem awareness, information search, evaluation of alternatives, purchase, and postpurchase behavior. Demographics, social factors, and psychological factors affect the consumer's decision process.
Stimulus	A cue (social, commercial, or noncommercial) or a drive (physical) meant to motivate or arouse a person to act.
Problem awareness	A stage in the consumer decision-making process during which the consumer recognizes that the product or service under consideration may solve a problem of shortage or unfulfilled desire.
Information search	Stage in the consumer's decision-making process that requires the assembly of a list of alternative products or services that will solve the problem at hand and a determination of the characteristics of each alternative. Information search may be either internal or external.
Evaluation of alternatives	Stage in the consumer's decision process in which criteria for a decision are set and alternatives ranked.
Purchase act	An exchange of money or a promise to pay for the acquisition of a product or service.
Postpurchase behavior	Stage in the consumer's decision process when further purchases or re-evaluation of the purchase are undertaken.
Cognitive dissonance	Doubt that the correct purchase decision has been made. To overcome cognitive dissonance and dissatisfaction, the firm must realize that the purchase process does not end with the purchase.

Extended consumer decision making Occurs when considerable time is spent on information search and evaluation of alternatives before a purchase is made. Expensive, complex products or services with which the consumer has had little or no experience require this form of decision making.

Limited consumer decision making Occurs when a consumer uses each of the steps in the purchase process but does not need to spend a great deal of time in each of them. The consumer has some past experience with the product or service under consideration.

Routine consumer decision making Occurs when the consumer buys out of habit and skips steps in the decision process. In this category are items that are purchased regularly.

Brand loyalty The consistent repurchase of and preference for a brand. The consumer attempts to minimize risk, time, and thought.

TRUE/FALSE

Circle the appropriate letter.

T   F   1. From a marketing viewpoint, social and psychological analysis are independent fields of inquiry that are exclusive of one another.

T   F   2. A group of people sharing a distinctive heritage is referred to as a social class.

T   F   3. A trend worth noting is that Americans are spending significantly more time on family care.

T   F   4. A self-confident and sociable person will purchase different products and services than an inhibited and aloof person.

T   F   5. When using attitude research, the attitude itself must be evaluated and then the purchase intent toward a company's brand must be ascertained.

T   F   6. An inner-directed person is interested in pleasing people around him or her, a fact marketers must take into consideration.

T   F   7. Communicating information is vital in lowering perceived risk.

T   F   8. Commercial sources of information are usually perceived as more credible than opinion leaders.

T   F   9. "Successful adapters" is a consumer profile developed by PRIZM.

T   F   10. Unlike demographics, many social and psychological factors are difficult to measures.

T   F   11. For every product or service bought, consumers go through all the stages of the decision process.

T   F   12. The distinguishing attribute of a social cue is that it comes from an interpersonal source not affiliated with the seller.

T   F   13. Many consumers are more hesitant to react to unfulfilled desires than to shortages.

T   F   14. A consumer with minimal purchasing experience will usually undertake an internal search to develop a list of alternatives.

T   F   15. Dissatisfaction with place of purchase, terms, or availability may cause a consumer to delay or not buy a product or service, even though there is contentment with the product or service itself.

T   F   16. Marketers must learn that their responsibility ends with the purchase of the product.

T   F   17. Cognitive dissonance can be reduced by a realistic promotion campaign and consumer aftercare.

T   F   18. Expensive, complex products or services with which the consumer has had little or no experience require limited decision making.

T   F   19. Brand loyalty is the consumer's attempt to minimize risk, time, and thought.

T   F   20. Drugstore shoppers make almost 60 per cent of final purchase decisions after entering the store.

COMPLETION

Fill in the missing word or words in the blanks provided.

[life-style, psychographics, AIO, pp. 151-152]

1. Social and psychological factors comprise a consumer's _____ _____, the pattern in which a person lives and spends time and money, which is measured by _____ through an _____ inventory.

[culture, social class, social performance, reference groups, family life cycle, time expenditures, pp. 152-156]

2. Social characteristics of consumers include _____, a group of people sharing a distinctive heritage; _____ _____, the ranking of people; _____ _____, how well roles are carried out; _____ _____, influencing thoughts and actions; the _____ _____ _____, evolving from bachelorhood to retirement; and _____ _____, involving the types of activities participated in and how long these last.

[personality, attitudes, opinions, class consciousness, motivation, pp. 156-158]

3. Psychological characteristics of consumers include _____, the sum total of traits making a person unique; _____ or _____, positive, negative, or neutral feelings; _____ _____, the extent to which social status is desired or pursued; and _____, the driving force impelling people to action.

[perceived risk, innovativeness, opinion leadership, importance of purchase, pp. 158-159]

4. Other psychological characteristics are _____ _____, the degree of uncertainty about the consequences or outcomes of specific purchase decisions; _____, the willingness to try new products or services

others perceive as risky; _____ _____ , in which people influence the purchasing behavior of others; and the _____ _____ _____ , which determines the time and effort consumers spend shopping for a product or service.

[Yankelovich Monitor, VALS, PRIZM, p. 160]

5. Three services that define and measure consumer life-styles are _____ _____ , _____ , and _____ .

[measure, self reports, hidden, pp. 161-163]

6. Unlike demographics, many social and psychological factors are difficult to _____ , somewhat subjective, usually based on _____ _____ of consumers, and sometimes _____ from view.

[stimulus, problem, information, alternatives, postpurchase, pp. 163-168]

7. The six stages of the consumer decision process are _____ , _____ awareness, _____ search, evaluation of _____ , purchase, and _____ behavior.

[stimulus, social, commercial, noncommercial, physical drives, p. 165]

8. A _____ is a cue or drive meant to motivate or arouse a person to act and includes _____ cues arising from interpersonal sources not affiliated with the seller; _____ cues, messages sponsored by sellers; _____ cues received from impartial sources; and _____ _____ originating in physical needs.

[shortage, unfulfilled desire, pp. 165-166]

9. When a consumer recognizes that a product or service under consideration may solve a _____ or an _____ _____ , he or she is aware of a need.

[internal search, external search, p. 166]

10. To assemble a list of alternatives, consumers usually conduct an _____ _____ for information when they have a lot of purchasing experience and an _____ _____ when they have minimal experience.

[Criteria for decisions, rank, p. 167]

11. _____ _____ _____ are those product or service features that consumers consider relevant to _____ alternatives from most to least desirable.

[purchase act, place, terms, availability, p. 167]

12. An exchange of money or a promise to pay for the acquisition of a product or service is a _____ _____ , which is affected by _____ of purchase, _____ , and _____ .

[cognitive dissonance, p. 168]

13. Doubt that the correct decision has been made is termed _____ _____ .

[extended, limited, routine, Brand loyalty, pp. 169-170]

14. Three types of consumer decision processes are _____ consumer decision making, used in purchasing expensive or complex products; _____ consumer decision making, for items not regularly purchased where moderate risk is involved; and _____ consumer decision making

for buying out of habit. _____ _____ is the method these consumers can use to minimize risk, time, and thought.

[hidden, subconscious, p. 171]   15. Limitations on the consumer decision process lie in the _____ nature of many elements of the process, the consumers' _____ performance, and the impact of demographic, social, and psychological factors.

DEFINITIONS

Match the terms and concepts with the appropriate definitions. Each term or concept may only be used once; there are more terms and concepts than definitions.

Column A	*Column B*
a. attitude	___ 1. Doubt that the correct purchase decision has been made.
b. brand loyalty	___ 2. The willingness to try a new product or service that others perceive as having a high degree of risk.
c. class consciousness	
d. cognitive dissonance	
e. consumer's decision process	___ 3. A reason for behavior.
f. culture	___ 4. A cue (social, commercial, or noncommercial) or a drive (physical) meant to motivate or arouse a person.
g. evaluation of alternatives	
h. extended consumer decision making	___ 5. Stage in the consumer's decision process that requires the assembly of a list of alternative products or services that will solve the problem at hand and a determination of the characteristics of each alternative.
i. family life cycle	
j. importance of purchase	
k. information search	___ 6. A person's positive, neutral, or negative feelings about products, services, companies, issues, and institutions.
l. inner-directed person	
m. innovativeness	___ 7. The extent to which social status is desired and pursued by a person.
n. joint decision making	___ 8. A technique with which life-styles can be measured using an AIO inventory.
o. life-style	
p. limited consumer decision making	___ 9. How a person carries out his or her roles as a worker, family member, citizen, and friend.
q. motivation	___ 10. One who is interested in pleasing the people around him or her.
r. motive	
s. opinion leader	___ 11. Person who influences the purchase behavior of other consumers through face-to-face interaction.
t. outer-directed person	
u. perceived risk	___ 12. A group of people sharing a distinctive heritage.
v. personality	___ 13. A group that influences a person's thoughts and actions.
w. postpurchase behavior	
x. problem awareness	___ 14. The process by which two or more consumers have input into purchases.

y. psychographics

z. purchase act

aa. reference group

bb. routine consumer decision
making

cc. social class

dd. social performance

ee. stimulus

ff. time expenditures

___ 15. Occurs when a consumer uses each step in the purchase process but does not need to spend a great deal of time in each of them. The consumer has some past experience with the product or service under consideration.

MULTIPLE CHOICE

Place the letter of the answer you think best in the blank provided.

_____ 1. Psychographics is a technique marketers can use for analyzing
   a. consumer demographics.
   b. geographic mobility.
   c. per capita income.
   d. consumer life-styles.

_____ 2. Individualism, freedom, achievement, and youthfulness are aspects of the distinctive heritage Americans call their
   a. reference groups.
   b. culture.
   c. social classes.
   d. time expenditures.

_____ 3. An example of a psychological characteristic of consumers is
   a. time expenditures.
   b. social class.
   c. performance.
   d. importance of purchase.

_____ 4. The type of person attracted by products that perform well functionally or products and services that are challenging is usually labeled
   a. class conscious.
   b. other directed.
   c. inner directed
   d. innovative.

_____ 5. When marketers remove a disputed ingredient from a product, they are attempting to deal with
   a. motivation.
   b. opinion leadership.
   c. perceived risk.
   d. innovativeness.

_____ 6. When introducing a new product or service, it is essential for marketers to identify and appeal to
   a. reference groups.
   b. inner-directed people.
   c. other-directed people.
   d. innovators.

_____ 7. The Yankelovich Monitor's consumer profiles include the category of
   a. resistant adapters.
   b. need driven.
   c. blue blood.
   d. outer directed.

_____ 8. In the early 1980s, most consumers
   a. thought owning an old car was socially unacceptable.
   b. were interested in auto model changes and styling.
   c. shifted their spending from autos to other items.
   d. increased their driving mileage.

_____ 9. Unlike demographics, many social and psychological factors are
   a. easy to measure.
   b. more objective.
   c. based on observer reports.
   d. subject to disputes.

_____ 10. The first step in the consumer's decision process is called
   a. problem awareness.
   b. stimulus.
   c. information search.
   d. evaluation of alternatives.

_____ 11. A message received from an impartial source that motivates or arouses a person to act is termed a
   a. noncommercial cue.
   b. personal cue.
   c. physical drive.
   d. commercial cue.

_____ 12. When a consumer becomes aware of a product or service that has not been purchased by that individual before, he or she is most likely to
   a. act promptly to make the purchase.
   b. recognize the existence of an unfulfilled desire.
   c. undertake an internal information search.
   d. experience cognitive dissonance.

_____ 13. When consumers evaluate alternatives, they
   a. become aware of shortages.
   b. engage in external information searches.
   c. establish criteria for decisions and rank their choices.
   d. decide on the terms of purchase.

14. Which of the following is *not* an important element during the purchase act phase of decision making?
    a. Place of purchase
    b. Terms of purchase
    c. Product attributes
    d. Availability

15. To overcome cognitive dissonance, firms are advised to
    a. provide follow-up telephone and service calls.
    b. conduct promotion campaigns that raise expectations.
    c. aim advertisements only at potential purchasers.
    d. recognize that the purchase process ends with the actual purchase.

16. In "fine tuning" marketing strategies to cater to target markets and their purchase behavior, marketers should realize that
    a. affluent consumers move through the decision-making process more quickly than do middle-income consumers.
    b. introverted consumers place heavy emphasis on social sources of information.
    c. insecure consumers tend to make quick, snap decisions.
    d. tight time schedules have little bearing on shopping decisions.

17. For the purchase of clothing, gifts, or home furnishings, consumers tend to engage in
    a. limited decision making.
    b. brand loyalty.
    c. extended decision making.
    d. routine decision making.

18. Problem awareness almost always leads to purchase in
    a. limited decision making.
    b. routine decision making.
    c. extended decision making.
    d. all consumer decision making.

19. Consumers who purchase a man's suit and spend a minimal amount of time seeking external information (and exhibit low store loyalty) are categorized as
    a. profashion shoppers.
    b. uninvolved shoppers.
    c. single shoppers.
    d. high-status shoppers.

20. A major limitation of the consumer's decision-making process for marketers is that it
    a. tells more about motives than actions.
    b. does not distinguish among different types of decision making.
    c. may conceal reasons why purchases are made.
    d. does not consider brand loyalty.

DISCUSSION QUESTIONS

1. From a marketing perspective, distinguish between culture and social class.

2. Draw up a consumer profile of a hypothetical outer-directed person. What social and psychological factors would be most likely to affect his or her consumer decision making?

3. What kinds of strategies may marketers use to lower the five major types of perceived risk?

4. Explain how consumer life-styles may be measured and defined for use by marketers.

5. Suppose you were considering becoming a first-time purchaser of a home computer. What steps in the consumer decision process would you take? Why?

6. Assume you bought a home videotape system. What postpurchase behavior might you engage in if you were pleased with your purchase? If you were displeased? What might you expect a marketer to do to reassure you?

7. Explain why the purchase of a man's suit has symbolic meaning for the purchaser.

EXERCISES

6-1.   Recently, the Home Testing Institute, in conjunction with *Progressive Grocer* magazine, studied the reasons why consumers choose a particular supermarket. Seven hundred households throughout the U.S. were surveyed via a mail question-naire; these households were considered to be representative of all households in the U.S. Table 1 shows the ten most important and ten least important supermarket characteristics from among the forty-two attributes examined.

The importance of supermarket characteristics varied by household income. While one-stop shopping and a good drug/toiletries section were important to lower-income households, a good selection of national brands and a good produce department were more valued by higher-income households.

Table 1
Supermarket Characteristics Affecting Store Choice,
Based on the Ratings of 42 Attributes

Most Important Characteristics
1. Cleanliness
2. All prices clearly labelled
3. Low prices
4. Accurate, pleasant checkout clerks
5. Freshness date marked on products
6. Good produce department
7. Good meat department
8. Shelves usually kept well stocked
9. Convenient store location
10. Good dairy department

Least Important Characteristics
33. Good assortment of nonfoods
34. Presence of in-store bakery
35. Presence of deli department
36. Presence of UPC scanning registers
37. Purchases carried to car by clerk
38. Eye-catching mass displays
39. Store employees know customer name
40. Hot foods (to take out or eat in store) sold
41. Trading stamps or other extras
42. Presence of money machine or automatic teller

Source: "42 Ways to Choose a Super," adapted from *Progressive Grocer* (May 1984), p. 58.

Questions

1.   Comment on Table 1. Which findings are most surprising to you?

2.   What life-style factors are likely to influence a consumer's choice of a supermarket? Explain your answer.

3.   Describe how the concept of perceived risk (functional, physical, financial, social, and psychological) may be applied to the purchase of supermarket products.

4.   Contrast the consumer's decision process used in the selection of a supermarket with that used in the purchase of products on a partricular shopping trip.

6-2.   In a recent series of advertisements, Prudential-Bache Securities used a slight variation of the traditional family life cycle to explain the need for financial planning.

Stage in Cycle	Financial Characteristics	Primary Financial Need
Bachelor	Greatest potential, fewest obligations	Definition of financial objectives for future
Newly married	Higher income, higher tax brackot	Saving for home
Full nest I and II	Concern for needs of children	Saving for college
Empty nest I and II	Higher disposable income as children's responsibilities lessen, spouse rejoins workforce, individuals progress in their careers	Saving for retirement, purchase of luxuries, lessening taxes
Empty nest III	Need to supplement social security and pension plans	Retirement

Questions

1.   What financial services should Prudential-Bache Securities attempt to market at different life-cycle stages?

2.   The family life cycle depicted in this exercise is a traditional one. However, a number of individuals do not marry, do not have children, or become divorced. What financial services should Prudential-Bache offer to these consumers?

3.   Why did Prudential base its advertising campaign on family life-cycle stage and not age?

4.   What are the potential disadvantages of a firm's using only the family life cycle to plan its marketing strategy?

6-3.   Outline the reference groups that influence your buying behavior. What types of product or service decisions are most affected? Which are affected the least? Why?

6-4.   Why would one person spend $400 for a watch while another would spend no more than $50? Describe the consumer's decision process for each person. What types of perceived risk affect each person? Explain your answers.

ANSWERS

True/False

1. F, pp. 151-152
2. F, p. 152
3. F, p. 155
4. T, p. 156
5. T, p. 157
6. F, pp. 157-158
7. T, p. 158
8. F, p. 159
9. F, p. 160
10. T, pp. 161-162
11. F, p. 165
12. T, p. 165
13. T, pp. 165-166
14. F, p. 166
15. T, p. 167
16. F, p. 168
17. T, p. 168
18. F, pp. 169-170
19. T, p. 170
20. T, p. 171

Multiple Choice

1. d, p. 151
2. b, pp. 152-153
3. d, p. 156
4. c, pp. 157-158
5. c, p. 158
6. d, pp. 158-159
7. a, p. 160
8. c, p. 161
9. d, pp. 161-162
10. b, p. 163
11. a, p. 165
12. b, pp. 165-166
13. c, pp. 166-167
14. c, p. 167
15. a, p. 168
16. a, p. 168
17. a, p. 170
18. b, p. 170
19. d, p. 171
20. c, p. 171

Definitions

1. d
2. m
3. r
4. ee
5. k
6. a
7. c
8. y
9. dd
10. t
11. s
12. f
13. aa
14. n
15. p

Discussion Questions

1. pp. 153-154
2. pp. 175-176
3. pp. 158-159
4. pp. 152-161
5. pp. 163-170
6. p. 168
7. p. 171

7

Organizational Consumers

CHAPTER OBJECTIVES

1. To examine the characteristics of organizational consumers and show how they differ from final consumers
2. To describe the different types of organizational consumers and their buying objectives, buying structure, use of purchase, and purchase constraints
3. To explain the organizational consumer's decision process
4. To consider the marketing implications of organizational buyer types, characteristics, and behavior

CHAPTER OVERVIEW

An organizational consumer is a formal entity that purchases products or services for further production, for use in operating the entity, or for resale to other consumers. Organizational consumers seek supplier reliability and consistency and specific product attributes. They are influenced by derived demand and utilize formal purchasing departments. They are geographically concentrated, expect sellers to visit them, use joint decision making, make large purchases, require personal selling, and look for favorable purchase terms.

Organizational consumers may be classified by area of specialization, size and resources, location, and products and services purchased. The major organizational consumers are manufacturers, wholesalers, retailers, government, and nonprofit. The SIC system provides much information on nongovernment consumers.

Organizational consumers can be characterized by buying objectives, buying structure, use of the purchase, and constraints. Their decision process includes buyer expectations, buying process, conflict resolution, and situational factors. Of prime importance is whether the organization uses joint decision making and, if it does, how. Some form of bidding, open or closed, is frequently employed with organizational consumers (most often with the government).

When conflicts arise under joint decision making, problem solving, persuasion, bargaining, or politicking is implemented to arrive at a purchase decision. Situational factors can intervene between decision making and a purchase. These factors include strikes, economic conditions, and organizational changes.

New task, modified rebuy, and straight rebuy are the different purchase situations facing organizational consumers. Organizational consumers and final consumers have many similarities and differences. It is important for marketers to understand and adapt to them. Dual marketing campaigns are necessary for manufacturers and wholesalers who sell to intermediate buyers and have their products resold to final consumers.

Purchasing agents and buyers have personal goals, such as status, promotion, and bonuses, which have a large impact on their decision making.

KEY TERMS AND CONCEPTS

Industrial marketing	Occurs when a firm deals with organizational consumers.
Product specifications	The minimum specifications set by organizational consumers. They deal with engineering and architectural guidelines, purity and grade standards, horsepower, voltage, type of construction, and materials employed in construction.
Multiple-buying responsibility	Two or more employees participating in joint decision making for complex or expensive purchases of organizational consumers.
Value analysis	A comparison of the benefits of different materials, components, and manufacturing processes in order to improve products, lower costs, or both.
Vendor analysis	The rating of specific suppliers in terms of quality (such as the per cent of defective merchandise), service (such as delivery speed and reliability), and price (such as credit and transportation terms).
Competitive bidding	Sellers asked to independently submit price bids for specific products, projects, and/or services.
Negotiation	Situation in which the buyer uses bargaining ability and order size to influence prices.
Derived demand	Bases organizational consumers' purchases on the demand of final consumers. Manufacturers must be aware that they are selling through wholesalers and retailers and not to them.
Accelerator principle	Final consumer demand affects several types of organizational consumers.
Buying specialists	Employees of organizational consumers who have technical backgrounds and are trained in supplier analysis and negotiation.

Systems selling	A combination of goods and services sold by a single source. This enables the buyer to have single-source accountability, one firm with which to negotiate, and assurance of the compatibility of various parts and components.
Reciprocity	A procedure by which organizational consumers select suppliers, who agree to purchase goods and services as well as sell them.
Standard Industrial Classification (SIC)	A coding system compiled by the U.S. Office of Management and Budget for which much data has been assembled. Manufacturers, wholesalers, and retailers are assigned SIC codes.
End-use analysis	A process by which a seller determines the proportion of its sales that are made to organizational consumers in different industries.
Manufacturer	A firm that produces for resale to other consumers.
Wholesaler	Buys or handles merchandise and its resale to retailers, organizational users, and/or other wholesalers but not the sale of significant volume to final consumers.
Retailer	An organization or individual that handles merchandise and services for sale to the ultimate (final) consumer.
Government	Uses products and services in the performance of its duties and responsibilities. There are 1 federal, 50 state, and 80,000 local government groups.
Nonprofit institution	Involved with nonprofit marketing.
Organizational buying objectives	Include the availability of items, reliability of sellers, consistency of quality, delivery, and price.
Buying structure of an organization	Refers to the level of formality and specialization used in the purchase process. It depends on an organization's size, resources, diversity, and level of specialization.
Organizational consumer's decision process	Consists of expectations, the buying process, conflict resolution, and situational factors.
Organizational consumer expectations	The perceived potential of alternative suppliers and brands to satisfy a number of explicit and implicit objectives.
Product-specific buying factors	Product-based variables which lead to either autonomous (independent) or joint decision making by organizational consumers. These variables include the degree of perceived risk, routineness of decision, and degree of time pressure.
Company-specific buying factors	Company-based variables which lead to either autonomous (independent) or joint decision making by organizational consumers. These variables include the degree of technology or production orientation, company size, and degree of centralization.
Conflict resolution	Procedure in organizational buying for resolving disagreements in joint-decision-making situations.

	The alternatives are problem solving, persuasion, bargaining, and politicking.
Situational factors	Those that can interrupt the organizational consumer's decision process and the actual selection of a supplier or brand. They can include strikes, machine breakdowns, organizational changes, and so on.
New task purchase process	A large amount of decision making undertaken by organizational consumers in the purchase of expensive products that have not been bought before.
Modified rebuy purchase process	A moderate amount of decision making undertaken by organizational consumers in the purchase of medium-priced products that have been bought infrequently before.
Straight rebuy purchase process	Routine reordering by organizational consumers for the purchase of inexpensive items bought on a regular basis.

TRUE/FALSE

Circle the appropriate letter.

T   F   1. Organizational consumers more often rely on product specifications in purchase decisions than final consumers who buy on the basis of description, style, and color.

T   F   2. Final consumers use multiple-buying responsibility more frequently and more formally than organizational consumers do.

T   F   3. Final consumers are more involved with leasing than organizational consumers are.

T   F   4. The demand of organizational consumers tends to be more volatile than that of final consumers.

T   F   5. Distribution channels for final consumers tend to be shorter than for organizational consumers.

T   F   6. For organizational consumers, including government, the *Standard Industrial Classification* is used to derive information.

T   F   7. Value analysis showing which sales are made to organizational consumers in different industries uses SIC data.

T   F   8. Industry groups differ by geographic area.

T   F   9. For new sellers, or those with new products, gaining wholesalers' cooperation may be difficult.

T   F   10. Private-label manufacturers may make products under a retailer's name.

T   F   11. Most government purchases are for specially made products rather than more standard products offered to traditional customers.

T   F   12. Manufacturer-consumers consider the further saleability of items as the highest priority.

T F 13. Retailer-consumers are usually unconcerned about exclusivity for the products they sell.

T F 14. Nonprofit consumers place most emphasis on price, availability, reliability, and consistency.

T F 15. Retailers have perceptions that suppliers oversell without regard to production and delivery capability.

T F 16. Product-specific factors leading to autonomous decision making are technology orientation, small size, and high centralization.

T F 17. Bids for government purchases are usually open, in the interest of fairness.

T F 18. The least desirable method of conflict resolution is persuasion, where each team member presents his or her own reasons why a particular brand or supplier should be selected.

T F 19. A straight rebuy purchase uses limited decision making, not reordering.

T F 20. Marketers need one set of marketing plans for the intermediate buyer and another for the final consumer.

COMPLETION

Fill in the missing word or words in the blanks provided.

[industrial marketing, organizational, multiple-buying, pp. 178-180]

1. Companies are said to be engaging in _____ _____ when they deal with _____ consumers. They often use _____ _____ responsibility for purchases, where two or more employees formally participate in decisions on complex and expensive products or services.

[Value analysis, vendor analysis, p. 180]

2. _____ _____ compares the benefits of different materials, components, and manufacturing processes in order to improve products, lower costs, or both while _____ _____ rates specific suppliers in terms of quality, service, and price.

[competitive bidding, negotiation, p. 181]

3. In _____ _____ , sellers are asked to submit independent price quotations for specific products, projects, and/or services; in _____ , the buyer uses bargaining ability and order size to set prices.

[derived, volatile, accelerator, pp. 182-183]

4. The nature of organizational consumer demand is _____ , and it tends to be more _____ than that of final consumers because of the _____ principle, in which final consumer demand affects several layers of organizational consumers.

[buying specialists, systems selling, reciprocity, p. 184]

5. In their purchases, many organizational consumers use _____ _____ , who have technical backgrounds and are trained in supplier analysis

and negotiations; organizational consumers also require special services such as _____ _____ , where a combination of goods and services is supplied by a single source, or _____ , a procedure by which organizational consumers select suppliers who agree to purchase goods and services as well as sell them.

[Standard Industrial Classification, end-use, p. 186]

6. For all but the government, the _____ _____ _____ , compiled by the U.S. Office of Management and Budget, can be used to derive information about organizational consumers and can be used in _____ _____ analysis so that a seller can determine the proportion of its sales made to organizational consumers in different industries.

[manufacturers, wholesalers, retailers, government, nonprofit institutions, p. 186]

7. Organizational consumers include _____ , firms that produce products for resale to other consumers; _____ , organizations that buy or handle merchandise and its resale; _____ , firms that handle merchandise and services for resale to the ultimate consumer; and _____ and _____ _____ , which also purchase products and services.

[availability, items, seller reliability, consistency, quality, delivery, price, p. 192]

8. Buying objectives for all types of organizational consumers consist of the _____ of _____ , securing an adequate supply; _____ _____ , involving the honesty and reputation of the firm making the sale; _____ of _____ , obtaining similar items on a continuous basis; _____ , minimizing or stabilizing the length of time between order placement and receipt of items; and _____ , concerning discounts and credits.

[saleability, exclusive buying arrangements, precise specifications, price, p. 192]

9. Because wholesaler-consumers consider further _____ of items of highest priority, where possible they seek _____ _____ _____ , which limits the number of wholesalers in each geographic area allowed to carry merchandise; government-consumers frequently require _____ _____ for products they purchase, and nonprofit consumers emphasize _____ .

[buying structure, purchasing department, buyers, General Services Administration, pp. 194-195]

10. The _____ _____ of large manufacturer-consumers consists of specialized purchasing agents; large wholesaler-consumers tend to have a single _____ _____ ; retailers have _____ for each specialized product category; and for government, the _____ _____ _____ is the federal office responsible for procurement.

[derived demand, budget, cash flow, p. 195]

11. For manufacturers, wholesalers, and retailers as consumers, _____ _____ is the major constraint on purchase behavior, whereas government is constrained by the _____ process and nonprofit institutions are constrained by _____ _____ .

[expectations, buying process, conflict resolution, situational, p. 196]

12. Four major components of the organizational consumer's decision process are _____ , _____ _____ , _____ _____ , and _____ factors.

[product-specific, company-specific, joint, p. 198]

13. In the buying process, _____ _____ factors and _____ _____ factors affect the type of organizational decision making that may be autonomous or _____ .

[problem solving, persuasion, bargaining, politicking, p. 198]

14. Four methods of conflict resolution are _____ _____ , _____ , _____ , and _____ .

[new task, modified rebuy, straight rebuy, p. 200]

15. Three types of purchase decisions are the _____ _____ , needed for an expensive product the firm has not bought before, involving a large amount of decision making; _____ _____ , used for medium-priced products the firm has bought infrequently, involving a moderate amount of decision making; and _____ _____ , used for inexpensive items bought regularly, involving reordering without decision making.

DEFINITIONS

Match the terms and concepts with the appropriate definitions. Each term or concept may only be used once; there are more terms and concepts than definitions.

Column A	*Column B*
a. accelerator principle	___ 1. An organization or individual which handles merchandise and services for sale to the ultimate (final) consumer.
b. buying specialists	
c. buying structure of an organization	___ 2. Situation in which the buyer uses bargaining ability and order size to influence prices.
d. competitive bidding	___ 3. Routine reordering by organizational consumers for the purchase of inexpensive items bought on a regular basis.
e. conflict resolution	
f. derived demand	___ 4. Employees of organizational consumers who have technical backgrounds and are trained in supplier analysis and negotiation.
g. end-use analysis	
h. government	___ 5. Occurs when a firm deals with organizational consumers.
i. industrial marketing	
j. manufacturer	___ 6. A comparison of the benefits of different materials, components, and manufacturing processes in order to improve products, lower costs, or both.
k. modified rebuy purchase process	
l. multiple-buying responsibility	___ 7. A procedure by which organizational consumers select suppliers who agree to purchase goods and services as well as sell them.
m. negotiation	
n. new task purchase	

o. nonprofit institutions

p. organizational buying objectives

q. organizational consumer's decision process

r. product-specific buying factors

s. product specifications

t. reciprocity

u. retailer

v. situational factors

w. Standard Industrial Classification (SIC)

x. straight rebuy purchase

y. systems selling

z. value analysis

aa. vendor analysis

bb. wholesaler

—— 8. A firm that produces for resale to other consumers.

—— 9. Final consumer demand affects several layers of organizational consumers.

—— 10. Bases organizational consumers' purchases on demand of final consumers.

—— 11. Refers to the level of formality and specialization used in the purchase process.

—— 12. A combination of goods and services sold by a single source, enabling the buyer to have single-source accountability, one firm with which to negotiate, and assurance of the compatibility of various parts and components.

—— 13. Two or more employees participating in joint decision making for complex or expensive purchases of organizational consumers.

—— 14. A process by which a seller determines the proportion of its sales that are made to organizational consumers in different industries.

—— 15. Buys or handles merchandise and its resale to retailers, organizational users, and/or others but not the sale of significant volume to final consumers.

MULTIPLE CHOICE

Place the letter of the answer you think best in the blank provided.

—— 1. Which of the following does *not* engage in industrial marketing?
a. Government
b. Nonprofit institutions
c. Manufacturers
d. Final consumers

—— 2. When organizational consumers compare the benefits of different materials, components, and manufacturing processes, they are engaging in
a. value analysis.
b. end-use analysis.
c. vendor analysis.
d. situational analysis.

—— 3. Derived demand tends to be
a. unrelated to the accelerator principle.
b. very volatile.
c. sensitive to price changes.
d. independent of final consumers.

4. Which of the following statements about organizational consumers is *false*?
    a. They are geographically concentrated.
    b. Their distribution channels tend to be longer than those of final consumers.
    c. They are fewer in number than final consumers.
    d. They may be able to produce goods and services for themselves.

5. Among the special services organizational consumers may require, the one that may be restricted by the Justice Department and the Federal Trade Commission is
    a. systems selling.
    b. reciprocity.
    c. extended warranties.
    d. free credit.

6. Information about which of the following is *not* likely to be found in the *Standard Industrial Classification?*
    a. Government
    b. Communication firms
    c. Sanitary services
    d. Financial institutions

7. A seller can determine the proportion of its sales made to organizational customers in different industries by using
    a. value analysis.
    b. end-use analysis.
    c. vendor analysis.
    d. cost-benefit analysis.

8. In selling to a manufacturer, it is important for the seller to know that
    a. industry groups differ by geographic area.
    b. store composition and atmosphere are critical concerns.
    c. most raw materials are purchased abroad.
    d. headquarters has little to do with purchasing decisions.

9. Most wholesale sales involve
    a. other wholesalers.
    b. foreign buyers.
    c. final consumers.
    d. industrial, commercial, or government users.

10. A major task for sellers in dealing with wholesalers is to
    a. get them to make products under the retailer's name.
    b. concentrate marketing efforts by geographic areas.
    c. place their items into the distribution system.
    d. sell to industrial, commercial, or government users.

11. Which of the following is *not* a seller concern in making sales to retailers?
    a. Legislative approval
    b. Floor space
    c. Private-label manufacturing
    d. Displays

_____ 12. When organizational buyers want to obtain similar items on a continuous basis, their buying objective may be termed
  a. availability of items.
  b. seller reliability.
  c. consistency of quality.
  d. delivery.

_____ 13. Exclusive buying arrangements are usually sought by
  a. manufacturer-consumers.
  b. wholesaler-consumers.
  c. the government.
  d. nonprofit institutions.

_____ 14. Buyers for each narrow product category are usually supervised by group managers and found among large
  a. manufacturer-consumers.
  b. wholesaler-consumers.
  c. governmental units.
  d. retailer-consumers.

_____ 15. The major constraint on the purchase behavior of wholesalers, manufacturers, and retailers is
  a. derived demand.
  b. profit margins.
  c. budget setting.
  d. cash flow.

_____ 16. Which of the following is *not* a component of the organizational consumer's decision process?
  a. Mergers among competing firms
  b. Conflict resolution
  c. Expectations
  d. Situational factors

_____ 17. Company-specific buying factors leading to autonomous decision making usually include
  a. low perceived risk.
  b. time pressures.
  c. routine products.
  d. technology orientation.

_____ 18. In government purchases,
  a. negotiation is most frequently used.
  b. open bidding is usually used.
  c. bargaining is preferred.
  d. closed bidding is customary.

_____ 19. Which of the following is *not* a method of resolving conflicts?
  a. Persuasion
  b. Projection
  c. Problem solving
  d. Politicking

_____   20. A modified rebuy purchase is needed when
   a. an expensive product is to be bought.
   b. the firm is reordering.
   c. items to be bought are inexpensive.
   d. the firm has bought the products infrequently.

DISCUSSION QUESTIONS

1. Which of the following techniques used by organizational consumers might be useful to final consumers: value analysis, vendor analysis, multiple-buying responsibility, competitive bidding? Why? Why not?

2. What is the accelerator principle and how does it affect organizational consumers?

3. If you were a supplier of steel to manufacturing companies, what kinds of information would you need to sell your product? Where would you go to get that information?

4. Describe the constraints on the purchases of manufacturers, wholesalers, retailers, and government and nonprofit institutions.

5. What are the psychological factors affecting organizational buyers and/or purchasing agents?

6. Why is conflict resolution necessary in purchase decisions? Compare and contrast the methods of resolution. Which of them is least desirable and why?

7. What types of purchase decisions do organizational buyers make? How do these compare to the types of decisions final consumers make?

EXERCISES

7-1.   Your supervisor has asked you, as the buyer responsible for cameras at a leading department store in Louisville, Kentucky, to rate three major camera vendors on a combination of quality, service, price, and product factors. The vendor analysis form to be used is shown in Figure 1.

Figure 1
Vendor Analysis Form,
Louisville Department Store

Vendor: _____   Department: _____ Cameras

Quality

1. Defect rate during seven-day customer return period
    ____ Excellent   ____ Good   ____ Poor

2. Defect rate during one-year warranty period
    ____ Excellent   ____ Good   ____ Poor

3. Overall value for money (quality per dollar) from consumer perspective
    ____ Excellent   ____ Good   ____ Poor

4. Overall product quality (reliability, durability, clarity)
    ____ Excellent   ____ Good   ____ Poor

Service

1. Salesperson training and motivation provided by vendor
    ____ Excellent   ____ Good   ____ Poor

2. Size of cooperative advertising allowance; providing retailers with point-of-purchase material
    ____ Excellent   ____ Good   ____ Poor

3. Providing rapid inventory replenishment when sales are very high
    ____ Excellent   ____ Good   ____ Poor

4. Quality of repair/adjustment service for store
    ____ Excellent   ____ Good   ____ Poor

5. Quality of repair/adjustment service for customer
    ____ Excellent   ____ Good   ____ Poor

Price

1. Gross profit margin on cameras and camera lines
    ____ Excellent   ____ Good   ____ Poor

2. Supplier restrictions on sales to price-cutting discount merchants
    ____ Excellent   ____ Good   ____ Poor

3. Attractiveness of price to consumers
    ____ Excellent   ____ Good   ____ Poor

4. Frequency of special deals, allowances, vendor-sponsored promotion
    ____ Excellent   ____ Good   ____ Poor

5. Prices compared to competitive suppliers
    ____ Excellent   ____ Good   ____ Poor

Figure 1 (continued)

Product

1. Image of product to consumers

 ____ Excellent ____ Good ____ Poor

2. Amount of sales assistance necessary to get customer to consider/purchase brand

 ____ Little ____ Moderate ____ Extensive

3. Compatibility of accessories (lenses, electronic flashes, lens caps) with other major brands

 ____ Excellent ____ Good ____ Poor

4. Differential advantage of product with respect to major competitors

 ____ Excellent ____ Good ____ Poor

5. Availability of accessories

 ____ Excellent ____ Good ____ Poor

Questions

1. Evaluate Figure 1. What important elements are missing from this vendor analysis form?

2. Under which specific conditions would you terminate dealing with a vendor? Explain.

3. As a full-service retailer, how would you respond to a camera wholesaler who also sold the same camera to discounters? The discounters are able to undercut your price by at least 20 per cent. Furthermore, many customers are learning about important camera product attributes in your store, but are buying this equipment elsewhere.

4. How would the form differ if the vendor is a high-fashion dress manufacturer?

7-2.　　　　Xerox embarked in 1984 on an aggressive systems selling program, called Team Xerox, in promotional and sales efforts. This program stresses the importance to customers of coordinating business machine purchases to develop a company-wide information-processing network. Xerox offers a wide variety of word processors, printers, typewriters, personal computers, and copiers, and servicing for all of its products. Its sales force sells to all types of business, government, and nonprofit organizations.

　　　　Through systems selling, the buyer gains single-source accountability, one firm with which to negotiate, and assurance that various parts and components are compatible. Xerox helps its clients determine their needs, satisfies these needs, and even provides financing, if necessary. The Xerox systems approach enables customers to get the right information to the right place at the right time.

　　　　The Sisters & Brothers (S&B) Company uses an entirely different marketing plan than Xerox. S&B, with annual sales of $2.5 million, manufactures, sells, and services word processors. Its sales force concentrates on small business accounts (firms with four or fewer typewriters). It does not sell to larger accounts nor offer any products besides word processors.

Questions

1.　　What are the advantages of systems selling to Xerox? The disadvantages?

2. Why might a company that is interested in buying three word processors, three personal computers, and one office copier buy the word processors from S&B?

3. What would be the most important organizational consumer buying objectives for information-processing equipment?

4. In general, what kinds of products are most suitable for systems selling? Least suitable?

7-3.   Substantial data regarding SIC classifications are available from the *Census of Business, Census of Manufactures, County Business Patterns, Dun & Bradstreet's Market Identifier, Sales & Marketing Management's Survey of Industrial and Commercial Buying Power, Standard & Poor's Register,* and *Dun & Bradstreet's Middle Market Directory.* Examine at least two of these publications and prepare an analysis of the food and kindred products industry (SIC Code 20) in your state or region.

7-4.   Clocks, insurance, and bookcases are items purchased by both final and organizational consumers. For each item, what would be the similarities and differences in the purchase process between final and organizational consumers?

ANSWERS

True/False

1. T, p. 180	11. F, p. 191
2. F, p. 180	12. F, p. 192
3. F, pp. 180-181	13. F, p. 192
4. T, pp. 183-184	14. T, p. 194
5. F, p. 184	15. T, p. 197
6. F, p. 186	16. F, p. 198
7. F, p. 186	17. F, p. 198
8. T, p. 187	18. F, pp. 198-199
9. T, p. 189	19. F, p. 200
10. T, p. 191	20. T, pp. 200-201

Multiple Choice

1. d, p. 178	11. a, pp. 190-191
2. a, p. 180	12. c, p. 192
3. b, pp. 182-184	13. b, p. 192
4. b, pp. 184-185	14. d, p. 195
5. b, p. 184	15. a, p. 195
6. a, p. 186	16. a, p. 196
7. b, 186	17. d, p. 198
8. a, p. 187	18. d, p. 198
9. d, p. 188	19. b, pp. 198-199
10. c, p. 189	20. d, p. 200

Definitions

1. u	9. a
2. m	10. f
3. x	11. c
4. b	12. y
5. i	13. l
6. z	14. g
7. t	15. bb
8. j	

Discussion Questions

1. pp. 180-181
2. pp. 183-184
3. pp. 186-188
4. p. 195
5. pp. 197-198
6. pp. 198-199
7. pp. 200, 169-170

8

Developing a
Target Market

CHAPTER OBJECTIVES

1. To explain and contrast mass marketing, market segmentation, and multiple segmentation and to describe the factors to be considered in selecting a target market strategy
2. To present several applications of each method for developing a target market
3. To discuss the bases of segmentation, steps in planning a segmentation strategy, organizational consumer segments, requirements for successful segmentation, and the limitations of segmentation
4. To examine sales forecasting and its role in developing a target market

CHAPTER OVERVIEW

Mass marketing (appealing to many customers through one basic marketing plan), market segmentation (appealing to one, well-defined consumer group through one marketing program), and multiple segmentation (appealing to two or more well-defined consumer groups through different marketing plans) are the alternative methods by which a firm can develop a target market. In choosing a method, the company must examine its resources and abilities, objectives, competition, consumer characteristics and needs, channel requirements, profits, and image. In recent years, pure mass marketing has declined, whereas market and multiple segmentation have grown.

When segmenting, a company must be careful to understand the majority fallacy: selecting the largest consumer segment, which also has the greatest number of competitors and brands. Untapped smaller segments may offer greater potential.

Segmentation can be used on one or a combination of geographic demographics, personal demographics, social factors, and psychological factors. The heavy-half theory, benefit segmentation, and the VALS classification are useful ways of defining market groups.

Six steps are necessary to create a segmentation strategy: determining consumer characteristics and needs, analyzing consumer similarities and differences, developing consumer group profiles, selecting consumer segment(s), positioning the company's offering in relation to competition, and establishing the marketing plan. Organizational consumer segments deserve separate analysis and planning by firms, even though the procedure for developing a target market is similar to that for final consumers. Successful segmentation planning requires large enough segments, differences among segments, similarities within segments, measurable consumer traits and needs, and efficiency in reaching segments.

Marketers should forecast short-run (one-year) and long-run (five-year) sales in conjunction with the development of target markets. This will enable them to pinpoint growth, compute budgets, allocate resources, measure success, analyze productivity, monitor the external environment and competition, and adjust marketing plans. A sales forecast describes the expected company sales of a specific product or service to a specific consumer group over a specific time period under a well-defined marketing program.

The company can obtain the data needed for sales forecasting from the government, industry trade associations, general publications, present and future customers, executives, experts, sales personnel, and internal records. A number of simple and complex methods are available for sales forecasting. These include simple trend analysis, market share analysis, jury of executive and expert opinion, sales force surveys, consumer surveys, chain-ratio method, market buildup method, and detailed statistical analyses. The best results are obtained when several methods and forecasts are combined.

The sales forecast should take into account the level of newness of the firm's offering, sales penetration, diminishing returns, and the changing nature of many variables.

KEY TERMS AND CONCEPTS

Mass marketing	An appeal to a broad range of consumers by utilizing a single basic marketing program.
Market segmentation	An appeal to one well-defined consumer group through one marketing plan.
Multiple segmentation	An appeal to two or more well-defined consumer groups through different marketing plans.
Majority fallacy	Concept stating that companies sometimes fail when they go after the largest market segment because competition is intense. A potentially profitable market segment may be the one that is ignored by other firms.
Geographic demographics	The basic identifiable characteristics of individual people.
Heavy-half	A market segmentation concept stating that for a wide variety of products a small proportion of total consumers may account for a large percentage of a product or service's total sales.
Benefit segmentation	Uses the benefits people seek in consuming a given product as a means of segmenting markets.
VALS (Values and Life-Styles) Program	A classification system for segmenting consumers in terms of a broad range of demographic and life-style factors. The VALS program, developed by the Stanford Research Institute, divides American life-styles into nine major categories.

Segmentation strategy	Consists of determining consumer needs and characteristics, analyzing consumer similarities and differences, developing consumer group profiles, selecting consumer segment(s), positioning the offering, and establishing a marketing plan.
Sales forecast	Projects expected company sales for a specific product or service to a specific consumer group over a specific period of time under a well-defined marketing program.
Simple trend analysis	A method of sales forecasting by which the firm forecasts future sales on the basis of recent or current performance.
Market share analysis	A method of sales forecasting that is similar to simple trend analysis, except that the company bases its forecast on the assumption that its share of industry sales will remain constant.
Jury of executive or expert opinion	A sales forecasting method by which the management of a company or other well-informed persons meet, discuss the future, and set sales estimates based on experience and intuition.
Sales force surveys	A method of sales forecasting that enables sales personnel to pinpoint coming trends, strengths, and weaknesses in the company's offering, competitive strategies, customer resistance, and the traits of heavy users.
Consumer surveys	A method of sales forecasting that obtains information about purchase intentions, future expectations, rate of consumption, brand switching, time between purchases, and reasons for purchases.
Chain-ratio method	A sales forecasting technique in which the firm starts with general information and then computes a series of more specific market information. These combined data yield a sales forecast.
Market buildup method	A sales forecasting technique in which the firm gathers data from small, separate market segments and aggregates them.
Sales penetration	The degree to which a company achieves its sales potential: Sales penetration = Actual sales $\div$ Sales potential.
Diminishing returns	Reduced productivity possible if a firm attempts to attract nonconsumers when its market is relatively saturated. In some cases, the costs of attracting additional consumers may outweigh the revenues.

TRUE/FALSE

Circle the appropriate letter.

T   F   1. During the last several years, as competition has grown, mass marketing has become a more and more popular method for developing a target market.

T   F   2. With mass marketing, the firm pursues an intensive channel strategy.

T   F   3. A mass marketing approach helps a company ensure a consistent, well-known image.

T   F   4. A market segmentation strategy is normally a sales maximization approach.

T   F   5. The best opportunity for firms engaged in segmentation is usually to select the largest market segment possible.

T   F   6. Market segmentation enables firms with low resources to compete effectively with larger firms for a specialized market.

T   F   7. Multiple segmentation means that a firm must enter markets where competitors are strongest.

T   F   8. Firms should note that the majority fallacy can work in reverse.

T   F   9. Channel members usually find multiple segmentation to be highly desirable.

T   F   10. Mass marketing strategies emphasize and cater to geographic differences.

T   F   11. Unisex products and services are examples of segmentation by gender.

T   F   12. The term *heavy-half* describes a market segment accounting for a large proportion of a product's total sales.

T   F   13. Negative attitudes toward products and services can readily be changed by product improvements and an upgraded company image.

T   F   14. According to the VALS classification, belongers and emulators fit into the need-driven category.

T   F   15. In developing a segmentation strategy, it is important to establish an appropriate marketing plan first and then to develop consumer profiles.

T   F   16. Selling to organizational and selling to final consumers require entirely different marketing approaches.

T   F   17. In order for segmentation planning to be successful, consumer groups must be different, yet reachable.

T   F   18. Market share analysis is similar to simple trend analysis, except that the company bases its forecast on recent or current performance.

T   F   19. The opposite approach to the chain-ratio method of sales forecasting is the market buildup method.

T   F   20. A sales forecast for a product or service that is new to both the firm and the industry needs to rely on trend analysis, market share, and trade association data.

COMPLETION

Fill in the missing word or words in the blanks provided.

[mass marketing, market segmentation, multiple segmentation, p. 207]

1. In _____ _____ , a company seeks to appeal to a broad range of consumers by utilizing a single marketing program; in _____ _____ , a company seeks to appeal to a well-defined consumer group via one marketing plan; and in _____ _____ , a company seeks to appeal to two or more well-defined consumer groups via different marketing plans.

[intensive, pp. 207, 209]

2. With mass marketing, a firm pursues an _____ channel strategy, selling its offerings at all possible outlets.

[majority fallacy, competition, pp. 210-211]

3. The company selecting the largest segment may regret it because of the _____ _____ , which stipulates that companies sometimes fail when they go after the largest market segment because _____ is too intense.

[mass marketing, market segmentation, multiple segmentation, pp. 207-208, 210, 212-213]

4. Under _____ _____ , a company can ensure a consistent, well-known image; under _____ _____ , the company can generate a specialized image; but with _____ _____ the company's image may suffer if it sells products and services to different segments under separate brands and consumers find out about it.

[geographic demographics, personal demographics, pp. 214-215]

5. When market segments are based on transportation networks, climate, media availability, and population size and density, _____ _____ are being used; when market segments are developed according to age, gender, educational level, occupation, and race or nationality, _____ _____ are being used.

[heavy-half, p. 222]

6. The term _____ _____ was coined to explain the purchases of the market segment representing a large percentage of total sales of a product.

[benefit segments, pp. 223-224]

7. Among the psychological factors useful in developing market segments are consumer motives and reasons for purchases, which can be broken down into _____ _____ .

[VALS, pp. 225-226]

8. _____ is an extremely useful classification system for segmenting consumers in terms of a broad range of demographic and life-style factors.

[characteristics, needs, similarities, differences, profiles, segments, pp. 228-229]

9. The first four steps in planning a segmentation strategy involve determining consumers' _____ and _____ for a product or service; analysis of consumer _____ and _____ ; development of consumer group _____ ; and selection of consumer _____ .

[positioning, competition, marketing plan, promotion, p. 229]

10. The last two steps in planning a segmentation strategy are _____ the company's offering in relation to the _____ and establishing a _____ _____ involving decisions about product, price, distribution, and _____ .

[differences, similarities, measure, large, reachable, pp. 233-234]

11. For segmentation to be successful, there must be _____ among consumers or else mass marketing would be the preferred strategy; within each segment there must be enough consumer _____ to develop an appropriate marketing plan; the firm must be able to _____ consumer characteristics and needs in order to establish groups; consumer groups must provide segments that are _____ enough to generate sales and cover costs; and the members of a segment must be _____ is an efficient manner.

[industry, sales potential, sales forecast, p. 235]

12. In order to estimate company sales, a firm should first look at _____ forecasts; next _____ _____ outlines the upper sales limit for a firm; then a _____ _____ details a firm's realistic sales level.

[simple trend, market share, jury of executive or expert opinion, sales force surveys, consumer surveys, p. 236]

13. Less sophisticated methods of sales forecasting include _____ _____ analysis, basing estimates on recent or current performance; _____ _____ analysis, basing estimates on a constant share of industry sales; _____ _____ _____ _____ _____ _____ , basing estimates on the intuition or experience of well-informed people; _____ _____ _____ , based on estimates of the firm's selling staff; and _____ _____ , finding out about consumers' attitudes and purchase behavior.

[chain-ratio, market buildup, test marketing, statistical, pp. 236-237]

14. Among the more complex methods of sales forecasting are the _____ _____ technique, developing a series of specific market factors from general data; the _____ _____ method, aggregating data from small, separate market segments; _____ _____ , estimating total future sales from short-run, geographically limited sales; and _____ analyses, such as simulation, complex-trend analysis, regression, and correlation.

[sales penetration, diminishing returns, pp. 239-240]

15. A firm with a high _____ _____ level has achieved its sales potential and must realize that _____ _____ may occur if it attempts to convert the remaining nonconsumers of its products.

DEFINITIONS

Match the terms and concepts with the appropriate definitions. Each term or concept may only be used once; there are more terms and concepts than definitions.

Column A

a. benefit segmentation

b. chain-ratio method

c. consumer survey

d. diminishing returns

e. geographic demographics

f. heavy-half

g. jury of executive or expert opinion

h. majority fallacy

i. market buildup method

j. market segmentation

k. market share analysis

l. mass marketing

m. multiple segmentation

n. personal demographics

o. sales force survey

p. sales forecast

q. sales penetration

r. segmentation strategy

s. simple trend analysis

t. VALS

Column B

____ 1. An appeal to two or more well-defined consumer groups through different marketing plans.

____ 2. Reduced productivity possible if a firm attempts to attract nonconsumers when its market is relatively saturated.

____ 3. A method of sales forecasting by which a firm forecasts future sales on the basis of recent or current performance.

____ 4. Concept stating that companies sometimes fail when they go after the largest market segment because competition is intense.

____ 5. The degree to which a company achieves its sales potential.

____ 6. A market segmentation concept stating that for a wide variety of products, a small proportion of total consumers may account for a large percentage of a product or service's total sales.

____ 7. An appeal to a broad range of consumers by utilizing a single basic marketing program.

____ 8. A sales forecasting technique in which the firm gathers data from small, separate market segments and aggregates them.

____ 9. Uses what people seek in consuming a given product as a means of segmenting markets.

____ 10. An appeal to one well-defined consumer group through one marketing plan.

____ 11. A method of sales forecasting that is similar to simple trend analysis, except that the company bases its forecast on the assumption that its share of industry sales will remain constant.

____ 12. A classification system for segmenting consumers in terms of a broad range of demographic and life-style factors.

____ 13. The basic identifiable characteristics of individual people.

____ 14. A method of sales forecasting that obtains information about purchase intentions, future expectations, rate of consumption, brand switching, time between purchases, and reasons for purchases.

___ 15. A method of sales forecasting by which the management of a company or other well-informed persons meet, discuss the future, and set sales estimates based on experience and intuition.

MULTIPLE CHOICE

Place the letter of the answer you think best in the blank provided.

_____ 1. With mass marketing, a company
   a. finds that channel members are very easily pleased.
   b. pursues an intensive channel strategy.
   c. ensures that channel members achieve levels of exclusivity for their products.
   d. often sets selling prices for channel members.

_____ 2. For a firm with limited resources and abilities, the most promising method of developing a target market is
   a. benefit segmentation.
   b. mass marketing.
   c. multiple segmentation.
   d. market segmentation.

_____ 3. A company is most likely to avoid the majority fallacy if it pursues
   a. a large market segment.
   b. a previously ignored market segment.
   c. a market segmentation strategy with many competitors.
   d. a large advertising campaign.

_____ 4. A company typically maximizes per unit profits, but not total profits, by using
   a. benefit segmentation.
   b. mass marketing.
   c. multiple segmentation.
   d. market segmentation.

_____ 5. Multiple segmentation involves
   a. a firm's entry into markets where competitors are strongest.
   b. mass marketing.
   c. distinctive strategies aimed at two or more segments.
   d. appealing to consumer groups with similar desires and financial resources.

_____ 6. Under multiple segmentation, the company's image
   a. is kept consistent and well known.
   b. is unimportant.
   c. may be endangered if consumers learn that dissimilar brands are made by the same manufacturer.
   d. encourages brand loyalty.

_____ 7. Which of the following is *not* a geographic demographic?
   a. Population size and density
   b. Media availability
   c. Transportation networks
   d. Nationalities

_____ 8. Personal demographics include
   a. benefit segments.
   b. gender.
   c. usage experience.
   d. class consciousness.

_____ 9. The term *heavy-half* is used to explain
   a. usage rate.
   b. usage experience.
   c. brand loyalty.
   d. usage attitudes.

_____ 10. Which of the following statements about psychological factors is true?
   a. Introverted consumers are more systematic in their purchases than are extroverted consumers.
   b. Consumers with negative attitudes require repetitive and follow-up advertising.
   c. Inner-directed consumers regularly buy items with fancy labels and pay higher prices than other-directed consumers do.
   d. Nonpersuasible persons can be convinced to buy items by means of a strong sales pitch.

_____ 11. According to Haley's study of benefit segmentation in the toothpaste industry, the group that used toothpaste heavily, bought the brand on sale, and was male, comprised the
   a. sensory segment.
   b. sociable segment.
   c. worrier segment.
   d. independent segment.

_____ 12. According to the VALS classification of American life-styles, among the outer-directed types are the
   a. survivors.
   b. achievers.
   c. experiential.
   d. societally conscious.

_____ 13. The first step in the development of a segmentation strategy is
   a. positioning a company's offering in relation to the competition.
   b. determining consumer characteristics and needs for a product or service.
   c. analyzing consumer differences and similarities.
   d. developing consumer profiles.

14. In dealing with organizational consumers, a company should use
    a. the same marketing plan as it does for final consumers.
    b. the same procedure for segmenting organizational consumers it uses for final consumers.
    c. different criteria for segmentation than it does for final consumers.
    d. geographic demographics but not personal demographics.

15. Which of the following is *not* necessary for segmentation planning to be successful?
    a. There must be differences among consumers.
    b. Members of a segment must be reachable.
    c. There must be differences within each segment.
    d. The segments must be large enough to generate sales and cover costs.

16. The upper sales limit for a company is defined as
    a. market segmentation.
    b. sales potential.
    c. market program.
    d. sales forecast.

17. The method of sales forecasting most similar to simple trend analysis is
    a. sales-force surveys.
    b. market share analysis.
    c. test marketing.
    d. time-series analysis.

18. Experience and intuition guide sales forecasting by
    a. sales force surveys.
    b. consumer surveys.
    c. test marketing.
    d. juries of executives.

19. The opposite approach to the chain-ratio method of sales forecasting is
    a. a jury of executive or expert opinion.
    b. a sales-force survey.
    c. a consumer survey.
    d. market buildup.

20. Which of the following statements about sales penetration is true?
    a. A firm with a low level of sales penetration must realize that it is likely to face diminishing returns if it attempts to convert more nonconsumers.
    b. With a sales penetration of 60 per cent, a firm has little room for future growth.
    c. Actual sales divided by sales potential yields sales penetration.
    d. Sales penetration is another word for sales potential.

DISCUSSION QUESTIONS

1. How does a multiple segmentation approach to developing a target market combine the best attributes of mass marketing and market segmentation?

2. If you were to base your market segmentation approach on geographic demographics, what five characteristics might you consider? What segments might be drawn from those characteristics?

3. Describe how usage rates, usage experience, and brand loyalty can become bases for market segmentation. What kinds of advertising appeals could be directed toward the various segments?

4. In planning a segmentation strategy, what is involved in positioning a company's offerings? Can you give examples of the kinds of information and decisions needed based on what you know about the automobile industry or the toothpaste industry or the jeans industry?

5. Apply the criteria used in segmenting the final consumer market to the organizational consumer market. If these criteria are the same, why do the two markets require entirely different approaches?

6. Which methods of sales forecasting are most appropriate to a continuing product or service? To a product or service new to both industry and firm? Which forecast would be the most accurate? Why?

7. How is sales penetration calculated? Explain why a firm with a high sales penetration level may need to exercise caution when forecasting future sales.

EXERCISES

8-1.   Yankelovich, Skelly & White, a large marketing research and public opinion polling organization, recently conducted a major study for the American Meat Institute and the National Live Stock and Meat Board.[1] This study separates meat purchases into five basic segments:

1.   Meat Lovers—those who feel meat must be included in a main meal

2.   Creative Cooks—those who enjoy preparing meals. This group enjoys meat but also uses other main dishes

3.   Price Driven—those who favor meat, but whose purchase decisions are based on price

4.   Active Life-Styles—those who seek convenience and eat away from home most frequently; they have a low level of commitment to meat.

5.   Health-Oriented—those who avoid eating meat for health reasons

Among the other major study findings are:

• Traditional households with large families and a female whose role is a homemaker are heavy meat users.

• Families with working wives and single-person households eat less meat.

• The average frequency of consumption of fresh beef is 3.4 times every two weeks. Heavy fresh beef users (those serving it at least twice per week) tend to be affluent, lack concern over price, and have low health concerns. Eighty-two per cent of U.S. households serve fresh beef at least once every two weeks.

• Ground beef is the most widely-used type of fresh meat in the U.S., being consumed in 89 per cent of U.S. households in a two-week period. Heavy users (those serving it twice a week or more) tend to be downscale and have larger households.

• Heavy hot-dog users are "price-driven" consumers in lower-income brackets, including single-parent households. The chief deterrent to hot-dog consumption is concern about additives, preservatives, and salt.

_____

[1] Mary Ann Linsen, "Changing Meat Preferences: Health or Price Driven?" *Progressive Grocer* (February 1984), pp. 99-105 ff.

Questions

1. Develop a marketing mix for meat aimed at each of the five identified segments.

2. Beef consumption can be raised by attempting to increase the rate of consumption of heavy users or by expanding overall (total) consumption rates. How would marketing strategies based on each of these alternatives differ? What are the advantages to each strategy?

3. Apply benefit segmentation to hot dogs.

4. What important bases of segmentation were not analyzed in the Yankelovich study? Discuss their importance.

8-2.   A medium-sized beef manufacturer has asked you to prepare a sales forecast for the firm, using information from the Yankelovich, Skelly & White study described in Exercise 8-1 and the 1984 *Statistical Abstract of the United States* (see Table 1). Although the company has had a 4 per cent growth rate in unit sales over the past five years, it is not certain that this trend will continue in the future. It does believe that per-capita meat consumption will stabilize at 1982 levels.

Table 1
Meat Industry Data,
1960-1982 (Selected Years)

Year	Per Capita Consumption- Meats (lbs.)	Per Capita Consumption- Beef (lbs.)	Per Capita Consumption- Veal (lbs.)	Per Capita Consumption- Lamb & Mutton (lbs.)	Per Capita Consumption- Pork (except lard) (lbs.)	Annual Price Index- Meat (June 1977- 100)	Civilian Population (millions)	GNP (billions)	Disposable Personal Income (billions)
1960	173.7	85.0	6.1	4.8	77.7	-	178.1	505.6	$ 352.0
1965	175.6	99.5	5.2	3.7	67.2	-	193.5	691.1	$ 475.8
1970	192.2	113.5	2.9	3.2	72.6	-	204.0	992.7	$ 695.3
1975	180.3	118.8	4.1	2.0	55.4	-	215.5	1,549.2	$1,096.1
1978	182.6	117.9	2.9	1.6	60.3	126.2	220.5	2,163.9	$1,474.0
1979	177.8	105.5	2.0	1.5	68.8	160.0	223.0	2,417.8	$1,650.2
1980	180.2	103.4	1.8	1.5	73.5	139.4	225.6	2,631.7	$1,828.9
1981	177.8	104.3	1.9	1.6	69.9	142.4	227.6	2,954.1	$2,047.6
1982 (prelim)	170.8	104.4	2.0	1.7	62.7	141.6	229.9	3,073.0	$2,176.5

Source: *Statistical Abstract of the United States, 1984* (Washington, D.C.: U.S. Bureau of the Census, 1983).

Questions

1.   What technique would you use to develop an industry sales forecast for beef (based on total pounds), using the data in Table 1? Why?

2. What technique would you use to develop a company sales forecast for beef (based on total pounds), using the data in Table 1? Why?

3. How could the data from the Yankelovich, Skelly & White study be incorporated into your forecasts?

4. What additional information is needed to improve the accuracy of your company sales forecast?

8-3. Select a product and then develop a short questionnaire testing the validity of the heavy-half theory for this product. Interview twenty people and explain your results.

8-4.   Table 8-7 in the text identifies seven market segments for the office photocopier market. Note that Xerox is the only company producing copiers for each segment and that (with the exception of Canon) no Japanese firm currently markets copiers for above $10,000—market segments 6 and 7 are controlled by U.S. firms.

Questions

1.   What difficulties may firms such as Sharp, Panasonic, Xerox, Savin, and Canon face by virtue of their having products in three or more successive market segments?

2.   What are the advantages of having products in successive market segments?

3.   What other means for segmenting the office photocopier market exist besides speed, volume, and price range?

4.   Describe IBM's market segmentation strategy for photocopiers.

ANSWERS

True/False

1. F, p. 210	11. F, pp. 218-219
2. T, p. 209	12. T, p. 222
3. T, p. 209	13. F, p. 223
4. F, p. 210	14. F, pp. 225-226
5. F, pp. 210-211	15. F, pp. 228-229
6. T, p. 210	16. T, pp. 229-231
7. F, p. 212	17. T, p. 233
8. T, pp. 210-211	18. F, p. 236
9. T, p. 213	19. T, p. 237
10. F, pp. 213-214	20. F, p. 239

Multiple Choice

1. b, p. 209	11. d, pp. 223-224
2. d, p. 210	12. b, pp. 225-228
3. b, pp. 210-211	13. b, p. 229
4. d, p. 211	14. b, pp. 222-223
5. c, pp. 212-213	15. c, pp. 233-234
6. c, p. 214	16. b, p. 235
7. d, pp. 214-215	17. b, p. 236
8. b, pp. 218-221	18. d, p. 237
9. a, p. 222	19. d, p. 237
10. a, p. 223	20. c, pp. 239-240

Definitions

1. m	9. a
2. d	10. j
3. s	11. k
4. h	12. t
5. q	13. n
6. f	14. c
7. l	15. g
8. i	

Discussion Questions

1. pp. 212-214
2. pp. 214-218
3. pp. 221-223
4. pp. 229-232
5. pp. 232-233
6. p. 239
7. p. 239

Part Two Review Quiz

DEFINITIONS

Define the following terms and concepts in your own words and then check your answers with the Key Terms and Concepts sections of the Study Guide, Chapters 5-8.

Consolidated Metropolitan Statistical Area
life-style
brand loyalty
competitive bidding
modified rebuy purchase process
market segmentation
chain-ratio method

SEQUENCES

For each of the following questions, arrange the events in chronological order by writing the numbers in the blanks provided, indicating the first in each series by 1.

1. The Consumer's Decision Process
   _____ information search
   _____ purchase
   _____ stimulus
   _____ evaluation of alternatives
   _____ postpurchase behavior
   _____ problem awareness

2.   The Organizational Consumer's Decision Process
      _____ situational factors
      _____ expectations
      _____ conflict resolution
      _____ buying process

3.   The Development of a Segmentation Strategy
      _____ positioning the company's offering relative to competitors
      _____ analyzing consumer similarities and differences
      _____ determining the characteristics and needs of consumers for the product or service category of the company
      _____ establishing an appropriate marketing plan
      _____ selecting consumer segments
      _____ developing consumer group profiles

SENTENCES

In each sentence, circle the word or phrase that is most appropriate.

1.   The [low/high] annual rate of U.S. population growth indicates that companies should focus on [general/specific] marketing opportunities.

2.   The mobility of the U.S. population is quite [high/low].

3.   Although incomes will [rise/fall] between 1980 and 1990, the real growth rate will be relatively [high/low].

4.   A [greater/smaller] number and percentage of the total population are working than ever before.

5.   Unemployment has less impact on [one/two] -earner families.

6.   Urban Americans are spending significantly [more/less] time on family care, and leisure-time activities are [increasing/decreasing] substantially.

7.   An [inner/outer] -directed person does not value prestige items.

8.   Opinion leaders normally have an impact over a [wide/narrow] range of products.

9.   Unlike demographics, many social and psychological factors are [easy/difficult] to measure.

10.   [Limited/Routine] consumer decision making takes place when a consumer uses each of the steps in the purchase process but does not need to spend a great deal of time on any of them.

11. The demand of organizational consumers tends to be [more/less] volatile than that of final consumers.

12. Reciprocity tends to [increase/decrease] competition.

13. [Manufacturers/Wholesalers] produce products for resale to other consumers.

14. The buying structure of large retailer-consumers tends to be [extremely/moderately] specialized with buyers for [broad/narrow] product categories.

15. For an inexpensive item bought on a regular basis, organizational consumers use the [modified/straight] rebuy purchase process.

16. [Market/Multiple] segmentation appeals to two or more well-defined consumer groups by different marketing plans.

17. A company is most likely to find an underdeveloped market in a [growing/declining] area.

18. In comparison to an extroverted consumer, an introverted shopper will be [more/less] systematic in making purchases.

19. When segmenting the organizational consumer market, a company should apply criteria that are [the same as/different from] those used in the final consumer market.

20. Consumer surveys and simulation are especially helpful in determining a sales forecast for products that are [new/continuing] on an industrywide basis.

ANSWERS

Sequences

1. 3,5,1,4,6,2, pp. 163-164
2. 4,1,3,2, p. 196
3. 5,2,1,6,4,3, p. 229

Sentences

1. low, specific, p. 129
2. high, p. 132
3. rise, low, pp. 133-134
4. greater, p. 137
5. two, p. 143
6. less, increasing, p. 155
7. inner, pp. 157-158
8. narrow, p. 159
9. difficult, pp. 161-169
10. Limited, p. 170
11. more, p. 183
12. decrease, p. 184
13. Manufacturers, p. 186
14. extremely, narrow, p. 195
15. straight, p. 200
16. Multiple, pp. 207, 212-214
17. growing, p. 217
18. more, p. 223
19. the same as, pp. 232-233
20. new, p. 239

Part
Three

Product Planning

9

An Overview of Product Planning

CHAPTER OBJECTIVES

1. To define product planning and differentiate among tangible, extended, and generic products
2. To examine the various types of consumer and industrial products, product mixes, and product management organization forms from which a firm may select
3. To discuss product positioning and its usefulness for marketers
4. To study the different types of product life cycles that a firm may encounter and the stages of the traditional product life cycle (introduction, growth, maturity, and decline)

CHAPTER OVERVIEW

Product planning is systematic decision making pertaining to all aspects of the development and management of a firm's products. It allows the firm to pinpoint opportunities, develop marketing programs, coordinate a product mix, maintain successful products, reappraise faltering products, and delete undesirable products.

Products should be defined in a combination of ways. A tangible product is the basic physical entity, service, or idea, which has precise specifications and is offered under a given description or model number. An extended product includes not only tangible elements, but also the accompanying cluster of image and service features. A generic product focuses on the benefits a buyer desires.

Consumer products are goods or services for the final consumer. They can be classified as convenience (staples, impulse, emergency), shopping, and specialty items. These are products that are differentiated on the basis of consumer awareness of alternatives and their characteristics prior to the shopping trip and the degree of search and time spent shopping. Consumer services can be categorized as rented-goods, owned-goods, or nongoods services.

Industrial products are goods or services used in the production of other goods or services, in the operation of a business, or for resale. Industrial goods are divided into installations, accessory equipment, raw materials, component materials, fabricated parts, and supplies. They are differentiated on the basis of decision making, costs, rapidity of consumption, role in production, and change in form. Industrial services are maintenance/repair and business advisory.

A product item is a specific model, brand, or size of a product that the company sells. A product line is a group of closely related items sold by the firm. A product mix consists of all the different product lines a firm offers.

A firm may choose from among or combine several product management organizations: marketing-manager system, product (brand) manager, product-planning committee, new-product manager, system, and venture team.

Product positioning enables the firm to map its offerings in terms of consumer perceptions, consumer desires (ideal points), competition, its own products within the same line, and the changing environment.

The product life cycle is a concept that seeks to describe a product's sales, profits, customers, competitors, and marketing emphasis from its inception until its removal from the market. Many firms desire a balanced product portfolio, with products in various stages of the life cycle. There are several derivations of the product life cycle: traditional, boom or classic, fad, extended fad, seasonal or fashion, revival or nostalgia, and bust. The traditional life cycle goes through four stages: introduction, growth, maturity, and decline. During each stage, the marketing objective, industry sales, competition, industry profits, profit margins, customers, and marketing plan change. Although the life cycle is useful as a planning tool, it should not be employed as a forecasting tool.

KEY TERMS AND CONCEPTS

Product planning
The systematic decision making pertaining to all aspects of the development and management of a firm's products, including branding and packaging.

Product
A basic offering that is accompanied by a set of image features that seeks to satisfy consumers' needs.

Tangible product
The basic physical entity, service, or idea which has precise specifications and is offered under a given description or model number.

Extended product
Includes not only the tangible elements of a product, service, or idea, but also the accompanying cluster of image and service features.

Generic product
The broadest definition of a product, which centers on customer need fulfillment. It focuses on what a product means to the customer, not the seller.

Consumer product
A good or service destined for the ultimate consumer's personal, family, or household use.

Convenience good
An item purchased with a minimum of effort, where the buyer has knowledge of product characteristics prior to shopping. Types are staples, impulse, and emergency goods.

Staples
Low-priced convenience goods that are routinely purchased.

Impulse goods	Convenience goods that the consumer did not plan to buy on a specific trip to the store.
Emergency goods	Convenience goods which are purchased out of urgent need.
Shopping good	An item for which consumers lack sufficient information about product alternatives and their attributes prior to making a purchase decision. The two major kinds of shopping goods are attribute-based and price-based.
Attribute-based shopping goods	Products/services for which consumers seek information and then evaluate product features, warranty, performance, options, and other factors.
Price-based shopping goods	Products/services for which consumers judge product attributes to be similar and look around for the least expensive item/store.
Specialty good	An item for which consumers are brand loyal. They are fully aware of product attributes prior to making a purchase decision and are willing to make a significant purchase effort to acquire the brand desired.
Rented-goods service	Involves the leasing of a product for a specified time period.
Owned-goods service	Involves an alteration or repair of a product owned by the consumer.
Nongoods service	Provides personal service on the part of the seller. It does not involve a product.
Industrial product	A good or service purchased for use in the production of other goods or services, in the operation of a business, or for resale to other consumers.
Installation	An industrial good capital item used in the production process that does not become part of the final product.
Accessory equipment	Industrial capital items, which require a moderate amount of decision making, are less expensive than installations, last a number of years, and do not change in form or become part of the final product.
Raw material	An unprocessed primary industrial material from extractive and agricultural industries. Raw material is considered an expense rather than a capital item.
Component material	Semimanufactured industrial good that undergoes further changes in form. A component material is considered as an expense rather than a capital item.
Fabricated part	Used in industrial goods without further changes in form. A fabricated part is considered as an expense rather than a capital item.
Industrial supplies	Convenience goods that are necessary for the daily operation of the firm.

Industrial services	Include maintenance and repair, and business advisory services.
Maintenance and repair services	Those industrial services which include painting, machinery repair, and janitorial services.
Business advisory services	Industrial services that include management consulting, advertising agency services, accounting services, and legal services.
Product item	A specific model, brand, or size of a product that the company sells.
Product line	A group of closely related items.
Product mix	Consists of all the different product lines that a firm offers.
Width of product mix	The number of different product lines a company has.
Depth of product mix	The number of product items within each product line.
Consistency of product mix	The relationship among product lines in terms of their sharing a common end use, distribution outlets, consumer group(s), and price range.
Marketing-manager system	A product management organization format under which all the functional areas of marketing report to one manager. These areas include sales, advertising, sales promotion, and product planning.
Product (brand) manager system	A product management organization format under which a middle manager focuses on a single product or a small group of products. This manager handles new and existing products and is involved with everything from marketing research to package design to advertising.
Product-planning committee	A product management organization staffed by executives from functional areas including marketing, production, engineering, finance, and research and development. It handles product approval, evaluation, and development on a part-time basis.
New-product manager system	A product management organization form which utilizes a product manager for existing products and a new-product manager for new products. After a new product is introduced, it is managed by the product manager.
Venture team	A product management organization form in which a small, independent department, consisting of a broad range of specialists, manages a new product's entire development process from idea generation to market introduction. Team members work on a full-time basis and function as a separate unit within the company.
Product positioning	Enables the firm to map its offerings in terms of consumer perceptions and desires, competition, and other company products, and environmental changes.

Ideal point	A product positioning concept which represents the combination of attributes consumers would like to see a product possess.
Product life cycle	A concept that attempts to describe a product's sales, profits, customers, competitors, and marketing emphasis from its inception until it is removed from the market. It is divided into introduction, growth, maturity, and decline stages.
Balanced product portfolio	A strategy by which a firm maintains a combination of new, growing, and mature products.
Introduction stage of the product life cycle	Period during which only one firm has entered the market and competition is limited. A consumer market must be developed.
Growth stage of the product life cycle	Period during which industry sales expand rapidly as a few more firms enter a highly profitable market that has substantial potential.
Maturity stage of the product life cycle	Period during which industry sales stabilize as the market becomes saturated and many firms enter to capitalize on the still sizable demand.
Decline state of the product life cycle	Period during which industry sales decline and many firms leave the market because customers are fewer and they have less income to spend.
Self-fulfilling prophecy	A situation in which a company predicts that sales will decline and ensures this by removing marketing support.

TRUE/FALSE

Circle the appropriate letter.

T   F   1. A tangible product focuses on the benefits a buyer desires and is the broadest view of a product.

T   F   2. The concept of an extended product is consistent with the marketing concept that considers the consumer as having a problem-solving orientation.

T   F   3. The initial decision in product planning is the choice of the type(s) of products to offer.

T   F   4. The tangible nature of a good or service designates it as a consumer product.

T   F   5. Two major categories of convenience goods are attribute-based and price-based.

T   F   6. Specialty goods are those for which consumers are brand loyal.

T   F   7. The consumer-goods classification system cannot be applied to consumer services.

T   F   8. Accounting, legal, and tutoring services are examples of nongoods services.

T   F   9. The marketing characteristics of services differ significantly from those of goods.

T   F   10. Installations and accessory equipment become part of the final product.

T   F   11. Raw materials, component materials, and fabricated parts are considered capital items.

T   F   12. Industrial supplies are convenience goods necessary for the daily operation of the firm.

T   F   13. A deep product mix enables a firm to diversify its products, appeals to different consumer needs, and encourages one-stop shopping.

T   F   14. The marketing-manager system may be costly, lead to conflicts, and cause discontinuity when a product is introduced.

T   F   15. The product-manager system faces two problems: lack of authority and inadequate attention to new products.

T   F   16. It is important that competitive and company product positioning distinguish among brands.

T   F   17. Product forms generally exhibit the traditional product life cycle more faithfully than product classes or brands.

T   F   18. During the growth stage of the product's life cycle, competition is at its highest level and the average mass market makes its purchases.

T   F   19. The product life cycle has proven useful in forecasting.

T   F   20. When companies engage in self-fulfilling prophecies, whereby they predict that sales will decline, they usually tend to increase marketing support.

COMPLETION

Fill in the missing word or words in the blanks provided.

[product planning, p. 253]

1. Systematic decision making pertaining to all aspects of the development and management of a firm's products is called _____ _____ .

[tangible, extended, generic, pp. 253-254]

2. Three distinct ways in which a firm should define its products are the _____ product, based on the physical entity, service, or idea; the _____ product, which also includes image and service features; and the _____ product, focusing on the benefits a buyer desires.

[convenience, staples, impulse, emergency shopping, specialty, pp. 255-256]

3. Three categories of consumer goods are (1) _____ goods, purchased with a minimum of effort and divided into _____ , low-priced routinely purchased items; _____ goods, items consumers do not plan to buy on a specific shopping trip; and _____ goods, purchased because of

urgency of need; (2) _____ goods, where consumers lack sufficient information about product alternatives and attributes before making a purchase decision; and (3) _____ goods, for which consumers are brand loyal.

[rented, owned, non, p. 258]

4. Three broad categories of consumer services are _____ goods involving leasing, _____ goods involving alterations and repairs, and _____ goods providing personal services, not products.

[installations, accessory equipment, raw, component, fabricated parts, pp. 258-260]

5. Industrial goods include _____ and _____ _____ , capital items used in the production process; and _____ materials, _____ materials, and _____ _____ used in the production of final products and considered as expenses.

[maintenance, repair, business advisory, p. 261]

6. Two general types of industrial services are _____ and _____ and _____ _____ .

[width, lines, depth, items, line, consistency, lines, p. 261]

7. A product mix can be described by its _____ , based on the number of different product _____ ; _____ , based on the number of product _____ within each product _____ ; and _____ , based on the relationship among product _____ .

[marketing-manager, product (brand) manager, pp. 263-264]

8. Under a _____ _____ system, all functional areas of marketing report to one manager; with a _____ _____ system, there is a middle manager who focuses on a single product or a small group of products.

[product-planning, new-product, venture team, pp. 264-265]

9. Other product management forms of organization are a _____ _____ committee, which is staffed by executives from functional areas and which disbands once a product is introduced in the market; a _____ _____ manager system, which has separate managers for new and existing products; and a _____ _____ , which is a small, independent department consisting of a broad range of specialists who disband once a product is introduced.

[perceptions, ideal points, p. 267]

10. Consumer _____ are images consumers have of products, whereas consumer _____ _____ refer to the attributes consumers would like products to possess.

[Competitive product positioning, company product positioning, p. 267]

11. _____ _____ _____ shows perceptions consumers have of a firm relative to competitors and _____ _____ _____ shows how consumers regard the firm's different brands within the same product line and their relation to each other.

[product life cycle, balanced product portfolio, pp. 269-270]

12. The _____ _____ _____ is a concept that attempts to describe a product's sales, profits, customers, competitors, and marketing emphasis from its inception until it is removed from the market; some marketers may seek to attain a _____ _____ _____ , whereby a combination of new, growing, and mature products is maintained.

[boom, fad, seasonal, pp. 270-271]

13. In contrasting selected life-cycle patterns, the _____ curve describes an extremely popular product receiving steady sales over a long time period; the _____ curve represents a product with quick popularity and a sudden decline; and the _____ , or fashion, curve results when a product sells well during nonconsecutive time periods.

[introduction, growth, maturity, decline, pp. 271-273]

14. Four stages in the traditional product life cycle are _____ , _____ , _____ , and _____ .

[self-fulfilling prophecies, pp. 273-274]

15. When companies predict that sales will decline and then remove marketing support, ensuring that this will occur, they are engaging in _____ _____ _____ .

DEFINITIONS

Match the terms and concepts with the appropriate definitions. Each term or concept may only be used once; there are more terms and concepts than definitions.

Column A

a. accessory equipment

b. attribute-based shopping good

c. balanced product portfolio

d. business advisory services

e. component material

f. consistency of product mix

g. consumer product

h. convenience good

i. decline stage of the product life cycle

j. depth of product mix

k. emergency goods

l. extended product

m. fabricated part

n. generic product

Column B

____ 1. A basic offering that is accompanied by a set of image features that seeks to satisfy consumers' needs.

____ 2. Low-priced convenience goods that are routinely purchased.

____ 3. Provides personal service on the part of the seller.

____ 4. A product positioning concept which represents the combination of attributes consumers would like to see a product possess.

____ 5. A strategy by which a firm maintains a combination of new, growing, and mature products.

____ 6. Period during which industry sales expand rapidly as a few more firms enter a highly profitable market that has substantial potential.

____ 7. An industrial-goods capital item used in the production process that does not become part of the final product.

o. growth stage of the product life cycle

p. ideal point

q. impulse goods

r. industrial product

s. industrial services

t. industrial supplies

u. installation

v. introduction stage of the product life cycle

w. maintenance and repair services

x. marketing-manager system

y. maturity stage of the product life cycle

z. new-product manager system

aa. nongoods service

bb. owned-goods service

cc. price-based shopping good

dd. product

ee. product item

ff. product life cycle

gg. product line

hh. product (brand) manager system

ii. product mix

jj. product planning

kk. product-planning committee

ll. product positioning

mm. raw material

nn. rented-goods service

oo. self-fulfilling prophecy

pp. shopping good

qq. specialty good

rr. staples

ss. tangible product

tt. venture team

uu. width of product mix

____ 8. The relationship among product lines in terms of their sharing a common end use, distribution outlets, consumer group(s), and price range.

____ 9. Enables the firm to map its offerings in terms of consumer perceptions and desires, competition, other company products, and environmental changes.

____ 10. Convenience goods that the consumer did not plan to buy on a specific trip to the store

____ 11. The number of different product lines a company has.

____ 12. A group of closely related items.

____ 13. Semimanufactured industrial good that undergoes further changes in form.

____ 14. A product-management organization staffed by executives from functional areas including marketing, production, engineering, finance, and research and development.

____ 15. An item for which consumers lack sufficient information about product alternatives and their attributes prior to making a purchase decision.

MULTIPLE CHOICE

Place the letter of the answer you think best in the blank provided.

_____ 1. The broadest definition of a product is
 a. tangible.
 b. convenience.
 c. extended.
 d. generic.

_____ 2. One category of consumer products is
 a. fabricated parts.
 b. staples.
 c. component materials.
 d. accessory equipment.

_____ 3. Impulse goods are a type of
 a. shopping goods.
 b. convenience goods.
 c. specialty goods.
 d. staples.

_____ 4. The marketing emphasis for shopping goods is on maintaining
 a. self-service.
 b. distinctive product features.
 c. intensive distribution.
 d. convenient location.

_____ 5. Specialty goods are those
 a. purchased with a minimum of effort.
 b. for which consumers lack sufficient information about product alternatives.
 c. for which consumers are brand loyal.
 d. purchased because of urgency of need.

_____ 6. Which of the following is *not* a marketing characteristic of consumer services that differs significantly from those of consumer goods?
 a. Intangibility
 b. Inseparability of producer from offering
 c. Perishability
 d. Accessibility

_____ 7. The type of industrial good requiring the least amount of decision making is
 a. installations.
 b. accessory equipment.
 c. industrial supplies.
 d. fabricated parts.

_____ 8. The width of a product mix is based on the
 a. number of different product lines.
 b. number of product items in each product line.
 c. relationship among product lines.
 d. relationship among product items.

_____ 9. Where resource shortages may be a significant problem, a firm should avoid a/an
   a. wide product mix.
   b. deep product mix.
   c. inconsistent product mix.
   d. consistent product mix.

_____ 10. The organizational system used when there are many distinct brands is the
   a. marketing-manager system.
   b. venture team.
   c. product-manager system.
   d. product-planning committee.

_____ 11. The organizational system that has many advantages yet may prove most costly, lead to conflicts, and cause discontinuity when a product is introduced is the
   a. marketing-manager system.
   b. new-product manager system.
   c. product-manager system.
   d. brand-manager system.

_____ 12. Competitive product positioning refers to
   a. the impact of environmental changes.
   b. how a firm's different brands within the same product line are perceived.
   c. consumer perceptions of the firm and its rivals.
   d. attributes consumers would like products to possess.

_____ 13. Demand is greatest for ice cream positioned as
   a. super premium.
   b. regular.
   c. low calorie.
   d. economy.

_____ 14. To achieve a balanced product portfolio, firms should focus on
   a. product positioning.
   b. the product life cycle.
   c. planned obsolescence.
   d. product management organization.

_____ 15. When a product receives steady sales over a long period of time, its life-cycle curve is described as
   a. extended.
   b. seasonal.
   c. nostalgic.
   d. classic.

_____ 16. A seasonal product life-cycle curve results when a product
   a. sells well during nonconsecutive time periods.
   b. has quick popularity and a sudden decline.
   c. receives steady sales over a long time period.
   d. achieves new popularity, although it is seemingly obsolete.

_____ 17. During which stage of the product life cycle does an affluent mass market buy distinctive products from a limited group of firms?
  a. Introduction
  b. Growth
  c. Maturity
  d. Decline

_____ 18. During the decline stage of the product life cycle, it is least advisable for firms to
  a. reposition their product.
  b. terminate their product.
  c. expand their promotion of the product.
  d. cut back their marketing program for the product.

_____ 19. Which of the following is _not_ a reason why marketers are interested in the product life-cycle concept?
  a. Life cycles are shorter now than previously.
  b. New products require heavier investments.
  c. Marketers can consider the mix of products a firm will offer.
  d. Marketers can accurately forecast changes.

_____ 20. Which of the following statements about the product life-cycle concept is true?
  a. The stages of the life cycle do not vary by product.
  b. External factors have little impact on product performance.
  c. Companies can extend a product's life cycle.
  d. The four major stages of the life cycle are clearly distinct from each other.

DISCUSSION QUESTIONS

1. Distinguish among tangible, extended, and generic products and explain their importance to the product-planning process.

2. Compare and contrast the marketing emphasis for convenience goods, shopping goods, and specialty goods.

3. Which industrial goods require the most decision making and which the least? Why?

4. Describe the elements of a product mix. Which type of product mix offers the greatest opportunity for diversification? Which is most vulnerable to environmental threats? Why?

5. Which product-management organizational form would you recommend for a firm that markets many distinct products and brands, each requiring individual expertise and marketing decisions? Choose two other organizational forms and explain why they would prove less satisfactory than the form you chose.

6. Describe the way Hasbro, Hewlett-Packard, and Chrysler have positioned their products.

7. Why hasn't the product life cycle proven useful in forecasting?

EXERCISES

9-1.   Figure 1 (Figure 9-11 in the text) contains a product positioning map generated by Chrysler Corporation. In total, sixteen brands are portrayed, ten American
(Lincoln, Cadillac, Chrysler, Buick, Oldsmobile, Ford, Dodge, Plymouth, Pontiac,
and Chevrolet), four German (Mercedes, Porsche, BMW, and Volkswagen), and
two Japanese (Toyota and Datsun).

Figure 1
Product Positioning Map
Generated by Chrysler

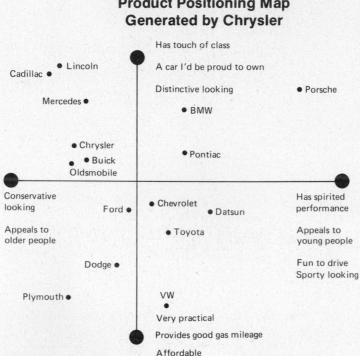

Source: John Koten, "Car Makers Use 'Image' Map as Tool to Position Products,"
Wall Street Journal (March 22, 1984), p. 33. Reprinted by permission of
Wall Street Journal, © Dow Jones & Company, 1984.

As noted in the text, after examining this map, Chrysler executives determined
that its car lines (Chrysler, Dodge, and Plymouth) needed to present younger images
and that Dodge and Plymouth needed to improve their rating for luxury ("a touch
of class").

Questions

1.   Describe the major market segments that are revealed in Figure 1.

2.   Evaluate Chrysler in terms of competitive product positioning.

3.   Evaluate Chrysler in terms of company product positioning.

4.   Where in Figure 4 should Chrysler seek to position its car lines? How should it try to accomplish this? What are the risks of that strategy?

9-2.　　　At one time, a toy had to sell well over a twenty-year period to be considered a classic. Now, because of the impact of television on new-product sales and because of shorter product life cycles, five years is often considered the industry criterion for a classic.[1] Three of the older toy classics flourishing in the 1980s are Erector sets (over 70 years old), Monopoly board games (over 50 years old), and Barbie dolls (over 25 years old).

　　　Often, it is difficult to anticipate what toys will become classics. For example, Slinky (a metal or plastic coil that can "walk" down stairs) was invented by a marine engineer in the early 1940s. Commented the president of the manufacturer of Slinky, "until our twenty-fifth year I thought Slinky was a novelty. Now I am convinced it is a staple." Etch-A-Sketch, introduced over 25 years ago, allows children to draw on a small screen by manipulating controls for horizontal and vertical lines. Said the president of Etch-A-Sketch's manufacturer, "Nobody goes to a store to buy an Etch-A-Sketch. It's the sort of thing that a mother sees when she is there, remembers she had fun with it, and buys one for her child."

---

[1] Paul B. Brown, "Staying Power," *Forbes* (May 26, 1984), pp. 186, 188.

Questions

1.　　Why is it difficult to anticipate which products will be classics?

2. Describe three toy classics that have been introduced since 1970. What has caused these toys to become classics?

3. The president of Etch-A-Sketch's manufacturer was asked if the product could survive for 25 years if it was introduced today. His response was, "I think Etch-A-Sketch would be an exciting product if we brought it out today, but my suspicion is that it might be blown out in five years." Comment on this reply.

4. How might the concept of self-fulfilling prophecy be a major cause of short product life cycles for toys?

9-3.　　　Explain how each of these products could be convenience goods for some consumers, shopping goods for others, and specialty goods for still others: telephone, magazine, used car.

9-4.   Identify the stage in the product life cycle for these products: eight-cylinder automobile engines, fountain pens, microwave ovens, smoke alarms, and video-cassette recorders. Be complete in your answer.

ANSWERS

True/False

1. F, p. 253	11. F, p. 260
2. F, pp. 253-254	12. T, p. 260
3. T, p. 255	13. F, p. 261
4. F, p. 255	14. F, p. 263
5. F, pp. 256-257	15. T, p. 264
6. T, p. 257	16. T, p. 267
7. F, p. 258	17. T, p. 270
8. T, p. 258	18. F, p. 272
9. T, p. 258	19. F, p. 273
10. F, p. 259	20. F, pp. 273-274

Multiple Choice

1. d, p. 254	11. b, p. 265
2. b, pp. 256-257	12. c, p. 267
3. b, p. 257	13. b, pp. 267-268
4. b, p. 257	14. b, p. 270
5. c, p. 257	15. d, pp. 270-271
6. d, p. 258	16. a, pp. 270-271
7. c, p. 260	17. b, p. 272
8. a, p. 261	18. c, pp. 272-273
9. d, p. 261	19. d, p. 273
10. c, p. 264	20. c, pp. 273-274

Definitions

1. dd	9. ll
2. rr	10. q
3. aa	11. uu
4. p	12. gg
5. c	13. e
6. o	14. kk
7. u	15. pp
8. f	

Discussion Questions

1. pp. 253-254
2. pp. 256-257
3. pp. 258-261
4. pp. 261-262
5. pp. 263-266
6. p. 268
7. pp. 273-274

10 Product Planning: From New Products to Product Deletion

CHAPTER OBJECTIVES

1. To examine the different types of new products available to a firm
2. To detail the importance of new products and determine why new products fail
3. To study the stages in the new-product planning process: idea generation, product screening, concept testing, business analysis, product development, test marketing, and commercialization
4. To analyze the growth and maturity of products, including the adoption process, the diffusion process, and extension strategies
5. To examine product deletion decisions and strategies

CHAPTER OVERVIEW

Management of the product life cycle deals with the creation and supervision of products over their life. A new product involves a modification or an innovation that the consumer perceives as substantive. A modification is an alteration in an existing product. A minor innovation is an item that has not been previously sold by the firm but has been sold by others. A major innovation is an item that is new to the firm and has not been sold by others.

Company objectives for introducing new products relate to sales, profits, less dependence on one product or product line, use of an established company distribution system, use of waste materials, and/or image.

When the company suffers a financial loss, a product is an absolute failure. When the company makes a profit but does not attain its objectives, a product is a relative failure. Failures occur because of a lack of a significant competitive advantage, poor planning, poor timing, and excessive enthusiasm by the product sponsor.

Proper new-product planning involves a comprehensive, seven-step process. During idea generation, new-product opportunities are sought and emphasis is placed on sources and methods. In product screening, unattractive ideas are weeded out by the use of a new-product screening checklist. At concept testing, the consumer reacts to the proposed idea and states a purchase intention. Business analysis requires a detailed evaluation of demand, costs, competition, investment, and profits. Product development converts an idea into a physical form and outlines a basic marketing strategy. Test marketing, a much-disputed technique, involves placing a product for sale in one or more selected areas and observing its performance under actual conditions. Commercialization is the sale of the product to the full target market. It should be noted that a new product can be aborted or modified at any point in the process.

The growth rate and level of a new product are highly dependent on the adoption process, which describes how a single consumer learns about and purchases a product, and the diffusion process, which describes how different members of the target market learn about and purchase a product. The adoption and diffusion processes are quicker for certain consumers, products, and marketing strategies.

Mature products provide companies with stable sales and profits and loyal consumers. They do not require the risks and costs of new products. There are several factors to consider and alternative strategies from which to choose when planning to sustain mature products. It may not be possible to retain these products if consumer needs disappear, new products make them obsolete, competitors exhibit too much strength, or the market becomes too saturated.

Product deletion is necessary for weak products. It may be difficult because of the interrelation of products, lost jobs, the impact on customers and channel members, and other factors. Product deletion should be conducted in a systematic manner.

KEY TERMS AND CONCEPTS

New product	A modification of an existing product or an innovation that the consumer perceives as meaningful.
Modification	A new product involving an alteration in a company's existing product. It can be a new model, style, color, product improvement, or new brand.
Minor innovation	A new product that has not been previously sold by the firm but has been sold by others.
Major innovation	A new product that has not been previously sold by the company or any other firm.
Absolute product failure	Occurs when a company is unable to regain its production and marketing costs. The firm incurs a financial loss.
Relative product failure	Occurs when the company is able to make a profit on an item but the product does not reach profit objectives and/or adversely affects image.
New-product planning process	Consists of seven basic steps: idea generation, product screening, concept testing, business analysis, product development, test marketing, and commercialization.
Idea generation	The stage in the new-product planning process which involves the continuous, systematic search for opportunities. It involves a delineation of the sources of new ideas and methods for generating them.

Product screening	Stage in the new-product planning process when poor, unsuitable, or otherwise unattractive ideas are weeded out from further consideration.
Patent	Awards exclusive selling rights for seventeen years to the inventor of a useful product or process.
Concept testing	Stage in the new-product planning process in which potential customers are asked to respond to a picture, written statement, or oral description of a new product, thus enabling the firm to determine attitudes prior to expensive, time-consuming prototype development.
Business analysis	The stage in the new-product planning process which projects demand, costs, competition, investment requirements, and profits for new products.
Product development	Converts a product idea into a physical form and identifies a basic marketing strategy.
Test marketing	The stage in the new-product planning process in which a product is placed for sale in one or more selected areas and its actual sales performance under the proposed marketing plan is observed.
Commercialization	The final stage in the new-product planning process. The firm introduces the product to its full target market. This corresponds to the introductory stage of the product life cycle.
Adoption process	The procedure an individual goes through when learning about and purchasing a new product. The adoption process consists of six stages: awareness, interest, evaluation, trial, adoption, and confirmation.
Diffusion process	Describes the manner in which different members of the target market often accept and purchase a product. The process spans the time from product introduction until market saturation.

TRUE/FALSE

Circle the appropriate letter.

T   **F**   1. Modifications are items that have not been previously sold by the firm but have been sold by others.

T   **F**   2. Vaseline is a product that was developed from waste materials of an existing product.

T   **F**   3. The failure rate of new products has declined over the past thirty years.

T   **F**   4. Relative product failure occurs when a company is unable to recoup its production and marketing costs.

T   **F**   5. The first step in new-product planning is product screening.

T F 6. Antifreeze, Teflon, and synthetic fibers evolved from laboratory-oriented sources of new product ideas.

T F 7. It is a wise policy to criticize foolish ideas during brainstorming sessions.

T F 8. During the idea-generation stage, the potential for product patentability must be determined.

T F 9. Concept testing is a quick and inexpensive tool for measuring consumer enthusiasm.

T F 10. Business analysis is much less time-consuming and detailed than product screening.

T F 11. Product construction decisions include promotion, storage, and trademark protection.

T F 12. Test marketing surveys consumer intentions toward a new product.

T F 13. Test marketing should be long enough to show sales after initial enthusiasm has worn off.

T F 14. Many firms now question the effectiveness of test marketing and downplay or skip this stage in the new-product planning process.

T F 15. Commercialization corresponds to the introductory stage of the product life cycle.

T F 16. The rate of product adoption will be slower if the product is a modification of an existing idea.

T F 17. In the diffusion process, a market segmenter might do well to concentrate on a line of products for laggards.

T F 18. More and more firms are placing their marketing emphasis on mature products.

T F 19. All mature products can be revitalized or extended.

T F 20. When a product shows poor current sales and profits, it should be quickly deleted.

COMPLETION

Fill in the missing word or words in the blanks provided.

[Modifications, minor innovations, major innovations, p. 282]

1. _____ are alterations in a company's existing products, whereas _____ _____ are items not previously sold by the firm that have been sold by others, and _____ _____ are items not previously sold by any company.

[Absolute product failure, relative product failure, p. 285]

2. _____ _____ _____ occurs when the company is unable to recoup its production and marketing costs; _____ _____ _____ occurs when the company is able to make a profit on an item but the product does not attain profit objectives and/or it adversely affects the firm's image.

[idea generation, commercialization, pp. 287-288]

3. The first step in the new-product planning process is _____ _____ ; the last is _____ .

[market-oriented, laboratory-oriented, p. 289]

4. Two sources of new product ideas are _____ _____ sources, which identify opportunities on the basis of consumer needs and wants, and _____ _____ sources, which identify opportunities on the basis of pure and applied research.

[new-product screening checklist, p. 289]

5. Many companies today use a _____ _____ _____ _____ for preliminary evaluation that allows product ideas to be measured against each other.

[patent, p. 290]

6. During the screening stage, firms look at the potential for obtaining a _____ on the product to gain exclusive selling rights for seventeen years.

[Concept testing, p. 292]

7. _____ _____ presents consumers with a proposed idea and measures purchase intention at an early stage of development.

[business-analysis, p. 292]

8. Demand projections, costs, competition, investment requirements, and profits constitute the _____ _____ phase of the new-product planning process.

[product-development, test marketing, pp. 292-293]

9. The _____ _____ stage converts a product idea into a physical form and identifies basic marketing strategy; _____ _____ involves placing a product for sale in a few selected areas to observe its performance.

[Commercialization, p. 296]

10. _____ involves implementation of a total marketing plan and mass production.

[awareness, interest, evaluation, trial, adoption, confirmation, p. 297]

11. The six stages of the adoption process are _____ , learning that a product exists; _____ , seeking information about it; _____ , deciding to try it; _____ , buying and testing it; _____ , using it regularly; and _____ , seeking reinforcement.

[innovators, adopters, majority, majority, laggards, p. 298]

12. The five stages of the diffusion process include _____ , the first consumers to accept the product; early _____ , the next group to accept a product; early _____ , the first part of the mass market to buy the product; late _____ , the second part of the mass market to purchase the product; and _____ , the last people to accept the product.

[mature, p. 299]

13. When products reach the latter two markets, they are in the _____ stage of the product life cycle.

[revitalized, extended, deleted, saturated, pp. 299-301]

14. Many products that are in this stage may be _____ or _____ , but others have to be _____ if consumers' needs disappear, better

products are developed, competitors secure a strategic advantage, or the market becomes _____ .

[replacement, notification, guarantees, p. 303] 15. When discontinuing a product, the firm must remember to consider _____ parts, _____ time for customers and channel members, and the honoring of _____ .

DEFINITIONS

Match the terms and concepts with the appropriate definitions. Each term or concept may only be used once; there are more terms and concepts than definitions.

Column A

a. absolute product failure

b. adoption process

c. business analysis

d. commercialization

e. concept testing

f. diffusion process

g. idea generation

h. major innovation

i. minor innovation

j. modification

k. new product

l. new-product planning process

m. patent

n. product development

o. product screening

p. relative product failure

q. test marketing

Column B

____ 1. A new product that has not been previously sold by the firm but has been sold by others.

____ 2. The final stage in the product planning process. The firm introduces the product to its full target market.

____ 3. Converts a product idea into a physical form and identifies a basic marketing strategy.

____ 4. The procedure an individual goes through when learning about and purchasing a new product.

____ 5. Occurs when a company is unable to regain its production and marketing costs.

____ 6. The stage in the new-product planning process which involves the continuous, systematic search for opportunities.

____ 7. A new product that has not been previously sold by the company or any other firm.

____ 8. The stage in the new-product planning process in which a product is placed for sale in one or more selected areas and its actual sales performance under the proposed marketing plan is observed.

____ 9. Stage in the new-product planning process in which potential customers are asked to respond to a picture, written statement, or oral description of a new product, thus enabling the firm to determine attitudes prior to expensive, time-consuming prototype development.

____ 10. Describes the manner in which different members of the target market often accept and purchase a product.

____ 11. The stage in the new-product planning process which projects demand, costs, competition, investment requirements, and profits for new products.

—— 12. A modification of an existing product or an innovation that the consumer perceives as meaningful.

—— 13. Occurs when a company is able to make a profit on an item but the product does not reach profit objectives and/or adversely affects image.

—— 14. Stage in the new-product planning process when poor, unsuitable, or otherwise unattractive ideas are weeded out from further consideration.

—— 15. Awards exclusive selling rights for seventeen years to the inventor of a useful product or process.

MULTIPLE CHOICE

Place the letter of the answer you think best in the blank provided.

—— 1. Which of the following statements about the prerequisites for a successful new product is *not* true?
a. It must have desirable attributes.
b. It must be developed within the company.
c. It must be unique.
d. It must communicate its features to consumers.

—— 2. An example of a minor product innovation is
a. the first home computer.
b. Kodak's self-developing camera.
c. Searle's aspartame.
d. Vaseline Petroleum Jelly.

—— 3. The failure rate of new products today, as compared with thirty years ago, has
a. increased.
b. decreased.
c. remained high.
d. remained low.

—— 4. In 1981, introduction of the Boeing 767 jet plane was hurt by
a. poor timing.
b. excessive enthusiasm.
c. poor planning.
d. lack of differential advantage.

—— 5. Which of the following products evolved from market-oriented sources?
a. Antifreeze
b. Teflon
c. Filter cigarettes
d. Synthetic fibers

_____ 6. When compiling ideas for new product opportunities,
   a. the ideas presented should not be criticized.
   b. a small number of ideas should be generated.
   c. the ideas of different people should be kept separate.
   d. concepts that are too creative should not be offered.

_____ 7. The potential for product patentability is determined during the
   a. test-marketing stage.
   b. product-screening stage.
   c. product-development stage.
   d. commercialization stage.

_____ 8. Which of the following is the least expensive stage in new-product development?
   a. Test marketing
   b. Concept testing
   c. Product development
   d. Commercialization

_____ 9. During the concept-testing stage,
   a. unattractive ideas are eliminated.
   b. a product is sold in a limited area.
   c. consumer purchase intentions are measured.
   d. costs and demand are projected.

_____ 10. The product first acquires a physical form during the
   a. product-screening stage.
   b. test-marketing stage.
   c. commercialization stage.
   d. product-development stage.

_____ 11. Which of the following is *not* a type of decision usually taken during the product development stage?
   a. Product construction
   b. Packaging
   c. Product positioning
   d. Product screening

_____ 12. Test marketing
   a. observes actual consumer behavior.
   b. inquires about customer intentions.
   c. is the full-scale introduction of the product.
   d. should show sales just during the period of initial enthusiasm.

_____ 13. Which of the following is *not* a source of dissatisfaction with test marketing?
   a. Competitors gain information.
   b. Firms are unable to predict national results.
   c. There are time delays before introduction.
   d. Tests measure intentions rather than actions.

_____ 14. Which of the following factors is least important during the commercialization stage?
   a. Trademark protection
   b. Intensity of distribution
   c. Production capabilities
   d. Speed of consumer acceptance

_____ 15. The first step in the adoption process is
   a. interest.
   b. evaluation.
   c. awareness.
   d. trial.

_____ 16. The rate of adoption is higher if the product
   a. is a major innovation.
   b. can be consumed quickly.
   c. is highly important.
   d. can be associated with a change in life-style.

_____ 17. The manner in which different members of the target market accept and purchase a product is called the
   a. adoption process.
   b. commercialization stage.
   c. test-marketing stage.
   d. diffusion process.

_____ 18. In the diffusion process, the late majority can be characterized as
   a. price-conscious, conservative, and low in income and status.
   b. past middle age and skeptical.
   c. gregarious, attentive to information cues, and having social status.
   d. socially aggressive, cosmopolitan, and communicative.

_____ 19. More and more firms are devoting a greater amount of their marketing emphasis to
   a. mature products.
   b. new products.
   c. growing products.
   d. product deletion.

_____ 20. It is wise to delete a product when it
   a. involves large amounts of management time.
   b. complements other company offerings.
   c. attracts a small, loyal market.
   d. shows poor sales and profits in the short run.

DISCUSSION QUESTIONS

1. Why is it important for a firm to develop new products?

2. What advice would you offer a company seeking to generate ideas for new products? Why?

3. Why is business analysis crucial to product development?

4. What kinds of test-marketing decisions must a firm make? How much latitude does the firm have?

5. Analyze your decision to purchase a 35mm camera in terms of the adoption process.

6. Who buys mature products? What strategies should marketers of mature products use?

7. What factors should a firm consider before it decides to delete a product?

EXERCISES

10-1.   An independent inventor has developed a prototype of a new type of bed mattress and is interested in selling the rights to this product to a large manufacturer, Sleep Well Mattress Corp. The product is a comfortable, seven-inch thick, air-filled, mattress suitable for use in a van, for camping, or for an overnight guest in a home. The mattress folds compactly when not in use and can be easily stored in a closet or under a regular bed. The mattress can easily be inflated with a hair dryer and uses standard-size mattress covers and sheets. Only one other firm currently offers a similar product, introduced recently.

      The inventor claims, and the mattress manufacturer has substantiated, that the product can be sold at retail for $50 (twin size) and $60 (queen size). This would provide the manufacturer and retailers with high profit margins, and compensate the inventor via a royalty fee.

      Before signing a contract for the product, Sleep Well's president wants to resolve several concerns about it:

- Can the product be patented?
- Can the product be successfully distributed through Sleep Well's customary outlets (such as department stores, specialty mattress stores, and furniture stores)?
- What affect will the product have on Sleep Well's other products?

Sleep Well's overall new-product screening checklist is contained in Figure 1 (Figure 10-4 in the text).

Figure 1
Sleep Well Mattress Corporation
New-Product Screening Checklist

General Characteristics of New Product	Rating*
Profit potential	_____
Existing competition	_____
Potential competition	_____
Size of market	_____
Level of investment	_____
Patentability	_____
Level of risk	_____
Marketing Characteristics of New Product	
Fit with marketing capabilities	_____
Effect on existing products (brands)	_____
Appeal to current consumer markets	_____
Potential length of product life cycle	_____
Existence of differential advantage	_____
Impact on image	_____
Resistance to seasonal factors	_____
Production Characteristics of New Product	
Fit with production capabilities	_____
Length of time to commercialization	_____
Ease of product manufacture	_____
Availability of labor and material resources	_____
Ability to produce at competitive prices	_____

   * Each characteristic is rated on a 1-10 scale.
     1 = outstanding; 10 = very poor.

Questions

1. What are the advantages and disadvantages of Sleep Well's turning to an outside inventor?

2. Evaluate the three major concerns expressed by Sleep Well's president.

3. How would you weight the items in Figure 1? What sources would you use to acquire the information needed to complete Figure 1?

4. Under what circumstances should Sleep Well market the new mattress? Not market it?

10-2.   Although some consumer-goods manufacturers introduce new products without test marketing, others subject their new products to extensive testing. For the latter companies, the length of a test market involves a series of trade-offs. Too short a test market may provide too little data. For example, if a product is purchased once every three months, a two-month test market would not test repurchasing. On the other hand, too long a test market involves heavy advertising and marketing research expenses, and gives competitors a chance to copy the new product prior to its national introduction.

Not long ago, A. C. Nielsen studied more than one hundred new product introductions to determine the ideal test-market length. Figure 1 was developed by comparing a firm's market share in a test-market situation at several two-month intervals with the share of market after an eighteen-month test. As an example, after two months, data for only 13 per cent of the products in test market could provide reliable estimates of market share at the end of eighteen months; after six months, data for 55 per cent of the products in test market could provide accurate forecasts.[1]

Figure 1
Advance Forecasting of Final Test Results, All Tests

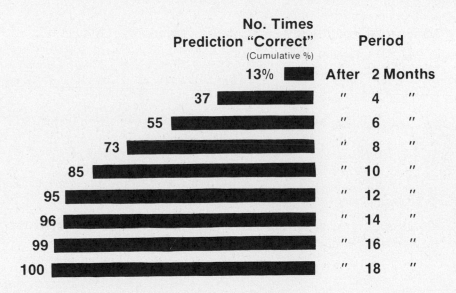

Source: "What Are the Odds in Test Marketing?" *The Nielsen Researcher* (Number 4, 1982), p. 21. Reprinted by permission.

_____

[1] "What Are the Odds in Test Marketing?" *The Nielsen Researcher* (Number 4, 1982), pp. 21-23.

Questions

1. What are the marketing implications of Figure 1?

2. Under what conditions would you conduct a two-month test market?

3. Under what conditions would you use a ten-month test market?

4. Describe several performance factors that could be measured via test marketing (in addition to market share).

10-3.   Develop a concept test for a new unisex perfume/cologne. Conduct your test with twenty university students. Explain your results.

Student's Name _____ **Class/Section** _____ **Instructor** _____

10-4. Outline five specific strategies for extending the mature stage of the product life cycle for dictionaries. Refer to Table 10-2 in the textbook.

ANSWERS

True/False

1. F, p. 282
2. T, p. 285
3. F, p. 285
4. F, p. 285
5. F, p. 287
6. T, p. 288
7. F, pp. 288-289
8. F, p. 289
9. T, p. 290
10. F, p. 292

11. F, p. 292
12. F, p. 293
13. T, p. 295
14. T, p. 296
15. T, p. 296
16. F, p. 297
17. T, p. 298
18. T, pp. 299-300
19. F, p. 300
20. F, p. 302

Multiple Choice

1. b, p. 282
2. b, p. 282
3. c, p. 283
4. a, p. 287
5. c, p. 288
6. a, pp. 288-289
7. b, p. 289
8. b, p. 290
9. c, pp. 290-292
10. d, p. 292

11. d, p. 292
12. a, p. 293
13. d, p. 293
14. a, pp. 296-297
15. c, p. 297
16. b, pp. 297-298
17. d, p. 298
18. b, p. 298
19. a, pp. 299-300
20. a, pp. 301-302

Definitions

1. i
2. d
3. n
4. b
5. a
6. g
7. h
8. q

9. e
10. f
11. c
12. k
13. p
14. o
15. m

Discussion Questions

1. pp. 283-285
2. pp. 287-289
3. p. 292
4. pp. 293-296
5. pp. 297-298
6. pp. 298-299
7. pp. 301-303

11

Branding and Packaging

CHAPTER OBJECTIVES

1. To define and distinguish among branding terms and to examine the importance of branding
2. To study the branding decisions a firm must consider regarding corporate symbols, branding philosophy, choice of brand names, and the use of trademarks
3. To define and distinguish among packaging terms and to examine the importance of packaging
4. To study the basic function of packaging, factors considered in packaging decisions, and criticisms of packaging

CHAPTER OVERVIEW

Branding is the procedure a firm follows in formulating its brand(s). A brand is a name, design, or symbol (or combination of these) that identifies a product or service. A brand name is a word, letter, or group of words or letters that can be spoken. A brand mark is a symbol, design, or distinctive coloring or lettering. A trade character is a personified brand mark. A trademark is a brand given legal protection.

Four decisions are necessary in branding. First, corporate symbols are determined and, if applicable, revised. The company name, logo, and trade characters set its overall image. Second, a branding philosophy is set, which includes the proper use of manufacturer, dealer, and/or generic brands as well as family or multiple branding. In addition, a mixed-brand strategy, the battle of the brands, and brand extension are assessed. Third, a brand name is chosen from one of several sources. A firm may license a name from another company. The consumer's brand decision process moves from nonrecognition to recognition to preference (dislike) to insistence (aversion). Fourth, the use of trademarks is evaluated and planned.

Packaging is the procedure a firm follows in formulating its package(s). A package consists of a product's physical container, label, and inserts. Packaging has six basic functions: containment and protection, usage, communication, market segmentation, channel cooperation, and new-product planning.

Packaging decisions involve image; family packaging; standardized packaging; package costs; packaging materials and innovativeness; package features; package size(s), color(s), and shape(s); the label and package inserts; multiple packaging; individual wrapping; package versatility; preprinted prices and inventory codes (such as UPC or OCR-A); reusable packages; and integration with the marketing plan. Packaging has been criticized on the basis of environmental, safety, and other issues.

KEY TERMS AND CONCEPTS

Brand
A name, design, or symbol (or combination of these) that identifies the products and services of a seller or group of sellers.

Brand name
A word, letter, or group of words or letters that can be spoken.

Brand mark
A symbol, design, or distinctive coloring or lettering.

Trade character
A brand mark that is personified.

Trademark
A brand name, brand mark, trade character, or combination thereof that is legally protected.

Corporate symbols
Firm's name, logo, and trade characters that play a significant role in the creation of overall company image.

Manufacturer (national) brand
An item that contains the name of the manufacturer. The major marketing focus on manufacturer brands is to attract and retain consumers who are loyal to a firm's offering and to control the marketing effort for the brands.

Dealer (private) brand
An item that contains the name of the wholesaler or retailer. Dealers secure exclusive rights for their brands and are responsible for their distribution.

Generic brand
An item that contains the name of the product itself and does not emphasize the manufacturer's or dealer's name.

Mixed-brand strategy
Occurs when a combination of manufacturer and dealer brands (and sometimes generic brands) are sold by manufacturers and retailers.

Battle of the brands
Manufacturer, dealer, and generic brands each attempting to increase their market share at the expense of the other. In particular, this is a battle between manufacturers and retailers.

Family (blanket) branding
A strategy in which one name is used for several products. It may be applied to manufacturer and dealer brands.

Brand extension
A strategy of applying an established brand name to new products.

Multiple (individual) branding	Separate brands used for each item or product category sold by the firm.
Licensing agreement	Permits a company to use another firm's trademark by paying a fee.
Brand decision process	Consists of nonrecognition, recognition, preference, and insistence stages that consumers pass through.
Package	Consists of a product's physical container, label, and inserts.
Packaging functions	Consist of containment and protection, usage, communication, market segmentation, channel cooperation, and new-product planning.
Universal Product Code (UPC)	Industrywide electronic system for coding information onto food and related merchandise. The UPC requires manufacturers to premark items with a series of thick and thin vertical lines; price and inventory data are contained but are not readable by employees and customers.
Optical Character Recognition (OCR-A)	Department store system for electronically coding information onto merchandise. OCR-A is readable by both machines and humans and can handle more information than the UPC.

TRUE/FALSE

Circle the appropriate letter.

T   F   1. Brand names, brand marks, and trade characters may have no legal protection against competitors.

T   F   2. In countries without brand names, both consumers and sellers suffer.

T   F   3. Corporate symbols play a minor role in the overall company image.

T   F   4. In contrast to manufacturer brands, dealer brands appeal to price-conscious consumers.

T   F   5. For most products, generic brands are of lower quality than are manufacturer or dealer brands.

T   F   6. Normally, a battle of the brands refers to a contest between competing manufacturers.

T   F   7. Family branding requires large promotional costs for new products.

T   F   8. Brand extension strategy promotes quick consumer acceptance of new products.

T   F   9. Multiple branding is particularly appropriate for specialized firms.

T   F   10. A surname by itself may be registered as a trademark.

T   F   11. The word *Teflon* is now considered generic and is therefore public property.

T   F   12. On the average, packaging costs 10 per cent of a product's retail price.

T   F   13. One of the functions of packaging is market segmentation.

T   F   14. Multiple packaging and larger sizes discourage increased product use.

T   F   15. A package can serve a promotional purpose after a purchase is made.

T   F   16. Many firms have been able to position existing products as new by changing their packages.

T   F   17. In the food industry, new and larger package sizes have recently captured high sales.

T   F   18. Multiple packaging can be used to get a consumer to try a new item.

T   F   19. Optical Character Recognition is slower to process than the Universal Product Code.

T   F   20. The consumer bears no responsibility for the negative results of packaging.

COMPLETION

Fill in the missing word or words in the blanks provided.

[brand name, brand mark, p. 310]
1. A _____ _____ is a word, letter, or group of words or letters that can be spoken; a _____ _____ is a symbol, design, or distinctive coloring or lettering.

[trade characters, trademarks, p. 310]
2. Ronald McDonald and Elsie the Cow are examples of _____ _____; Coca-Cola and MasterCard are examples of _____ .

[Trademarks, p. 310]
3. _____ provide their owners with exclusive brand privileges and allow them to prosecute those who use the brands without permission.

[Middle Ages, quality, quantity, p. 310]
4. Branding started in the _____ _____ to control the _____ and the _____ of products.

[corporate symbols, p. 312]
5. A firm's name, logo, and trade characters are considered _____ _____ .

[Manufacturer, dealer, generic, p. 314]
6. _____ brands are items containing the name of the producer; _____ brands are those containing the name of the wholesaler or retailer; and _____ brands are items containing the names of the products themselves.

[battle of the brands, mixed-brand, pp. 316-317]
7. Manufacturer, dealer, and generic brands frequently engage in a _____ _____ _____ _____ in which each attempts to obtain a greater share of the consumer's dollar; however, more and more manufacturers and retailers are using a _____ _____ strategy, selling a combination of manufacturer and dealer brands.

[family, brand-extension, p. 317]

8. Under _____ branding, one name is used for several products; a _____ _____ strategy applies this name to the new products the firm introduces.

[multiple branding, p. 317]

9. For firms that use a mixed-brand strategy, _____ _____ , separate brands for each item or product category, are necessary to secure control and secrecy.

[trademark, p. 321]

10. When brands become too popular, they run the risk of becoming public property; then a firm loses its _____ position.

[label, inserts, p. 328]

11. In packaging, a _____ contains the product's brand name, the company logo, and ingredients, and _____ comprise coupons, recipes, prizes, and instructions or safety information.

[containment, protection, usage, communication, market segmentation, channel cooperation, new-product planning, pp. 324-325]

12. Six main functions of packaging are _____ and _____ , to protect the product; _____ , to allow the product to be handled and restored; _____ , to promote the item; _____ _____ , to appeal to particular consumers; _____ _____ , to satisfy wholesaler and retailer needs; and in _____ _____ _____ , to serve as an innovation for the firm.

[standardized, p. 327]

13. An international or multinational firm may decide to use a _____ package to increase worldwide recognition.

[Universal Product Code, Optical Character Recognition, p. 329]

14. Two premarked inventory codes used in packaging are the _____ _____ _____ for the food industry and the _____ _____ _____ for department stores.

[Packaging, p. 330]

15. _____ has been criticized and regulated in recent years because of its impact on the environment and because of scarce resources, rising costs, and inadequate safety.

DEFINITIONS

Match the terms and concepts with the appropriate definitions. Each term or concept may only be used once; there are more terms and concepts than definitions.

Column A

a. battle of the brands

b. brand

c. brand decision process

d. brand extension

e. brand mark

Column B

____ 1. A strategy of applying an established brand name to new products.

____ 2. Department store system for electronically coding information onto merchandise.

____ 3. Firm's name, logo, and trade characters that play a significant role in the creation of an overall image.

f. brand name

g. corporate symbols

h. dealer brand

i. family branding

j. generic brand

k. licensing agreement

l. manufacturer brand

m. mixed-brand strategy

n. multiple branding

o. Optical Character Recognition

p. package

q. packaging functions

r. trade character

s. trademark

t. Universal Product Code

____ 4. A brand name, brand mark, trade character, or combination thereof that is legally protected.

____ 5. A symbol, design, or distinctive coloring or lettering.

____ 6. A strategy in which one name is used for several products.

____ 7. Consists of a product's physical container, label, and inserts.

____ 8. Separate brands used for each item or product category sold by the firm.

____ 9. An item that contains the name of the product itself and does not emphasize the manufacturer's or the dealer's name.

____ 10. A brand mark that is personified.

____ 11. Permits a company to use another firm's trademark by paying a fee.

____ 12. An item that contains the name of the wholesaler or retailer.

____ 13. Occurs when a combination of manufacturer and dealer brands (and sometimes generic brands) are sold by manufacturers and retailers.

____ 14. Manufacturer, dealer, and generic brands each attempting to increase their market share at the expense of the other.

____ 15. Consist of containment and protection, usage, communication, market segmentation, channel cooperation, and new-product planning.

MULTIPLE CHOICE

Place the letter of the answer you think best in the blank provided.

_____ 1. A brand name is defined as a
   a. brand mark that is personified.
   b. symbol or design that is distinctive.
   c. word or letters that can be spoken.
   d. corporate symbol that is legally protected.

_____ 2. The earliest and most aggressive promoters of brands in the United States were
   a. cereal companies.
   b. patent medicine manufacturers.
   c. soap producers.
   d. clothing makers.

_____   3. Which of the following is *not* a reason why the Exxon name developed?
  a. Its old name infringed on another firm's trademark.
  b. It had no clear corporate identity.
  c. Some of its brand names had unfortunate foreign connotations.
  d. It could not use the name Esso nationwide.

_____   4. Manufacturer brands appeal to those who
  a. accept some risk regarding quality.
  b. purchase for larger families.
  c. are loyal to specific stores.
  d. prefer convenience shopping.

_____   5. Generic brands started in
  a. the drug industry.
  b. the grocery business.
  c. motor oil production.
  d. small appliance manufacture.

_____   6. The major marketing goal of generics is to
  a. attract consumers loyal to a firm's offering.
  b. serve economy-minded consumers.
  c. control the marketing effort for brands.
  d. retain customers loyal to the store.

_____   7. In a mixed-brand strategy,
  a. there is no control over the brand bearing the seller's name.
  b. brand and store loyalty decline.
  c. channel-member competitiveness increases.
  d. two or more market segments can be reached.

_____   8. Which of the following is *not* an advantage of family branding?
  a. Uniformity of a company's image
  b. Lower promotion costs
  c. Ease of introduction of new products
  d. Maximization of multiple segmentation

_____   9. For firms that use a mixed-brand strategy, it is advisable to pursue a
  a. brand-extension strategy.
  b. generic brand strategy.
  c. multiple-branding strategy.
  d. family-branding strategy.

_____   10. With multiple branding,
  a. manufacturers secure less shelf space in a retail store.
  b. appeals to different market segments can be made.
  c. promotional costs are lower.
  d. new products benefit from an established identity.

_____   11. Under a licensing agreement, a firm
  a. gets a trademark from the government.
  b. carries generic products.
  c. pays fees to use a company's trademarked name.
  d. changes its corporate symbols.

_____ 12. During which phase of the consumer's brand decision process does the seller emphasize persuasion?
   a. Nonrecognition
   b. Recognition
   c. Preference
   d. Insistence

_____ 13. Under the Lanham Act of 1946, firms
   a. receive trademark protection.
   b. must list package ingredients.
   c. are responsible for package safety.
   d. can no longer engage in the battle of the brands.

_____ 14. An aspect of a product or its package can be registered as a trademark if
   a. the feature is functional.
   b. a surname is used.
   c. the brand describes a product category.
   d. it is nonfunctional.

_____ 15. The single-serving container illustrates the function of a package for purposes of
   a. market segmentation.
   b. channel cooperation.
   c. new-product planning.
   d. communication.

_____ 16. Campbell uses
   a. glass containers for soup.
   b. family packaging for soup.
   c. paper soup bottles.
   d. generic soup packaging.

_____ 17. To increase worldwide recognition, a firm is well advised to use
   a. family packaging.
   b. standardized packaging.
   c. multiple packaging.
   d. individual packaging.

_____ 18. Multiple packaging is known to
   a. increase consumption.
   b. lengthen shelf life.
   c. be quite costly.
   d. promote a lower quality image.

_____ 19. The Universal Product Code
   a. is readable by humans and by machines.
   b. is slower to process than OCR-A.
   c. requires prices to be marked on merchandise.
   d. can handle less information than OCR-A.

_____ 20. Lever Brothers' introduction of Sunlight dishwashing liquid was criticized
because of its
a. packaging.
b. trademark violations.
c. branding.
d. negative connotations abroad.

DISCUSSION QUESTIONS

1. Describe how brand names, brand marks, and trade characters can receive legal protection.

2. Why is branding important? Provide specific examples in your answer.

3. Why do some companies change their corporate symbols? Provide specific examples in your answer.

4. What is a branding philosophy? What kinds of strategy decisions should a company manufacturing high-quality athletic equipment make in outlining its own philosophy?

5. How may packaging affect market segmentation?

6. Why are the color and shape of a package important?

7. Enumerate some of the recent criticisms of packaging. What can consumers and manufacturers do to remedy these complaints?

EXERCISES

11-1.   In 1983, a record number (1,055) of U.S. firms changed their company names. Fifty-two per cent of the changes were the result of mergers and acquisitions; 25 per cent were due to straight name changes; 23 per cent were impelled by divestitures and other corporate reorganizations. The industries in which the greatest number of company name changes took place were financial institutions, 502; manufacturing and industrial firms, 127; and communication firms, 92 (many due to the breakup of AT&T).[1]

Sometimes, companies change their names for the wrong reasons. Explained Edwin Lefkowith, chief executive of a communications strategy consulting firm:

> A name change can be a symptom of other problems. The name may not be well known or well regarded, but the fault may be in how it is being used, not the name itself. Underfunding of promotions of the corporate name, lack of exposure, or not giving the public enough time to get used to the name are examples of situations where the problem appears to be with the name itself, when in fact the problem lies elsewhere.[2]

Table 1 contains ten pitfalls that Lefkowith recommends firms avoid when contemplating a name change.

Table 1
Pitfalls to Avoid When Considering a Company Name Change

1. Don't consider changing the name if it is really the company which needs rehabilitation. The corporation's faults must be corrected first.
2. Don't consider a change if higher visibility and recognition are the goals. The short-range result of a name change is zero awareness of the company.
3. Don't approach a name change lightly. There must be significant weaknesses in the existing name before this path is taken.
4. Don't be influenced by competitors' name changes. Each company faces unique circumstances and should relate its name requirements to its own objectives, not industry trends.
5. Don't undertake a change under a tight time deadline. The creative, evaluative, and planning processes suffer when rushed.
6. Don't approach a change with the goal of finding a name that will "ring your chimes." There is no perfect name, only the best available option.
7. Don't seize the first suggestion or limit yourself to a short list of options. Everyone involved should be advised of the need to generate a large group of names for consideration.
8. Don't become emotionally attached to a name before a legal evaluation has been made. A group of candidate names should be kept moving forward.
9. Don't think the job ends with the selection of a new name. Graphic presentations and a total plan of introducing and using the name must be prepared.
10. Don't try to do everything at once. The logistics and inventory of communications require careful planning to keep nonrecurring costs of new materials to a minimum. More importantly, the recognition level and reputation of the previous name must be transferred to the new name. A well conceived and sustained transition plan is crucial for success.

Source: "Some Corporate Name Changes Made for Wrong Reason," *Marketing News* (March 2, 1984), p. 17. Reprinted by permission of the American Marketing Association.

---

[1] "All-Time Record Is Set for Corporate Name Changes," *Marketing News* (March 2, 1984), p. 17.

[2] "Some Corporate Name Changes Made for Wrong Reason," *Marketing News* (March 2, 1984), p. 17.

Questions

1. Why do you think so many companies are changing their names?

2. Under what conditions should a company change its name? Retain its name? Refer to Table 1 in your answer.

3. Many companies are changing their names to initials (e.g., National Cash Register to NCR, Addressograph-Multigraph Corporation to AM International). Evaluate this approach.

4. What are the pros and cons of marketing products under the company name?

11-2.   In aseptic packaging, aluminum foil is sandwiched between paperboard and plastic laminates to create an airtight container. Aseptic "paper bottle" packaging has a number of significant advantages over traditional beverage cans and bottles:[1]

- One-liter aseptic containers are about half as costly as cans and cost only 30 per cent as much as bottles.
- Since aseptic beverages are subjected to a briefer heating period during sterilization than canned goods, their flavors are more natural.
- Aseptic containers do not require refrigerated shipment or storage by retailers or consumers.
- The 250 milliliter (8.4 oz.) box, which comes with a drinking straw, is especially suitable for lunch boxes.
- Milk can be placed in aseptic packaging and kept unrefrigerated for months. This makes milk appropriate for lunch boxes and for home emergency use.

Aseptic containers also have some disadvantages:

- The filling process is complicated, since both the container and its contents must be sterilized.
- Many marketers believe that consumers will not purchase or use milk which is months old and unrefrigerated.
- Currently, aseptic boxes cannot hold carbonated beverages (they lack the necessary rigidity).

---

[1] "'Paper Bottles' Are Coming on Strong," *Business Week* (January 16, 1984), pp. 56-57.

Questions

1.   Evaluate aseptic containers based upon the six basic packaging functions: containment and protection, usage, communication, market segmentation, channel cooperation, and new-product planning.

2. Many marketers use multiple-unit packaging for aseptic packages, combining three units, rather than sell individual units. What are the advantages and disadvantages of this strategy?

3. Explain how aseptic packaging can be used to extend a fruit juice's maturity stage of the product life cycle.

4. What will be the impact of aseptic packaging on vending machine operators? On soda manufacturers? Why?

11-3.   Develop a short questionnaire on manufacturer, dealer, and generic brands of canned vegetables. The questionnaire should cover product quality and value perceptions, and product uses (for family use, for guest use, and so on). Administer the questionnaire to twenty people at your local supermarket. What do you conclude from the results?

11-4.   You have been employed to develop a package for the Commercial Tape Division of Scotch® brand transparent tape. Outline your packaging decisions. Should the Consumer Tape Division use the same package? Why or why not?

ANSWERS

True/False

1. T, p. 310
2. T, p. 311
3. F, p. 312
4. T, pp. 315-316
5. T, p. 316
6. F, p. 317
7. F, p. 317
8. T, pp. 318-319
9. F, p. 318
10. F, p. 321
11. F, p. 321
12. T, p. 322
13. T, p. 326
14. F, p. 325
15. T, pp. 322, 324
16. T, p. 326
17. T, p. 328
18. T, p. 328
19. T, p. 329
20. F, p. 330

Multiple Choice

1. c, p. 310
2. b, p. 310
3. a, p. 313
4. d, p. 315
5. a, p. 316
6. b, p. 316
7. d, p. 317
8. d, p. 317
9. c, pp. 317-318
10. b, pp. 317-318
11. c, p. 319
12. b, p. 320
13. a, p. 321
14. d, p. 321
15. a, p. 326
16. b, p. 326
17. b, p. 327
18. a, p. 328
19. c, p. 329
20. a, p. 330

Definitions

1. d
2. o
3. g
4. s
5. e
6. i
7. p
8. n
9. j
10. r
11. k
12. h
13. m
14. a
15. q

Discussion Questions

1. pp. 310, 321-322
2. pp. 311-312
3. pp. 312-313
4. pp. 314-318
5. p. 326
6. pp. 326-327
7. p. 330

Part Three Review Quiz

DEFINITIONS

Define the following terms and concepts in your own words and then check your answers with the Key Terms and Concepts sections of the Study Guide, Chapters 9-11.

product
product positioning
maturity stage of the product life cycle
modification
commercialization
manufacturer brand
packaging

SEQUENCES

For each of the following questions, arrange the events in chronological order by writing the numbers in the blanks provided, indicating the first in each series by 1.

1. Stages in the Traditional Product Life Cycle
   _____ decline
   _____ introduction
   _____ growth
   _____ maturity

2. The New-Product Planning Process
   _____ test marketing
   _____ idea generation
   _____ concept testing
   _____ commercialization
   _____ product screening
   _____ product development
   _____ business analysis

3. The Consumer's Adoption Process
   _____ adoption
   _____ interest
   _____ confirmation
   _____ trial
   _____ awareness
   _____ evaluation

4. The Brand Decision Process
   _____ preference
   _____ recognition
   _____ insistence
   _____ nonrecognition

SENTENCES

In each sentence, circle the word or phrase that is most appropriate.

1. A generic brand focuses on what the product means to the [customer/seller].

2. Most services are [tangible/intangible], which makes the consumer's choice [more/less] difficult than with goods.

3. Installations and accessory equipment are [capital/expense] items.

4. A [wide/deep] product mix can satisfy the needs of several consumer segments, maximize shelf space, prevent competitors, cover a range of prices, and sustain dealer support.

5. With a [new-product/product] manager system, there is often conflict and discontinuity.

6. [Competitive/Company] product positioning refers to how consumers perceive the firm's different brands within the same product line and the relationship of those brands to each other.

7. The boom curve type of product life cycle describes an extremely popular product that receives steady sales over a [long/short] period of time.

8. [Major/Minor] innovations are items that have not been previously sold by the firm but have been sold by others.

9. Concept testing is a [quick/slow] and [expensive/inexpensive] method of measuring consumer enthusiasm.

10. For [frequently/seldom] purchased items, a six-month period of test marketing is normal.

11. The rate of adoption will be [faster/slower] if consumers have high discretionary income.

12. Members of the [early/late] majority are usually past middle age and have low economic and social status.

13. The most successful companies and industries generate products that remain in maturity for [long/short] time periods.

14. A personified brand mark is known as a trade [character/mark].

15. Turnover of dealer brands is [higher/lower] than that of manufacturer brands.

16. A mixed-brand strategy [encourages/discourages] brand and store loyalty.

17. Family branding is [most/least] effective for specialized firms or those with specialized product lines.

18. Multiple packaging and larger sizes [increase/decrease] product usage.

19. The Universal Product Code is [faster/slower] to process than the Optical Character Recognition system.

20. Throwaway bottles use [more/less] energy than returnable bottles.

ANSWERS

Sequences

1. 4,1,2,3, pp. 271-273
2. 6,1,3,7,2,5,4, pp. 287-288
3. 5,2,6,4,1,3, p. 297
4. 3,2,4,1, p. 320

Sentences

1. customer, p. 254
2. intangible, more, p. 258
3. capital, p. 259
4. deep, p. 261
5. new-product, p. 265
6. Company, p. 267
7. long, pp. 270-271
8. Minor, p. 282
9. quick, inexpensive, p. 290
10. frequently, p. 295
11. faster, p. 297
12. late, p. 298
13. long, p. 300
14. character, p. 310
15. lower, p. 316
16. encourages, p. 316
17. most, p. 317
18. increase, p. 325
19. faster, p. 329
20. more, p. 330

Part
Four

Distribution
Planning

12

An Overview of Distribution Planning and Physical Distribution

CHAPTER OBJECTIVES

1. To define distribution planning, examine distribution functions, describe the different types of distribution channels, and consider the factors used in selecting a channel of distribution
2. To consider cooperation and conflict in a channel of distribution
3. To show the special considerations relating to a distribution channel for industrial products
4. To discuss physical distribution and demonstrate its significance for marketing
5. To study transportation alternatives and inventory management

CHAPTER OVERVIEW

Distribution planning is systematic decision making relating to the physical movement and transfer of ownership of a product or service from producer to consumer. A channel of distribution contains the organizations or people involved with the movement and exchange of products or services.

Regardless of who performs them, channel functions include marketing research, buying, promotion, customer services, product planning, price planning, and distribution. Independent channel members can play an important role by performing various functions and resolving the differences between manufacturers' and consumers' goals.

A direct channel requires the manufacturer to perform all distribution functions, while in an indirect channel these activities are carried out by both the manufacturer and independent middlemen. In comparing the two methods, the firm must balance its costs and abilities against control and total sales. An indirect channel may use a contractual arrangement or an administered agreement.

A long channel has a number of levels of independent middlemen; it can be shortened if the firm increases the functions it performs. A wide channel has a large number of firms at any stage in the channel, such as retailers. The distribution channel may be exclusive, selective, or intensive, depending on the firm's goals, channel members, customers, and marketing emphasis. A dual channel allows a company to operate through two or more distribution methods.

In contracts between manufacturers and other channel members, price policy, conditions of sale, territorial rights, services/responsibility mix, and contract length and conditions of termination are specified. Cooperation and conflict both occur in a channel of distribution. Conflicts need to be settled fairly, since confrontation leads to hostility and negative actions by all parties. A pushing strategy, based on channel cooperation, is available to established, successful firms. A pulling strategy, based on proving the existence of consumer demand prior to channel support or acceptance, must be used by many new companies.

The channel of distribution for industrial products normally does not use retailers but tends to be direct, involve few transactions and large orders, require specification selling and knowledgeable channel members, utilize team selling and different channel members, and include leasing arrangements.

Physical distribution is involved with getting goods delivered to the designated place, at the designated time, and in proper condition. There are a number of reasons for studying physical distribution: costs, importance of customer service, and its relationship with other functional areas of the organization.

In a physical distribution strategy, decisions are made regarding transportation, inventory levels, warehousing, and location of facilities. Railroads typically carry goods for long distances and ship bulky items that are low in value in relation to their weight. Motor trucks dominate in transporting small shipments over short distances. Waterways are used primarily for the shipment of low-value freight. Pipelines provide reliable and continuous movement of liquid, gaseous, and semiliquid products. Airways offer fast, expensive movement of perishables and high-value items.

Inventory management is needed to regulate product supplies and distribution. Stock turnover is the number of times during a year that the average inventory on hand is sold. The reorder point is based on a pre-established minimum inventory level at which merchandise must be reordered. The economic order quantity formula determines the optimal quantity of goods to order based on total order-processing and holding costs. Warehousing decisions include selecting a private or public warehouse and examining the availability of public warehouse services.

KEY TERMS AND CONCEPTS

Distribution planning	The systematic decision making regarding the physical movement and transfer of ownership of a product or service from producer to consumer. It includes transportation, storage, and customer transactions.
Channel of distribution	All the organizations or people involved with the movement and exchange of products or services.
Channel member (middleman)	An organization or person in the distribution process.
Channel functions	The functions completed by some member of the channel: marketing research, buying, promotion, customer services, product planning, pricing, and distribution.

Sorting process	The distribution activities of accumulation, allocation, sorting, and assorting necessary to resolve the differences in the goals of manufacturers and final consumers.
Direct channel of distribution	Involves the movement of goods and services from manufacturer to consumers without the use of independent middlemen.
Indirect channel of distribution	Involves the movement of goods and services from manufacturer to independent channel member to consumer.
Contractual channel arrangement	Specifies in writing all the terms regarding distribution functions, prices, and other factors for each channel member in an indirect channel.
Administered channel	One in which the dominant firm in the distribution process plans the marketing program and itemizes responsibilities.
Channel length	Refers to the number of independent members along the channel.
Vertical integration	When a firm shortens its channel by acquiring a company at another stage in the channel.
Channel width	Refers to the number of independent members at any stage of the distribution process.
Horizontal integration	The practice of a firm acquiring other businesses like itself.
Exclusive distribution	A policy in which a firm severely limits the wholesalers and retailers it utilizes in a geographic area, perhaps employing only one or two retailers within a specific shopping district.
Selective distribution	A policy by which the firm employs a moderate number of wholesalers and retailers.
Intensive distribution	A policy in which a firm uses a large number of wholesalers and retailers in order to obtain widespread market coverage, channel acceptance, and high-volume sales.
Dual channel of distribution	A strategy whereby the firm appeals to different market segments or diversifies its business by selling through two or more different channels.
Manufacturer/channel member contract	A written agreement that focuses on price policy, conditions of sale, territorial rights, services/responsibility mix, and contract length and conditions of termination.
Pushing strategy	Dealer support and cooperation are first attained; then advertising is addressed to customers.
Pulling strategy	Demand is first generated through direct advertising to customers, then dealer support is obtained.
Physical distribution	The broad range of activities concerned with the efficient movement of finished goods from the end of

the production line to the consumer. In some cases it includes the movement of raw materials from the source of supply to the beginning of the production line.

Order cycle

The period of time from when the customer places an order until it is received.

Distribution standards

Clever and measurable goals regarding customer service levels in physical distribution.

Total-cost approach

Determines the distribution service level with the lowest total costs, including freight, warehousing, and the cost of lost business. The ideal system seeks a balance between low distribution costs and high opportunities for sales.

Physical distribution strategy

Includes the transportation form or forms to be used, inventory levels and warehouse form(s), and the number and locations of plants, warehouses, and retail locations.

Railroad

A transportation form that usually carries heavy, bulky items that are low in value (relative to their weight) over long distances.

Motor truck

A transportation form that predominantly transports small shipments over short distances.

Waterway

A transportation form that involves the movement of goods on barges via inland rivers and on tankers and general merchandise freighters through the Great Lakes, incoastal shipping, and the St. Lawrence Seaway.

Pipeline

A transportation form that involves continuous movement, with no interruptions, inventories, and intermediate storage locations.

Airway

The fastest, most expensive form of transportation.

Transportation service company

Handles the shipments of moderate-sized packages. The three kinds of companies are government parcel post, private parcel service, and express service.

Containerization

A coordinated transportation practice that allows goods to be placed in sturdy containers, which serve as mobile warehouses. Containers can be placed on trains, trucks, ships, and planes.

Freight forwarder

A transportation service firm which consolidates small shipments (usually less than 500 pounds each) from several companies, picks up merchandise at the shipper's place of business, and arranges for delivery at the buyer's door.

Common carrier

A company that must transport the goods of any firm interested in its services; it cannot refuse any shipments unless its rules are broken. Common carriers provide service on a fixed and publicized schedule between designated points. A regular fee schedule is published.

Contract carrier	A company that provides one or a few shippers with transportation services based on individual agreements. Contract carriers are not required to maintain rules or schedules and rates may be negotiated.
Exempt carrier	A transporter that is excused from legal regulations and must only comply with safety requirements. Exempt carriers are specified by law.
Private carrier	A shipper possessing its own transportation facilities.
Inventory management	Concerned with ensuring the continuous flow of goods and matching the quantity of goods in inventory with sales demand.
Just-in-time (JIT) inventory system	A procedure by which the purchasing firm reduces the amount of inventory it keeps on hand by ordering more frequently and in greater quantity.
Stock turnover	Represents the number of times during a specified period (usually one year) that the average inventory on hand is sold. Stock turnover is calculated in units or dollars.
Reorder point	Establishes an inventory level at which new orders must be placed. The reorder point depends on order lead time, usage rate, and safety stock.
Order size	The appropriate amount of merchandise, parts, etc. to purchase at one time. Depends on the availability of quantity discounts, the resources of the firm, inventory turnover, the costs of processing each order, and the costs of maintaining goods in inventory.
Economic order quantity (EOQ)	The order volume corresponding to the lowest sum of order processing and holding costs.
Warehouse	Receives, identifies, and sorts merchandise. It stores goods, implements product-recall programs, selects goods for shipment, coordinates shipments, and dispatches orders.
Bonded warehouse	A public storage facility used to store imported or taxable merchandise, wherein goods are released only after appropriate taxes are paid. Allows firms to postpone tax payments until goods are ready to be shipped to customers.
Field warehouse	A public warehouse which issues a receipt for goods stored in a private warehouse or in transit to consumers. The field warehouse receipt can serve as collateral for a loan.
Physical distribution system	The coordination of a firm's transportation and inventory management strategies.

TRUE/FALSE

Circle the appropriate letter.

T   F   1. A firm that uses channel members increases its per unit distribution costs, but also increases its per unit profits.

T   F   2. Assorting is a wholesaler function, whereas accumulation is a retailer function.

T   F   3. Channel members have little discretion is setting prices and arranging purchasing terms.

T   F   4. An indirect channel is usually employed by a company that wants to enlarge its market and increase its sales volume.

T   F   5. In an administered channel, channel leadership is usually specified in writing.

T   F   6. In the distribution process, length refers to the number of independent channel members at any stage in the process.

T   F   7. With horizontal integration, a firm acquires companies at different stages in the channel.

T   F   8. In intensive distribution, the firm severely limits the wholesalers and retailers it uses in a geographic area.

T   F   9. Channel members usually have the same general objectives.

T   F   10. In a pushing strategy the company first generates consumer demand and then secures dealer support.

T   F   11. Greater variety means lower volume per item, which increases unit warehousing costs.

T   F   12. Low average inventories in stock enable companies to reduce finance charges.

T   F   13. Since 1950 the relative importance of pipelines has decreased, while the relative importance of railroads has increased substantially.

T   F   14. Trucks are less flexible than railroads.

T   F   15. Pipelines minimize handling and labor costs.

T   F   16. United Parcel Service is a government transportation service company.

T   F   17. Freight forwarders prosper because less-than-carload rates are sharply higher than carload rates.

T   F   18. Contract carriers are required to maintain fixed routes, schedules, and rates.

T   F   19. The reorder point is calculated by dividing the number of units sold by the average inventory on hand.

T   F   20. A bonded warehouse allows firms to increase their working capital by coordinating tax payments with deliveries to customers.

COMPLETION

Fill in the missing word or words in the blanks provided.

[sorting process, accumulation, allocation, sorting, assorting, p. 347]

1. The _____ _____ consists of the wholesaler function of collecting small shipments from several manufacturers to be transported more economically, known as _____ ; the wholesaler/retailer function of distributing items to various consumer markets, known as _____ ; the wholesaler/retailer function of separating merchandise into grades, colors, and sizes, known as _____ ; and the retailer function of acquiring a broad range of merchandise, known as _____ .

[direct, indirect, p. 348]

2. Two basic types of channels of distribution are _____ and _____ .

[length, vertical integration, width, horizontal integration, p. 351]

3. The number of independent members along a channel constitutes its _____ ; when firms acquire companies at different stages in the channel, _____ _____ is said to have taken place. The number of independent channel members at any stage of the distribution process constitutes its _____ ; and when a firm acquires other businesses like itself in the channel, _____ _____ is said to have taken place.

[dual channels of distribution, pp. 351-352]

4. Under a system of _____ _____ _____ _____ , a firm appeals to different market segments or diversifies its business by selling through more than one channel.

[Exclusive distribution, selective distribution, intensive distribution, p. 351]

5. _____ _____ is a policy by which a firm severely limits the wholesalers and retailers it utilizes in a geographic area; _____ _____ is a policy by which a firm employs a moderate number of wholesalers and retailers; and _____ _____ is a policy by which a firm uses a large number of wholesalers and retailers.

[pushing, pulling, pp. 355-356]

6. In a _____ strategy an established manufacturer is able to secure immediate dealer suport when introducing a new product; in a _____ strategy, an unfamiliar company must first generate consumer demand and then secure dealer support.

[physical distribution strategy, p. 361]

7. Choices of transportation forms and inventory management decisions constitute two central components of _____ _____ _____ .

[government parcel post, private parcel, express companies, p. 364]

8. Three types of transportation service companies are _____ _____ _____ , for example, express mail; _____ _____ services, for example, United Parcel Service; and _____ _____ , for example, Federal Express.

[containerization, freight forwarding, p. 364]

9. Two major innovations that improve a firm's ability to coordinate shipments are _____ and _____ _____ .

[common contract, exempt, private, pp. 364-365]

10. Transportation firms can be categorized according to their legal status as _____ carriers, providing space between designated points on a fixed schedule; _____ carriers, providing services by agreement; _____ carriers, having no economic regulations but having safety regulations and being specified by law; and _____ carriers, posessing their own transportation facilities.

[just-in-time, p. 365]

11. With a_____ _____ _____ inventory system, the purchasing firm can reduce the amount of inventory it keeps on hand by ordering more frequently and in lower quantity.

[stock turnover, pp. 365-366]

12. The balance between sales and inventory on hand is expressed by _____ _____ , the number of times during a specified period that the average inventory on hand is sold.

[reorder point, order lead time, usage rate, safety stock, p. 368]

13. The _____ _____ establishes a stock level at which new orders must be placed; _____ _____ _____ specifies the time from when an order is placed until it is ready for sale; _____ _____ describes the average sales in units per day or the rate at which a product is used in a production process; and _____ _____ is the extra merchandise kept on hand to protect against out-of-stock conditions.

[Order processing, inventory holding, economic order quantity, p. 369]

14. _____ _____ costs are associated with filling out order forms, computer time, and merchandise handling; _____ _____ costs are composed of warehouse expenses, investment expenses, insurance, deterioration, and pilferage; the _____ _____ _____ is the order volume corresponding to the lowest sum of these costs.

[Private warehouses, public warehouses, p. 370]

15. _____ _____ are owned and operated by firms for the purpose of storing and distributing their own products; _____ _____ provide storage and related physical distribution services to any interested individual or firm on a rental basis.

DEFINITIONS

Match the terms and concepts with the appropriate definitions. Each term or concept may only be used once; there are more terms and concepts than definitions.

Column A	*Column B*
a. administered channel	____ 1. The period of time from when the customer places an order until it is received.

b. airway

c. bonded warehouse

d. channel functions

e. channel length

f. channel member

g. channel of distribution

h. channel width

i. common carrier

j. containerization

k. contract carrier

l. contractual channel arrangement

m. direct channel of distribution

n. distribution planning

o. distribution standards

p. dual channel of distribution

q. economic order quantity

r. exclusive distribution

s. exempt carrier

t. field warehouse

u. freight forwarder

v. horizontal integration

w. indirect channel of distribution

x. intensive distribution

y. inventory management

z. just-in-time inventory system

aa. manufacturer/channel member contract

bb. motor truck

cc. order cycle

dd. order size

ee. physical distribution

ff. physical distribution strategy

gg. physical distribution system

hh. pipeline

____ 2. Occurs when the dominant firm in the distribution process plans the marketing program and itemizes responsibilities.

____ 3. Dealer support and cooperation first attained; then advertising is addressed to customers.

____ 4. Represents the number of times during a specified period that the average inventory on hand is sold.

____ 5. A strategy whereby the firm appeals to different market segments or diversifies its business by selling through two or more different channels.

____ 6. A transportation form that involves continuous movement, with no interruptions, inventories, and intermediate storage locations.

____ 7. Concerned with ensuring the continuous flow of goods and matching the quantity of goods in inventory with sales demand.

____ 8. Refers to the number of independent members along the channel.

____ 9. When a firm shortens its channel by acquiring a company at another stage in the channel.

____ 10. A company that must carry the goods of any firm interested in its services; it cannot refuse any shipments unless the carrier's rules are broken.

____ 11. A transportation form that predominantly transports small shipments over short distances.

____ 12. Involves the movement of goods and services from manufacturer to consumers without the use of independent middlemen.

____ 13. An organization or person in the distribution process.

____ 14. The practice of a firm acquiring other businesses like itself.

____ 15. The order volume corresponding to the lowest sum of order processing and holding costs.

  ii. pulling strategy

  jj. pushing strategy

 kk. railroad

  ll. reorder point

mm. selective distribution

 nn. sorting process

 oo. stock turnover

 pp. total-cost approach

 qq. transportation service company

 rr. vertical integration

 ss. warehouse

 tt. waterway

MULTIPLE CHOICE

Place the letter of the answer you think best in the blank provided.

_____ 1. Which of the following is *not* an aspect of distribution planning?
    a. Transportation
    b. Manufacture
    c. Storage
    d. Customer transactions

_____ 2. Which of the following statements about channels of distribution is *false*?
    a. It is usually easy for new firms to enter established channels.
    b. Relations with channel members are difficult to change.
    c. It is usually easy to place new products into distribution for established firms.
    d. Channel members need to coordinate planning and the implementation of their strategies.

_____ 3. When goods and services move from manufacturer to independent channel members to consumers, there is said to exist
    a. horizontal integration.
    b. an indirect channel of distribution.
    c. selective distribution.
    d. a dual channel of distribution.

_____ 4. Direct channels of distribution are most frequently used by companies that
    a. service limited target markets.
    b. want to increase sales volume.
    c. wish to relinquish customer contact.
    d. give up many distribution costs.

_____ 5. In an administered channel,
   a. terms regarding prices and distribution functions are clearly specified in writing and are legally binding.
   b. a channel member distributes its own products or services directly to the consumer.
   c. a dominant firm in the distribution process plans the marketing program and itemizes responsibility.
   d. companies appeal to different market segments by selling through more than one distribution system.

_____ 6. In describing a channel of distribution, width refers to
   a. the number of independent members along the channel.
   b. ownership of companies at different stages in the channel.
   c. the number of independent channel members at any stage of the distribution process.
   d. acquisition of businesses at the same stage in the channel.

_____ 7. Horizontal integration
   a. enables a firm to be more self-sufficient.
   b. lowers middleman costs.
   c. coordinates the timing of products through the channel.
   d. improves bargaining power with outside channel members.

_____ 8. With intensive distribution, a firm
   a. increases per unit profits.
   b. emphasizes good service and pleasant shopping conditions.
   c. maintains its channel control.
   d. aims at the mass market.

_____ 9. In comparison with the distribution of consumer products, industrial product distribution
   a. uses more indirect channels.
   b. involves smaller orders and greater transactions.
   c. does not require cooperative selling.
   d. does not usually employ retailers.

_____ 10. Which of the following statements about transportation modes is _false_?
   a. The volume of waterway shipments has remained stable.
   b. Freight deliveries by airways remain low despite airline growth.
   c. The relative importance of railroads has declined substantially.
   d. The share of ton-miles shipped by pipelines has declined since 1950.

_____ 11. Most trucking involves
   a. long distances.
   b. less flexibility than rail shipments.
   c. small shipments.
   d. less speed than rail shipments for short runs.

_____ 12. The type of freight carried by railroads most closely resembles that carried by
   a. pipelines.
   b. waterways.
   c. trucks.
   d. airways.

13. Which of the following is *not* an express company?
    a. Emery Air Freight
    b. Purolator Courier Corporation
    c. Western Union
    d. Burlington Northern Air Freight

14. Exempt carriers
    a. possess their own transportation facilities.
    b. cannot refuse to transport the goods of any shipper.
    c. are specified by law.
    d. maintain fixed routes, rates, and schedules.

15. Which of the following is *not* an aspect of inventory management?
    a. Stock turnover
    b. Reorder timing
    c. Warehousing
    d. Product planning

16. Stock turnover is the balance between
    a. reorder point and economic order quantity.
    b. usage-rate and order-processing costs.
    c. order lead time and safety stock.
    d. sales and inventory on hand.

17. Which of the following is *not* used to calculate the reorder point?
    a. Order lead time
    b. Inventory holding costs
    c. Safety stock
    d. Usage rate

18. The economic order quantity is calculated by summing
    a. usage rates and order lead time.
    b. inventory holding costs and order-processing costs.
    c. safety stock and stock turnover.
    d. average inventory on hand and number of units sold.

19. Companies with stable inventory levels and long-run expectations to serve the same geographic markets tend to use
    a. private warehousing.
    b. public warehousing.
    c. bonded warehousing.
    d. field warehousing.

20. Which of the following is a specific advantage of field warehousing?
    a. Firms can increase their working capital by coordinating tax payments with deliveries to customers.
    b. The warehouse receipt can serve as collateral for a loan.
    c. It can provide transportation economies by allowing carload shipments to local markets before warehouse distribution to customers.
    d. It offers additional services such as inventory control and order processing.

DISCUSSION QUESTIONS

1. Why are middlemen necessary?

2. What are the different types of channels of distribution? How can they be described?

3. How can channels of distribution be controlled?

4. How does the use of the total cost approach determine the optimal customer service level?

5. You are shipping fruit and vegetables from the Southeast to the Northeast. Which transportation mode would you select from among the following: railroad tank cars, trucks, pipelines, waterways? Why?

6. What are the goals of inventory management in determining stock turnover, when to reorder, and how much to reorder? How can they be achieved (given optimum conditions)?

7. Why is it sometimes preferable to use a combination of private and public warehousing? Be specific.

EXERCISES

12-1.   A vacuum cleaner manufacturer sells its consumer products (portable vacuums, uprights, and power-head machines) using a strategy of selective distribution. In each geographic area, a moderate number of retailers sells its products. A line of commercial vacuums (for hotels, motels, and other businesses) is sold through industrial supply wholesalers.

Lately, the manufacturer and some of its retailers have had substantial conflicts:

- Many of the smaller retailers have formed informal buying groups. One store submits an order for a number of retailers, qualifies for quantity and other discounts, and splits the vacuum order with buying group members. The vacuum cleaner manufacturer does not like dealing with these buying groups; the small retailers claim this helps them compete more effectively with department stores.

- Many of the smaller retailers also sell used vacuum cleaners, typewriters, and sewing machines, and repair small appliances. Their store appearance is generally unattractive and cluttered. They cannot use display materials provided by the manufacturer because of their lack of space. The vacuum cleaner manufacturer is concerned that its products are being given inadequate attention.

- The small retailers are upset that the manufacturer is designating several of its models with special colors and model numbers for department-store chains. While the chains desire this to limit price competition, the small retailers are displeased.

- The manufacturer feels it has little control over its retailers in general. They all carry competing lines, set their own selling prices, and in many cases totally disregard cooperative promotions (wherein the manufacturer partially reimburses retailers for promotional expenses for its items). In one instance, while the vacuum cleaner manufacturer had a national promotion on a new high-power unit, many small retailers stressed used typewriters or reconditioned Electrolux (a competing manufacturer) vacuums with higher profit margins.

Questions

1.   Are all or most of these conflicts inevitable? Explain your answer.

2.   How can each of these conflicts be minimized?

3.   Why should a manufacturer be upset by price-cutting retailers, since it sells more units at the same profit margin? Explain.

4.   Why would the manufacturer use wholesalers to distribute commercial vacuums to large hotel chains rather than sell directly to the hotels?

12-2.   In greater numbers, U.S. manufacturers are beginning to improve their operations by adopting just-in-time (JIT) inventory control systems. With a JIT system, a firm keeps a minimum level of inventory on hand and relies on suppliers to provide parts, etc. on an "as needed" basis. The advantages of a JIT system are higher attention to quality control, greater coordination between vendors and buyers, and lower inventory costs.

Although the first JIT system was developed in the U.S., Japanese firms have been much quicker to apply the technique. The Japanese view large inventories as wasteful; many American companies have regarded large inventories as required in order to meet unanticipated high consumer demand or resolve quality control problems.

Converting from a traditional inventory system to a JIT system is complex:

- Typically, just-in-time systems utilize only one supplier. This is necessary to coordinate production and delivery schedules, and insure necessary quality control. Many U.S. firms use multiple suppliers to foster competition and ensure supply (in case of labor disruptions at one supplier).
- In just-in-time systems, parts are shipped directly to the factory floor. Traditional warehouses are not used. Workers need to quickly verify correctness of shipping quantities.
- Suppliers must be located near their major users to provide fast delivery. This involves considerable fixed costs to the supplier.
- Railroads are not well suited to just-in-time. Their delivery schedules often are inflexible; they also cannot load deliveries directly on the factory floor.
- Strict quality control is necessary. With little safety stock, a poor-quality parts shipment can close an entire factory.

Questions

1.   What kinds of production processes are most easily adapted to a just-in-time system?

2.   A vendor desires a long-term contract prior to agreeing to a just-in-time replenishment system. What factors should the contract include?

3.   What are the other major ramifications of just-in-time inventory systems to suppliers? To product users?

4.   Explain why a just-in-time inventory system may not always result in a lower total cost of distribution.

12-3.   A manufacturer of videocassette recorders wants to evaluate its current channel coverage strategy. What are the specific advantages and disadvantages of
exclusive, selective, and intensive coverage for this firm?

12-4.   Develop a checklist for a bakery servicing supermarkets to evaluate its physical
distribution system.

ANSWERS

True/False

1. F, p. 343	11. T, p. 360
2. F, p. 347	12. T, p. 361
3. F, p. 347	13. F, pp. 362-363
4. 1, pp. 348-349	14. F, p. 362
5. F, p. 351	15. T, p. 363
6. F, p. 351	16. F, p. 364
7. F, p. 351	17. T, p. 364
8. F, p. 351	18. F, p. 364
9. T, p. 353	19. F, p. 368
10. F, pp. 355-356	20. T, p. 371

Multiple Choice

1. b, p. 342	11. c, p. 362
2. a, p. 343	12. b, p. 362
3. b, p. 348	13. c, p. 364
4. a, pp. 348-349	14. c, p. 364
5. c, p. 351	15. d, p. 365
6. c, p. 351	16. d, pp. 365-366
7. d, p. 351	17. b, p. 368
8. d, p. 351	18. b, p. 369
9. d, pp. 356-357	19. a, p. 370
10. d, p. 361	20. b, p. 371

Definitions

1. cc	9. rr
2. a	10. i
3. jj	11. bb
4. oo	12. m
5. p	13. f
6. hh	14. v
7. y	15. q
8. e	

Discussion Questions

1. pp. 343, 345-348
2. pp. 348, 351-352
3. pp. 350-355
4. p. 359
5. pp. 359, 361-364
6. pp. 365-370
7. pp. 370-371

13

Wholesaling

CHAPTER OBJECTIVES

1. To define wholesaling and show its importance
2. To describe the three broad categories of wholesaling (manufacturer wholesaling, merchant wholesaling, and agents and brokers) and the specific types and firms within each category
3. To examine recent trends in wholesaling

CHAPTER OVERVIEW

Wholesaling is the buying or handling of merchandise and its resale to retailers, organizational users, and/or other wholesalers but not the sale of significant volume to final consumers. Approximately 600,000 wholesalers sell over $1 trillion of merchandise annually.

Wholesale functions encompass distribution, personal selling, marketing and technical assistance, financial assistance, recordkeeping, returns and allowances, and risk taking. These functions may be assumed by the manufacturer or shared with an independent wholesaler. Wholesalers are sometimes in a precarious position because they are located between manufacturers and retailers and must determine their responsibilities to each.

Manufacturer wholesaling can be conducted through sales or branch offices. The sales office carries no inventory. Through either or both offices, manufacturers carry out all wholesale functions.

Merchant wholesalers buy, take title, and possess products for their own accounts. Full-service merchant wholesalers assemble an assortment of products, provide trade credit, store and deliver merchandise, offer merchandising and promotion assistance, provide a personal sales force, and offer research and planning support. Full-service merchant wholesalers fall into general merchandise, specialty merchandise, rack jobber, franchise, and cooperative types. Limited-service merchant wholesalers take title to merchandise but do not provide all wholesale functions. Limited-service merchant wholesalers are divided into cash and carry, drop shipper, truck/wagon, and mail order types.

Agents and brokers negotiate purchases and expedite sales but do not take title to goods. Agents are used on a more permanent basis than brokers. Types of agents are manufacturers' agents, selling agents, and commission (factor) merchants. Food brokers dominate brokerage.

Competition among independent wholesalers has grown over the last several years. To protect their place in the channel, some wholesalers are diversifying their markets and product mixes, while others are specializing more. To reduce costs, telephone sales are rising.

KEY TERMS AND CONCEPTS

Wholesaling
Involves the buying and handling of merchandise and its resale to retailers, organizational users, and/or other wholesalers but not the sale of significant volume to final consumers.

Manufacturer wholesaling
Occurs when the producer undertakes all wholesaling functions itself. Includes manufacturer's sales offices and manufacturer's branch offices.

Manufacturer's sales office
A form of manufacturer wholesaling that assigns selling tasks to a sales office but maintains inventory only at production facilities.

Manufacturer's branch office
A form of manufacturer wholesaling that assigns warehousing and selling tasks to a branch office.

Merchant wholesaler
Buys, takes title, and takes possession of products for its own accounts. Merchant wholesalers may be full service or limited service.

Full-service merchant wholesaler
Assembles products, provides trade credit, stores and delivers merchandise, offers merchandise and promotion assistance, provides a personal sales force, offers research and planning support, makes information available, provides installation and repair services, and acts as the sales arm for its manufacturer.

Limited-service merchant wholesaler
Buys and takes title to merchandise but does not perform all of the functions of a full-service merchant wholesaler. May not provide credit, merchandise assistance, or market research data.

General merchandise (full-line) wholesaler
A full-service merchant wholesaler which carries a wide assortment of products, nearly all the items needed by the retailer to which it caters.

Specialty merchandise (limited line) wholesaler
A full-service merchant wholesaler that concentrates its efforts on a relatively narrow range of products and has an extensive assortment within that range.

Rack jobber
A full-service merchant wholesaler that furnishes the racks or shelves on which merchandise is displayed. The rack jobber owns the merchandise on its racks, selling the items on a consignment basis.

Franchise wholesaling
A full-service merchant wholesaling format whereby independent retailers affiliate with an existing wholesaler in order to use a standardized storefront design, business plan, name, and purchase system.

Wholesale cooperative
A full-service merchant wholesaler owned by member firms which seeks to economize functions and offer broad support. There are producer-owned and retailer-owned wholesale cooperatives.

Cash-and-carry wholesaler
A limited service merchant wholesaler which enables a small businessperson to drive to a wholesaler, order products, and take them back to his/her store or business. No credit, delivery, and merchandise and promotional assistance are provided.

Drop shipper (Desk jobber)
A form of limited-service merchant wholesaler which purchases goods from manufacturers/suppliers and arranges for their shipment to retailers or industrial users.

Truck/wagon wholesaler
A limited-service merchant wholesaler which has a regular sales route, offers items from a truck or wagon, and delivers goods as they are sold.

Mail order wholesaler
A limited-service merchant wholesaler which uses catalogs instead of a personal sales force to promote products and communicate with customers.

Agent
A wholesaler that does not take title to goods and is compensated through payment of a commission or a fee. It may be a manufacturers' agent, selling agent, or commission (factor) merchant.

Broker
A temporary wholesaler, paid by commission or fee. The most common is a food broker, who introduces buyers and sellers, and helps complete transactions.

Manufacturers' agent
An agent who works for several manufacturers and carries noncompetitive, complementary products in exclusive territories. A manufacturer may employ many agents, each with a unique product-territorial mix.

Selling agent
An agent that assumes responsibility for marketing the entire output of a manufacturer under a contractual agreement. It performs all wholesale functions except taking title to merchandise.

Commission (factor) merchant
An agent who receives goods on consignment, accumulates them from local markets, and arranges for their sale in a central market location.

Food broker
A middleman involved with food and related general merchandise items who introduces buyers and sellers to one another and brings them together to complete a sale.

TRUE/FALSE

Circle the appropriate letter.

T   F   1. Wholesaling involves sales of significant volume to final consumers.

T   F   2. All independent wholesalers take title to or physical possession of goods.

T   F   3. Although wholesale revenues are higher than those for retailing, there are more than four times as many retailers as wholesalers.

T   F   4. An item may be sold twice at the wholesale level.

T   F   5. Wholesalers may offer financial assistance for the manufacturer or supplier and retail or business customer.

T   F   6. Selling to the wholesaler means the retailer or final consumer is the object of the manufacturer's or supplier's interest.

T   F   7. A manufacturer's sales office usually carries inventory.

T   F   8. Direct selling typically occurs when there are few customers to service and orders are large.

T   F   9. The largest category of wholesalers in terms of sales is manufacturer wholesalers.

T   F   10. Limited-service merchant wholesalers do not take title to merchandise.

T   F   11. Limited-service merchant wholesalers can be divided into general merchandise, specialty merchandise, rack jobber, franchise, and cooperative types.

T   F   12. Rack jobbers will take back unsold merchandise.

T   F   13. Producer cooperatives not only market, transport, and process farm products, they also manufacture and distribute farm supplies.

T   F   14. Retail-owned wholesale cooperatives are used by hardware and grocery stores.

T   F   15. Cash-and-carry wholesaling involves items sold from wagons that have a regular sales route.

T   F   16. Because they have legal ownership of products, drop shippers take physical possession of goods and have facilities for storing them.

T   F   17. The principal difference between agents and brokers is that brokers tend to be used on a permanent basis and agents are employed temporarily.

T   F   18. Selling agents are more likely to work for small manufacturers than for large ones.

T   F   19. Commission (factor) merchants normally assist in merchandising and promotion.

T   F   20. Competition among independent wholesalers has increased dramatically over the last several years.

COMPLETION

Fill in the missing word or words in the blanks provided.

[Wholesalers, retailers, p. 378]

1. _____ deal with fewer, larger, and more geographically concentrated customers than _____ do.

[local, financial assistance, p. 378]

2. Wholesalers enable a manufacturer or supplier to have _____ distribution and offer _____ _____ to them by paying for goods when they are shipped, not when they are sold.

[to, through, p. 380]

3. Selling _____ the wholesaler means the distributor is viewed as a customer, while selling _____ the wholesaler means the retailer or final consumer is the object of interest.

[manufacturer wholesaling, merchant wholesaling, agents, brokers, p. 380]

4. Three broad categories of wholesaling are _____ _____, _____ _____, and _____ and _____ .

[manufacturer wholesalers, p. 381]

5. When producers undertake all wholesale functions themselves they can be called _____ _____ .

[manufacturer's sales, manufacturer's branch, p. 383]

6. A _____ _____ office is located at the company's facilities and does not carry inventory, whereas a _____ _____ office includes facilities for both warehousing and selling goods.

[merchant wholesalers, p. 383]

7. Full-service wholesalers and limited-service wholesalers are two types of _____ _____ .

[general merchandise, specialty merchandise, rack jobbers, franchise wholesalers, cooperatives, pp. 383-384]

8. Five types of full-service wholesalers are _____ _____ wholesalers, carrying a wide assortment of products; _____ _____ wholesalers, concentrating on a relatively narrow range of products; _____ _____ , owning merchandise on their display shelves; _____ _____ , offering a standardized storefront design, business format, name, and purchase system; and _____ , owned by member firms to economize functions and offer broad support.

[Producer-owned, retailer-owned, pp. 384-386]

9. _____ _____ wholesale cooperatives are popular in farming, while _____ _____ wholesale cooperatives are used by hardware and grocery stores.

[cash-and-carry, drop shippers, truck/wagon, mail order, pp. 387-388]

10. Four types of limited-service wholesalers are _____ _____ _____ wholesalers, offering small retailers neither credit nor delivery; _____ _____ , purchasing goods from manufacturers/suppliers and arranging for their shipment to retail or industrial users; _____ _____ wholesalers, having regular sales routes and offering goods from their

vehicles; and _____ _____ wholesalers, utilizing catalogs instead of a personal sales force.

[Mail-order, pp. 389-390] 11. _____ _____ wholesaling is often found with jewelry, cosmetics, and auto parts.

[manufacturers', selling, commission merchants, p. 390] 12. Three types of agents are _____ agents, selling noncompetitive items and complementary products; _____ agents, assuming responsibility for marketing the entire output of a manufacturer under contractual agreement; and _____ _____ , receiving goods on consignment and arranging for their sale at a central location.

[Manufacturers' agents, pp. 390-392] 13. _____ _____ are organizations that work for several manufacturers and carry noncompetitive, complementary products in exclusive territories.

[food, pp. 390-391] 14. Brokers are very common in the _____ industry.

[increased costs, p. 392] 15. Because of _____ _____ , many wholesalers have begun to service small accounts through telephone selling and automatic reorder systems.

DEFINITIONS

Match the terms and concepts with the appropriate definitions. Each term or concept may only be used once; there are more terms and concepts than definitions.

Column A	Column B
a. agent	___ 1. A temporary wholesaler paid by commission or fee.
b. broker	
c. cash-and-carry wholesaling	___ 2. Buys and takes title to merchandise but does not perform all functions such as providing credit or market research data.
d. commission merchant	
e. drop shipper	___ 3. A full-service merchant wholesaler that furnishes shelves on which merchandise is displayed.
f. food broker	
g. franchise wholesaling	___ 4. A wholesaler that does not take title to goods and is compensated through payment of a fee or commission.
h. full-service merchant wholesaler	
	___ 5. Occurs when the producer undertakes all wholesaling functions itself.
i. general merchandise wholesaler	
j. limited-service merchant wholesaler	___ 6. A full-service merchant wholesaler owned by member firms which seeks to economize functions and offer broad support.

k. mail order wholesaler

l. manufacturer wholesaling

m. manufacturer's branch office

n. manufacturer's sales office

o. merchant wholesaler

p. rack jobber

q. selling agent

r. specialty merchandise wholesaler

s. truck/wagon wholesaler

t. wholesale cooperative

u. wholesaling

_____ 7. A full-service merchant wholesaler that concentrates its efforts on a relatively narrow range of products and has an extensive assortment within that range.

_____ 8. An agent that assumes responsibility for marketing the entire output of a manufacturer under a contractual agreement.

_____ 9. A limited-service merchant wholesaler which has a regular sales route and delivers goods as they are sold from its vehicle.

_____ 10. A limited-service merchant wholesaler which enables a small businessperson to drive to a wholesaler, order products, and take them back to his/her store or business.

_____ 11. An agent who receives goods on consignment, accumulates them from local markets, and arranges for their sale in a central market location.

_____ 12. A form of limited-service merchant wholesaler which purchases goods from manufacturers/suppliers and arranges for their shipment to retailers or industrial users.

_____ 13. A form of manufacturer wholesaling that assigns selling tasks to an office but maintains inventory only at production facilities.

_____ 14. A full-service merchant wholesaler which carries a wide assortment of products, nearly all the items needed by the retailer to which it caters.

_____ 15. A full-service merchant wholesaling format whereby independent retailers affiliate with an existing wholesaler in order to use a standardized storefront design, business plan, name, and purchase system.

MULTIPLE CHOICE

Place the letter of the answer you think best in the blank provided.

_____ 1. High wholesale sales occur because
   a. there are so many retailers.
   b. there is only one level of retailing.
   c. items can be sold twice on the wholesale level.
   d. wholesalers service small, final consumer groups.

2. Which of the following statements about the functions of wholesalers is *false?*
   a. They enable a manufacturer or supplier to have national distribution with a maximum of customer contacts.
   b. They provide a ready-made sales force.
   c. They provide warehouse, field storage, and delivery facilities.
   d. They handle returns and allowances and adjusting for defective merchandise.

3. Wholesalers prefer manufacturers to
   a. shrink territories.
   b. add new distributors to cover existing territories.
   c. sell through the wholesaler.
   d. provide training and technical assistance.

4. Selling to the wholesaler means that the customer to be researched and satisfied is the
   a. retailer.
   b. distributor.
   c. final consumer.
   d. manufacturer.

5. Coca-Cola's past practices in dealing with its wholesalers illustrate
   a. how valued domestic operations were.
   b. the effects of direct selling.
   c. the conflicts that can occur among channel members.
   d. the importance of training.

6. Manufacturers are less likely to engage in direct selling when
   a. there are no middlemen available.
   b. average purchases are high.
   c. customers are geographically concentrated.
   d. there are a large number of customers.

7. The largest category of wholesalers in terms of sales is
   a. manufacturer wholesalers.
   b. agents.
   c. merchant wholesalers.
   d. brokers.

8. Which of the following is *not* a full-service wholesaler?
   a. Specialty merchant wholesalers
   b. Rack jobbers
   c. Drop shippers
   d. Franchise wholesalers

9. General merchandise wholesalers
   a. do not have much depth in any specific product line.
   b. offer standardized storefront designs, business formats, and names and purchase systems.
   c. have an extensive assortment within their range of products.
   d. furnish display cases for the merchandise they carry.

_____ 10. Walgreen's, Ben Franklin Stores, and Western Auto are examples of
   a. rack jobbers.
   b. wholesale cooperatives.
   c. franchise wholesaling.
   d. cash-and-carry wholesaling.

_____ 11. To economize functions and obtain broad support firms may
   a. affiliate with an existing wholesaler in franchise wholesaling.
   b. form producer-owned and retailer-owned cooperatives.
   c. rely on rack jobbers.
   d. buy directly from many manufacturer/wholesalers.

_____ 12. Which of the following is _not_ a limited-service wholesaler?
   a. General merchandise wholesaler
   b. Cash-and-carry wholesaler
   c. Truck/wagon wholesaler
   d. Mail order wholesaler

_____ 13. Drop shippers do not provide
   a. merchandising.
   b. trade credit.
   c. a personal sales force.
   d. research and planning assistance.

_____ 14. Truck/wagon wholesalers usually deal with
   a. building materials.
   b. automobile parts.
   c. hardware products.
   d. perishables.

_____ 15. Agents and brokers
   a. receive profits from sales of goods they own.
   b. are the largest category of wholesalers.
   c. take title to goods.
   d. work for commissions or fees.

_____ 16. Which of the following is _not_ a type of agent?
   a. Manufacturers' agent
   b. Selling agent
   c. Commission merchant
   d. Mail order merchant

_____ 17. Which of the following receives goods on consignment from producers and arranges for their sale at a central market location?
   a. Selling agents
   b. Manufacturers' agents
   c. Food brokers
   d. Commission merchants

_____ 18. Selling agents
   a. assume responsibility for marketing the entire output of a manufacturer.
   b. are able to eliminate conflict-of-interest situations by selling noncompetitive items.
   c. are likely to work for large manufacturers.
   d. receive goods on consignment from producers for sale at a central market location.

_____ 19. Food brokers usually
   a. complete a transaction on their own authority.
   b. provide credit.
   c. can store and deliver goods.
   d. take title to goods.

_____ 20. Which of the following is *not* a recent trend in wholesaling?
   a. A decline in competition among independent wholesalers
   b. Diversification of the markets served
   c. Broadened product mixes
   d. Telephone selling to small accounts

DISCUSSION QUESTIONS

1. Why are wholesale sales so high?

2. What would an industry be like without wholesalers?

3. On what grounds do wholesalers feel they receive inadequate support from manufacturers/suppliers? What kinds of support would they like?

4. When is a manufacturer most likely to engage in direct selling?

5. Compare and contrast full-service and limited-service merchant wholesalers. Provide specific examples from the subtypes provided in the text.

6. Describe the functions performed by brokers and agents.

7. Explain the advantages and disadvantages of wholesalers servicing small accounts by telephone selling and automatic reorder systems.

EXERCISES

13-1.   A burglar-alarm products manufacturer has traditionally sold its products through its own sales force (manufacturer wholesaling). Burglar-alarm installers purchased their products directly from the manufacturer (either by phone, by visiting the manufacturer's showroom, or through visits by the manufacturer's sales force).

The manufacturer has now begun to test market a wireless burglar and fire alarm aimed at do-it-yourself consumers and at consumers who have been reluctant to spend the $1,500-$3,000 generally required to buy an effective home burglar-alarm system and have it installed. The product would use the manufacturer's well-known brand name and would be sold through department stores, full-line discount stores, retail catalog showrooms, and other retailers.

The firm is contemplating whether to utilize a new sales force for this product or to use manufacturer's agents. The firm is convinced that its existing sales force could not handle the new product for several reasons. One, it will be sold through entirely different channels. Two, installers see the new alarm as a competitive threat. The manufacturer is concerned about hostility towards it. This will be intensified if the same sales force sells products to installers and to do-it-yourself consumers. Three, the current sales force has little additional time to serve new customers.

Questions

1.   What are the advantages and disadvantages of each option?

2. Which option should the manufacturer use? Explain your answer.

3. Can the manufacturer use manufacturers' agents to develop a territory and then switch to its own sales force? Explain your answer.

4. How can the manufacturer make sure that by using manufacturers' agents it will lose only a minimal amount of control?

13-2.　　　　Food brokers are becoming increasingly important. One estimate is that as much as 50 per cent of all the food sold at retail is distributed via food brokers. Not long ago, Anheuser-Busch, Chesebrough-Pond's, and Hershey Foods signed on food brokers to either replace or supplement their own direct sales forces.

　　　　Recently, an associate editor of a leading business publication spent a day in the field with a food broker specializing in dairy products to get a better glimpse of his activities.[1]

- A total of five supermarkets were visited.
- Among the nonselling functions performed were refastening loose price labels, issuing credits for defective products, checking for recalled items, verifying compliance with manufacturer display requirements to obtain deals, setting up displays, and checking prices with competitors.
- In many cases, the tasks performed had no short-run profit impact on the food broker. For example, food brokers receive no commission on spoiled goods.
- The broker was concerned about one store ordering too much of a single yogurt flavor (he assumed that different flavors had equal popularity). He also was concerned that an order for his brand of orange juice was not properly filled out; as a result it was out-of-stock. In another instance, the broker noted that a salami manufacturer had shipped an order too close to the product's expiration date.

---

[1] Steven Mintz, "S&MM Spends a Day in the Field with a Food Broker," *Sales & Marketing Management* (June 1982), Special Report.

Questions

1.　Under what circumstances would a food manufacturer choose to use its own sales force to call on retailers? When would it use food brokers?

2. Why do you think that firms such as Anheuser-Busch are turning to food brokers?

3. One store dairy manager stated that service from a manufacturer's direct sales-person was better than that from a broker. The "broker is worried about too many items," and has too many channels to go through to rectify a problem. Evaluate this statement.

4. Food brokers are often seen as a useful source of marketing information for manufacturers. List some of the information they can provide.

13-3.   According to the text, wholesalers are very much "in the middle," not fully knowing whether their allegiance should be to the manufacturer or supplier or their own customers. Interview a wholesaler in your community concerning his or her attitudes toward this statement.

13-4.   Interview a hospital purchasing agent concerning his or her experience with a merchant wholesaler. Refer to Table 1. What conclusions do you reach?

Table 1
Contrasting Strategies of Full-Service and Limited-Service Medical-Supply Merchant Wholesalers

Full-Service Medical-Supply Wholesaler
- Provides special services for physicians, such as frequent sales calls, emergency and small-order delivery, and liberal credit terms
- Guarantees zero out-of-stock policy for key health care items through an inventory control system
- Prepares an ideal inventory model for accounts and agrees to manage inventory to maintain appropriate stock levels
- Uses a sales contract or prime vendor contract whereby the hospital agrees to do the majority of its purchasing through the contracting wholesaler
- Maintains an inventory of 8,000-10,000 items
- Is paid, on average, every 50 days

Limited-Service Medical-Supply Wholesaler
- Offers the lowest market price as the primary means of generating sales; gross profit margin is 10% of sales, compared with the industry average of 20%
- Uses multiyear supply contracts with hospitals, reducing need for field sales support; average selling costs as a per cent of new sales are 2.0%, compared with the industry average of 5.5%
- Seeks sales contracts only from largest-volume hospitals
- Deals only in high-volume medical commodities
- Uses high levels of computer cost controls and accounting controls
- Maintains an inventory of 1,500-3,000 items
- Is paid, on average, in fewer than 30 days

Source: Adapted from P. Ronald Stephenson, "Wholesale Distribution: An Analysis of Structure, Strategy and Profit Performance," in Arch G. Woodside *et al.* (Editors), *Foundations of Marketing Channels* (Austin, Texas: Lone Star Publishers, 1978), pp. 103-107. © Lone Star Publishers, 1978; reprinted with permission.

ANSWERS

True/False

1. F, p. 377	11. F, p. 384
2. F, p. 377	12. T, pp. 385-386
3. T, p. 378	13. T, p. 387
4. T, p. 378	14. T, pp. 387-388
5. T, p. 378	15. F, pp. 388-389
6. F, p. 380	16. F, p. 390
7. F, p. 383	17. F, p. 390
8. T, p. 383	18. T, p. 392
9. F, p. 383	19. F, p. 392
10. F, p. 384	20. T, p. 393

Multiple Choice

1. c, p. 378	11. b, p. 387
2. a, p. 378	12. a, pp. 388-389
3. d, p. 380	13. a, p. 390
4. b, p. 380	14. d, p. 390
5. c, p. 380	15. d, p. 390
6. d, p. 383	16. d, p. 390
7. c, p. 383	17. d, p. 392
8. c, p. 384	18. a, p. 392
9. a, p. 385	19. c, p. 392
10. c, p. 387	20. a, p. 393

Definitions

1. b	9. s
2. j	10. c
3. p	11. d
4. a	12. e
5. l	13. n
6. t	14. i
7. r	15. g
8. q	

Discussion Questions

1. p. 378
2. pp. 378-379
3. p. 380
4. p. 383
5. pp. 384-390
6. pp. 390-392
7. pp. 393-394

14

Retailing

CHAPTER OBJECTIVES

1. To define retailing and show its importance
2. To examine the different types of retailing categorized by ownership, strategy mix, and nonstore operations
3. To describe four major considerations in retail planning: store location, atmosphere, scrambled merchandising, and the wheel of retailing
4. To explore recent trends in retailing

CHAPTER OVERVIEW

Retailing encompasses those business activities involved with the sale of goods and services to the ultimate (final) consumer for personal, family, or household use. Average retail sales are small, yet the use of credit is widespread. Final consumers make many unplanned purchases and generally visit a retail store to make a purchase.

Retailing has an impact on the economy because of its total sales and the number of people employed. Retailers provide a variety of functions, including gathering a product assortment, providing information, handling merchandise, and completing transactions. Retailers deal with one group of suppliers that sell products the retailers use in operating their businesses and a second group selling items the retailers will resell.

Retailers may be categorized in several ways. Ownership types are independent, chain, franchise, leased department, and cooperative. The ease of entry into retailing fosters competition and results in many new firms failing. Different strategy mixes are used by convenience stores, supermarkets, superstores, specialty stores, variety stores, department stores, full-line discount stores, and retail catalog showrooms. Nonstore retailing involves vending machines, direct-to-home, and mail order. Service retailing includes rental goods, owned goods, and nongoods (discussed in Chapters 9 and 22).

In retail planning, store location, atmosphere, scrambled merchandising, the wheel of retailing, and technological advances need to be considered. Locational alternatives are isolated stores, unplanned business districts, and planned shopping centers. Only the planned centers utilize balanced tenancy. Atmosphere is the sum total of a store's physical characteristics that help develop an image and attract customers. Scrambled merchandising is the addition of products unrelated to the retailer's original business. The wheel of retailing explains low-end and high-end retail strategies and how they emerge.

Retailers have adapted their strategies in response to recent trends regarding consumer demographics and life-styles, costs and price levels, and technological advances.

KEY TERMS AND CONCEPTS

Retailing	Encompasses those business activities that involve the sale of goods and services to the ultimate (final) consumer for personal, family, or household use. Retailing is the final stage in the channel of distribution.
Independent retailer	A retailer operating only one outlet.
Chain retailer	Involves common ownership of multiple retailing units.
Retail franchising	A contractual arrangement between a franchisor who may be a manufacturer, wholesaler, or service sponsor and a retail franchisee, which allows the franchisee to conduct a certain form of business under an established name and according to a specific set of rules.
Leased department	A department in a retail store (usually a department, discount, or specialty store) that is rented to an outside party.
Retail cooperative	A format that allows independent retailers to share purchases, storage, and shipping facilities, advertising, planning, and other functions.
Consumer cooperative	A form of retailer owned and operated by consumer members.
Retail strategy mix	The combination of prices, products, sales personnel, hours, and other factors that a retailer employs.
Convenience store	A retail store featuring food items that is open long hours and carries a limited number of items. Consumers typically use a convenience store for fill-in merchandise, often at off-hours.
Supermarket	A departmentalized food store with minimum annual sales of $2 million.
Superstore	A large food-based retailer that is much more diversified than a supermarket.
Specialty store	A retailer which concentrates on the sale of one merchandise line.
Variety store	A retailer which sells a wide assortment of low and popularly priced merchandise.

Department store	A large retailer, employing 25 plus people and usually selling a general line of apparel for the family, household linens, and dry goods, and furniture, home furnishings, appliances, radios, and televisions. It is organized into separate departments for purposes of buying, promotion, service, and control.
Full-line discount store	A retailer characterized by low prices, a broad merchandise assortment, low-rent location, self-service, brand-name merchandise, wide aisles, use of shopping carts, and most merchandise displayed on the selling floor.
Retail catalog showroom	A warehouse-type outlet at which consumers select merchandise from a catalog. Customers frequently write up their own orders, products are usually stored in a back room, and there are limited displays.
Nonstore retailing	Retail form which does not utilize conventional store facilities. Includes vending machines, direct-to-home sales, and mail order.
Vending machine	A nonstore retail operation which involves coin-operated machinery, eliminates the use of sales personnel, allows around-the-clock sales, and can be placed outside rather than inside a store.
Direct-to-home retailer	A nonstore retail operation which sells directly to consumers in their homes.
Mail order retailing	A nonstore retail operation which seeks customers through television, radio, printed media, or the mail, receives orders through the mail or telephone, and ships merchandise to the customer's home.
Isolated store	A free-standing retail outlet located on either a highway or a side street.
Unplanned business district	A retail location form in which a group of stores are located close to one another and the combination of stores is not based on prior planning. There are four types of unplanned business districts: central business district, secondary business district, neighborhood business district, and string.
Planned shopping center	A retail location that is centrally owned or managed, planned and operated as an entity, surrounded by parking, and based on balanced tenancy. The types are regional, community, and neighborhood.
Balanced tenancy	Relates the type and number of stores within any planned center to the overall needs of the surrounding population. To ensure balance a shopping center may limit the merchandise lines any store carries.
Atmosphere	The sum total of the physical characteristics of a retail store that are used to develop an image and draw customers.
Scrambled merchandising	Occurs when a retailer adds products or product lines that are unrelated to each other and the retailer's original business.

Wheel of retailing
A concept describing how low-end (discount) strategies can turn into high-end (high price) strategies, thus providing opportunities for new firms to enter as discounters.

TRUE/FALSE

Circle the appropriate letter.

T   F   1. Those who buy for resale or use in manufacture are more systematic in their purchasing than final consumers are.

T   F   2. The gross margin for department stores is higher than for supermarkets.

T   F   3. There are many independent retailers because of ease of entry.

T   F   4. Only a few hundred chains operate a hundred or more units; yet they are responsible for one quarter of total store sales.

T   F   5. Franchising is a form of independent retailing.

T   F   6. The goal of retail cooperatives is to offer reduced prices to customers.

T   F   7. Consumer cooperatives are a fast-growing form of retail enterprise.

T   F   8. Newspapers, ice cream, and gasoline are popular items at convenience stores.

T   F   9. A superstore is a departmentalized food store with minimum annual sales of $1 million.

T   F   10. With the growth of other retail strategy mixes, variety stores have fallen on hard times.

T   F   11. Discount stores are the largest retailers of general merchandise and housewares.

T   F   12. A department store has the greatest assortment of any retailer.

T   F   13. Catalog showrooms specialize in national brands.

T   F   14. With a cold canvass system of direct-to-home sales, one consumer acts as a host and invites friends to an at-home sales demonstration.

T   F   15. Discount or warehouse stores are usually best suited for an isolated location.

T   F   16. A string is a group of stores based on balanced tenancy.

T   F   17. A neighborhood shopping center sells mostly convenience products.

T   F   18. Scrambled merchandising decreases impulse purchasing.

T   F   19. The slowdown in overall population growth in the U.S. and geographic population shifts are causing a number of retailers to close down more regional and cross-country branches.

T   F   20. A computerized checkout system improves inventory control.

COMPLETION

Fill in the missing word or words in the blanks provided.

[Retailing, p. 400]

1. _____ encompasses those business activities that involve the sale of goods and services to the ultimate consumer for personal, family, or household use.

[sales, employment, distribution, suppliers, pp. 400-402]

2. Retailing is important to study because it contributes substantially to the total amount of U.S. _____ and _____ , performs essential functions in _____ by collecting assortments of products for sale and deals with _____ , with whom there may be differences of viewpoint.

[independent, chain, franchising, pp. 403-404]

3. An _____ retailer operates only one retail outlet, whereas a _____ operates many. A form of the latter is _____ , where a contract allows a certain form of business under an established name according to a specified set of rules.

[leased department, p. 405]

4. A _____ _____ in a retail store is rented to an outside party.

[retail cooperative, consumer cooperative, p. 406]

5. In a _____ _____ , independent retailers form an organization to share purchases, advertising, and other functions; a _____ _____ is a retailer owned by consumer members.

[convenience, super-markets, superstore, pp. 407-408]

6. A _____ store carries a limited number of items and is open for long hours; its success has encouraged _____ to lengthen their hours of operation for the sale of food. A larger version of the supermarket is the _____ , which carries more diversified goods.

[specialty, variety, pp. 408-409]

7. A _____ store concentrates on the sale of one merchandise line, whereas a _____ store sells a wide assortment of low and popularly priced merchandise.

[discount, department, retail catalog showroom, p. 409]

8. A full-line _____ store is characterized by broad merchandise assortments and self-service; a _____ store is a retailer employing at least 25 people and is organized into separate divisions for purposes of buying, promotion, service, and control; and a _____ _____ _____ is an establishment where consumers can shop at a warehouse location.

[vending machines, direct-to-home, mail-order, pp. 409-411]

9. Three types of nonstore retailing operations are _____ _____ , which are coin operated; _____ _____ _____ sales, involving selling directly to the consumer at home; and _____ _____ sales, involving soliciting through the media and shipping products to the consumer at home.

[isolated store, unplanned business district, planned shopping center, pp. 412-414]

10. Three basic types of retail location are the _____ _____ , a free-standing outlet located either on a highway or side street; the _____

_____ _____ , where a group of stores is spontaneously located in close proximity; and the _____ _____ _____ , which is centrally owned and managed and based on balanced tenancy.

[central, secondary, neighborhood, string, p. 414]

11. Four types of unplanned shopping areas are the _____ business district, synonymous with the term downtown; the _____ business district, usually bounded by the intersection of two major streets; the _____ business district, located on a major street in a residential area; and the _____ , composed of a group of stores with similar or compatible product lines.

[planned, regional, community, neighborhood, pp. 414-415]

12. Balanced tenancy characterizes the _____ shopping center. The _____ form sells predominantly shopping goods; the _____ types sell both shopping goods and convenience items; and the _____ type sells mostly convenience items.

[exterior, general interior, store layout, interior displays, p. 415]

13. Four components of a store's atmosphere are the _____ , for example, a storefront; the _____ _____ , for example, lighting; the _____ _____ , for example, floor space allocated for customers; and _____ _____ , for example, mannequins.

[Scrambled merchandising, wheel of retailing, p. 416]

14. _____ _____ occurs when a retailer adds products or product lines that are unrelated to each other and to the retailer's original business. When retail innovators first appear as low-price operators and then gradually upgrade their offerings, thereby eventually developing into traditional retailers, the _____ _____ _____ may be occurring.

[slowdown, saturation, time, sophistication, price, technological, pp. 417-420]

15. Retailers are responding to a _____ in the overall U.S. population growth, the _____ of many prime markets, the _____ constraints of a growing number of working women, the increased _____ of consumers with regard to their purchases, the _____ levels confronting consumers especially during inflationary times, and _____ advances such as the computerized-checkout system.

DEFINITIONS

Match the terms and concepts with the appropriate definitions. Each term or concept may only be used once; there are more terms and concepts than definitions.

Column A	Column B
a. atmosphere	___ 1. A retailer which concentrates on the sale of one merchandise line.

b. chain retailer

c. consumer cooperative

d. convenience store

e. department store

f. direct-to-home retailer

g. full-line discount store

h. independent retailer

i. isolated store

j. leased department

k. mail order retailing

l. nonstore retailing

m. planned shopping center

n. retail catalog showroom

o. retail cooperative

p. retail franchising

q. retail strategy mix

r. retailing

s. scrambled merchandising

t. specialty store

u. supermarket

v. superstore

w. unplanned business district

x. variety store

y. vending machine

z. wheel of retailing

____ 2. The sum total of the physical characteristics of a retail store that are used to develop an image and draw customers.

____ 3. The combination of prices, products, sales personnel, hours, and other factors that a retailer employs.

____ 4. Common ownership of multiple retailing units.

____ 5. Retailing form which does not utilize conventional store facilities.

____ 6. A retailer which sells a wide assortment of low and popularly priced merchandise.

____ 7. A free standing retail outlet located on either a highway or a side street.

____ 8. Occurs when a retailer adds products or product lines that are unrelated to each other and the retailer's original business.

____ 9. A retailer operating only one outlet.

____ 10. A retail form owned and operated by consumer members.

____ 11. A format that allows independent retailers to share purchases, storage and shipping facilities, advertising, planning, and other functions.

____ 12. A concept describing how low-end strategies can turn into high-end strategies, thus providing opportunities for new firms to enter as discounters.

____ 13. A nonstore retail operation which involves coin-operated machinery, eliminates the use of sales personnel, allows around-the-clock sales, and can be placed outside rather than inside a store.

____ 14. A departmentalized food store with minimum annual sales of $2 million.

____ 15. A retail store featuring food items that is open long hours and carries a limited number of items.

MULTIPLE CHOICE

Place the letter of the answer you think best in the blank provided.

____ 1. Which of the following is *not* a way in which retailers can increase sales in their stores?
a. Broadened merchandise assortments
b. Limiting parking time
c. Attracting more family members to shop
d. Increasing the frequency of shopping

2. Many final consumers do *not*
   a. patronize stores.
   b. make unplanned purchases.
   c. make many small purchases.
   d. shop systematically.

3. Which of the following is *not* a way in which 7-Eleven stores can be classified?
   a. Chain
   b. Variety store
   c. Franchise
   d. Isolated store

4. Independent retailers
   a. have the greatest survival rate.
   b. comprise the bulk of retailers.
   c. require consumers to take lots of initiative.
   d. face little competition.

5. Safeway, K mart, and Sears are examples of
   a. independent retailers.
   b. leased departments.
   c. retail cooperatives.
   d. chains.

6. Popular for beauty salons, jewelry, photographic studios, shoe repairs, and cosmetics are
   a. independent retailers.
   b. leased departments.
   c. retail cooperatives.
   d. chains.

7. A store classified by retail strategy mix is a/an
   a. retail catalog showroom.
   b. insolated store.
   c. franchise.
   d. independent retailers.

8. Which of the following is *not* a reason why more and more supermarkets are becoming superstores?
   a. Self-service operation
   b. An interest in one-stop shopping
   c. Higher margins on general merchandise
   d. Improved transportation networks

9. The retail strategy mix currently facing hard times is that used by a
   a. specialty store.
   b. variety store.
   c. full-line discount store.
   d. department store.

_____ 10. Both discount and department stores feature
   a. self-service.
   b. limited inventories.
   c. fashion leadership.
   d. brand name merchandise.

_____ 11. Which of the following is *not* a form of direct-to-home retailing?
   a. Cold canvass
   b. Referral system
   c. Scrambled merchandising
   d. Party method

_____ 12. Where there are no adjacent stores with which a firm must compete, the location is most appropriately described as a/an
   a. string.
   b. isolated store.
   c. planned shopping center.
   d. unplanned business district.

_____ 13. Which of the following is a type of unplanned business district?
   a. Trading area
   b. String
   c. Isolated stores
   d. Community shopping center

_____ 14. Balanced tenancy characterizes
   a. chains.
   b. planned shopping centers.
   c. nonstore retailing.
   d. superstores.

_____ 15. A neighborhood shopping center sells mostly
   a. shopping goods.
   b. convenience products.
   c. discount items.
   d. catalog merchandise.

_____ 16. Atmosphere is most closely related to the store's
   a. nonstore operations.
   b. ownership.
   c. advertisements.
   d. interior displays.

_____ 17. Which of the following is *not* a reason for the popularity of scrambled merchandising?
   a. One-stop shopping
   b. High profit margins
   c. Improved store image
   d. Increased impulse purchasing

_____ 18. Differences between department-store and discount-store strategies are explained by the
   a. scrambled merchandising idea.
   b. referral method.
   c. wheel-of-retailing notion.
   d. balanced tenancy approach.

_____ 19. Baskin-Robbins outlets in U.S. Navy exchange facilities and Burger King stores inside Woolworth outlets are examples of retailers' response to
   a. the slowdown in overall population growth.
   b. time constraints on working women.
   c. increased consumer sophistication about purchases.
   d. the saturation of many prime markets.

_____ 20. Computer-based checkouts
   a. improve ordering decisions.
   b. increase employee training time.
   c. require price marking on merchandise.
   d. increase checkout time.

DISCUSSION QUESTIONS

1. Final consumers make many unplanned purchases. How may retailers capitalize on this tendency?

2. What is the impact of retailing on the economy? What is the impact of the economy on retailing? What conclusions, if any, can you draw?

3. Why are variety stores in trouble? What is the status of retail catalog showrooms? What strategies might reverse the trends you discern?

4. Compare discount-store and department-store strategies.

5. Why are large retailers usually best suited for isolated store locations?

6. Design an atmosphere suitable for a specialty store. Include in your answer all of the four components listed in the text.

7. What are the advantages and disadvantages of scrambled merchandising? How does this concept help you to understand the shift from supermarkets to superstores?

EXERCISES

14-1.   A department store chain has hired you as a retail consultant and asked you to examine the data contained in Tables 1 and 2. Table 1 measures retail performance over a recent five-year period by store category. It describes several firms in each category. Table 2 projects 1985 retail sales by store category on the basis of actual 1983 sales.

Table 1
Yardsticks of Retail Performance for Selected Retail Store Categories
(ranked by return on equity)

	Annual Return on Equity (5-year average)	Net Profit Margin (latest 12 mos.)	Annual Sales Growth (5-year average)
MAJOR SUPERMARKET CHAINS			
American Stores	23.6%	1.3%	52.8%
Albertson's	22.4	1.5	16.9
Lucky Stores	22.0	1.4	14.9
Supermarkets General	21.0	1.2	11.3
Winn-Dixie Stores	20.2	1.6	12.1
DEPARTMENT STORES			
R. H. Macy	20.0%	5.4%	12.8%
Dayton-Hudson	17.9	3.4	19.1
Mercantile Stores	15.8	5.0	12.1
Dillard Department Stores	15.1	3.7	19.6
May Department Stores	14.5	4.2	9.8
DISCOUNT and VARIETY STORES			
Wal-Mart Stores	33.1%	4.0%	37.3%
SCOA Industries	27.5	3.0	11.7
Heck's	14.6	1.6	16.8
Rose's Stores	14.0	2.5	7.0
Zayre	13.6	2.1	9.8
FAST-FOOD CHAINS			
Wendy's International	24.8%	7.8%	42.0%
McDonald's	22.8	11.4	15.9
Marriott	21.0	3.8	18.6
Jerrico	17.8	4.6	22.0
Denny's	17.5	3.8	18.3
OTHER SPECIALISTS			
Tandy	45.2%	11.2%	19.2%
Limited	33.2	5.1	31.8
Toys "R" Us	25.5	6.2	27.9*
Melville	25.3	4.2	18.0
Avon Products	23.5	6.0	12.1

*Four-year growth

Data from Richard Greene, "Supermarkets," *Forbes* (January 2, 1984), pp. 228-230; and Howard Rudnitsky, "Retailing," *Forbes* (January 2, 1984), pp. 231-234.

Table 2
Retail Sales Outlook, 1983-1985
for Selected Store Categories

Store Category	1983 Sales $ Billion	1985 Sales Projection $ Billion	Per Cent Change
Automotive dealers	$ 199.8	$ 247.5	+ 23.9
Department stores	115.3	132.7	+ 15.1
Variety stores	9.1	10.3	+ 13.2
Food stores	263.1	297.2	+ 13.0
Men's apparel stores	8.5	9.6	+ 12.9
Women's apparel stores	21.0	23.8	+ 13.3
Shoe stores	10.7	12.3	+ 15.0
Eating and drinking places	118.8	136.9	+ 15.2
Total retail sales	$1,170.0	$1,350.5	+ 15.4

Data from "Retail Sales Outlook 1983-85," *Sales & Marketing Management* (October 31, 1983), p. 18.

Questions

1. Offer at least five conclusions that can be reached by studying Tables 1 and 2.

2. The department store hiring you as a consultant has an annual net profit margin of 6.2 per cent and it has had a five-year average sales growth of 4.0 per cent. Compare this store's performance with that of the department stores shown in Table 1. Explain how its performance could be different from those in Table 1.

3. What other data are needed to get a clearer picture of the department store chain's performance?

4. According to Table 1, leading fast-food chains are quite profitable and have grown substantially over the last several years. Would you recommend that the department store chain consider opening fast-food outlets in its stores? What are the pros and cons of this strategy?

14-2.   Site selection practices can have a long-term effect on profitability. Aside from costing about $100,000 to open a store (such as Wendy's), choosing the wrong site can involve additional operating losses of between $60,000 and $100,000 per year.

Accordingly, site selection experts have developed a variety of methodologies for conducting a site evaluation analysis. The first step in any evaluation is to find out who customers are and where they reside in relation to the store site. This requires conducting exit interviews with a random group of customers in existing stores. One expert recommends sampling 1,000 customers per store to delineate a trading area. A sample of 300 to 400 interviews "would suffice," however. If a firm only desires a demographic profile, 150 to 200 customers per store may be adequate.

Demographic data obtained in an interview should include family income, family size, age, education, occupation, and housing type. The interviewer should also record the general area in which the respondent lives, the amount spent in the store, and the customer's attitudes toward the store and its competition.[1]

Among the guidelines in site selection used by large retail chains are:[2]

- Looking for parallel businesses that attract a similar target market
- Using advertising to lower operating costs, and to more favorably negotiate terms
- Using space as efficiently as possible
- Negotiating to receive an excessive vacancy clause. With such a clause, a lease can be broken if too much space in a shopping area is unfilled
- Avoiding locations dominated by stores with little or no customer interchange with adjacent retailers
- Trying to position the store location in the exact center of a market
- Analyzing nearby tenants for affinities with the store

---

[1] "Why Site Selection; Methodology: The First Step in a Program for Self-Analysis," *Chain Store Age Executive* (January 1983), pp. 30-31.

[2] John R. Dorfman, "Sense of Site," *Forbes* (February 14, 1983), pp. 122-123.

Questions

1.   Why is site selection so costly? Be complete in your answer.

2.   What are the advantages and disadvantages of conducting exit interviews with customers in existing stores?

3.   How would an independent retailer differ from a chain retailer in its site selection criteria?

4.   What other locational factors, besides those mentioned in the exercise, should be considered before choosing a site?

14-3.   Visit a small grocery store and ask the owner how he or she is able to compete with larger supermarkets. Determine the grocer's major differential advantages and disadvantages.

14-4.　　　Select a franchisor of interest to you and determine the provisions with which its franchisees must comply. Evaluate this information.

ANSWERS

True/False

1. T, p. 400
2. T, p. 401
3. T, p. 403
4. T, p. 404
5. F, pp. 404-405
6. F, p. 406
7. F, p. 406
8. T, p. 407
9. F, pp. 407-408
10. T, pp. 408-409
11. T, p. 409
12. T, p. 409
13. T, p. 409
14. F, p. 410
15. T, pp. 412-413
16. F, p. 414
17. T, p. 415
18. F, p. 416
19. F, p. 417
20. T, p. 419

Multiple Choice

1. b, p. 400
2. d, p. 400
3. b, p. 403
4. b, p. 403-404
5. d, p. 404
6. b, p. 405
7. a, p. 406
8. a, pp. 407-408
9. b, pp. 408-409
10. d, p. 409
11. c, p. 410
12. b, pp. 412-414
13. b, p. 414
14. b, p. 414
15. b, p. 415
16. d, p. 415
17. c, p. 416
18. c, p. 416
19. d, pp. 417-418
20. a, p. 419

Definitions

1. t
2. a
3. q
4. b
5. l
6. x
7. i
8. s
9. h
10. c
11. o
12. z
13. y
14. u
15. d

Discussion Questions

1. p. 400
2. p. 401
3. pp. 408-409
4. p. 409
5. pp. 412-414
6. p. 415
7. p. 416

Part Four Review Quiz

DEFINITIONS

Define the following terms and concepts in your own words and then check your answers with the Key Terms and Concepts sections of the Study Guide, Chapters 12-14.

channel of distribution
physical distribution
just-in-time inventory system
franchise wholesaling
manufacturers' agent
full-line discount store
planned shopping center

SEQUENCES

For each of the following questions, arrange the events in chronological order by writing the numbers in the blanks provided, indicating the first in each series by 1.

1. The Sorting Process
   _____ assorting
   _____ allocation
   _____ accumulation
   _____ sorting

2. The Order Cycle
   _____ packaging and shipping
   _____ warehousing and storage
   _____ customer order
   _____ transportation to a warehouse
   _____ order entry
   _____ transportation to a customer

3.   Wheel of Retailing from Low End to High End
     _____ full-line discount stores
     _____ prestige department stores
     _____ retail catalog showrooms
     _____ traditional department stores
     _____ factory outlets

SENTENCES

In each sentence, circle the word or phrase that is most appropriate.

1.   A firm that uses independent channel members is likely to [increase/decrease] its per-unit distribution costs and [increase/decrease] its per-unit profits.

2.   A/An [direct/indirect] channel of distribution involves the movement of goods and services from manufacturer to independent channel member to consumer.

3.   [Vertical/Horizontal] integration enables a firm to shorten its channel by acquiring a company at another stage in the channel.

4.   With [exclusive/selective] distribution, the firm employs a moderate number of wholesalers and retailers, trying to combine channel control and a prestige image with good sales volume.

5.   Greater product variety tends to mean [higher/lower] volume per item, which [increases/decreases] overall shipping and warehousing costs.

6.   Over the last several years, deregulation of transportation industries has greatly [expanded/reduced] competition in and among these industries.

7.   The just-in-time inventory system encourages firms to order [more/less] frequently and in [higher/lower] quantity.

8.   Selling [to/through] the wholesaler means the retailer or final consumer is the object of the manufacturer's/supplier's interest.

9.   Manufacturer wholesaling is most likely when there are [few/many] customers to service, the product is considered a [major/minor] purchase by customers, and orders are [large/small].

10.   [Full/Limited]-service merchant wholesalers provide the most functions.

11.   [Producer/Retailer]-owned wholesale cooperatives are popular in farming.

12.   Drop shippers [do/do not] have legal ownership of products and [do/do not] take physical possession of them.

13.   Brokers are usually employed on a [permanent/temporary] b

14.   Over the last several years, competition among indeper
        [increased/decreased] dramatically.

15.   Average retail sales are [low/high] and most are [for cash/on

16.   The most common form of retail operation is the [chain/inde

17.   A super [store/market] is a large food-based retailer that stocks garden supplies,
        household appliances, and clothing as well.

18.   A string occurs in a/an [planned/unplanned] business district.

19.   Scrambled merchandising frequently [increases/decreases] competition among
        unrelated stores.

20.   Computerized checkouts [raise/lower] costs, [increase/decrease] checkout time, and
        [require/eliminate] price marking on merchandise.

SWERS

Sequences

1. 4,2,1,3, p. 347
2. 3,5,1,4,2,6, p. 358
3. 3,5,2,4,1, pp. 416, 418

Sentences

1. decrease, decrease, p. 343
2. indirect, p. 348
3. Vertical, p. 351
4. selective, p. 351
5. lower, increases, p. 360
6. expanded, p. 361
7. more, lower, p. 365
8. through, p. 380
9. few, major, large, p. 383
10. Full, p. 383
11. Producer, p. 387
12. do, do not, p. 390
13. temporary, p. 390
14. increased, p. 393
15. low, on credit, p. 400
16. independent, p. 403
17. store, pp. 407-408
18. unplanned, p. 414
19. increases, p. 416
20. lower, decrease, eliminate, p. 419

Part
Five

Promotion Planning

15 An Overview of Promotion Planning

CHAPTER OBJECTIVES

1. To define promotion and show its importance
2. To describe the general characteristics of advertising, publicity, personal selling, and sales promotion
3. To explain the channel of communication and how it functions
4. To examine the components of a promotion plan: objectives, budget, and mix of elements
5. To study the legal environment and the criticisms and defenses of promotion

CHAPTER OVERVIEW

Promotion informs, persuades, or reminds people about a firm's products, services, ideas, community involvement, or impact on society. Its major elements are advertising, publicity, personal selling, and sales promotion.

Through the channel of communication, a source sends a message to its audience. The channel consists of source, encoding, message, medium, decoding, audience, feedback, and noise. The source is the company, independent institution, or opinion leader that seeks to present a message to an audience. In choosing a source, credibility, expertise, and other factors must be considered.

Encoding is the process by which a thought or an idea is translated into a message by the source. The message is the combination of words and symbols transmitted to the audience; it must be presented in a desirable, exclusive, and believable manner. Timing must be carefully planned. The medium is the personal or nonpersonal channel used to convey a message. Decoding is the process through which the message sent by the source is translated by the audience.

The audience is the object of the source's message. Although it is usually the target market, it may also be stockholders, consumer groups, independent media, the public, or government officials. Feedback is the response the audience makes to the firm's message: purchase, attitude change, or nonpurchase. Noise is the interference at any stage along the channel of communication.

Promotion objectives may be demand- or image-oriented. Demand objectives should parallel the hierarchy-of-effects model, moving from awareness to purchase. Primary demand is total product demand; selective demand is for the company's brand. Institutional advertising is used to enhance company image.

There are five methods for setting a promotion budget: all you can afford, incremental, competitive parity, percentage of sales, and objective and task. The weakest is the all-you-can-afford technique. The best is the objective-and-task technique. The S-curve effect and marginal return should be considered when setting a budget.

The promotion mix is the overall and specific communication program of the firm, combining advertising, publicity, personal selling, and/or sales promotion. Consumer, budget, product, competition, media, and place-of-purchase factors should be considered in the development of a promotion mix.

There are many laws and rules affecting promotion. The major ways unsatisfactory promotion is guarded against are full disclosure, substantiation, cease-and-desist orders, corrective advertising, and fines. Critics are strong in their complaints about promotion. Marketers are equally firm in their defenses.

KEY TERMS AND CONCEPTS

Promotion planning	Systematic decision making pertaining to all aspects of the development and management of a firm's promotional effort.
Promotion	Any form of communication used by a firm to inform, persuade, or remind people about its products, services, image, ideas, community involvement, or impact on society.
Word-of-mouth communication	The process by which people express their opinions and product-related experiences to one another.
Advertising	Any paid form of nonpersonal presentation and promotion of ideas, goods, and services by an identified sponsor.
Publicity	Nonpersonal stimulation of demand for a product, service, or business by placing commercially significant news about it in a published medium or obtaining favorable presentation upon radio, television, or stage that is not paid for by an identified sponsor.
Personal selling	An oral presentation in a conversation with one or more prospective buyers for the purpose of making sales.
Sales promotion	Involves marketing activities, other than advertising, publicity, or personal selling, that stimulate consumer purchases and dealer effectiveness. Included

	are shows, demonstrations, and various nonrecurrent selling efforts not in the ordinary routine.
Channel of communication (Communication process)	The mechanism through which a source sends a message to its audience. It consists of source, encoding, message, medium, decoding, audience feedback, and noise.
Source of communication	The company, independent institution, or opinion leader that seeks to present a message to an audience. Part of the channel of communication.
Two-step flow of communication	Theory stating that a message goes from the company to opinion leaders and then to the target market.
Multistep flow of communication	The communication theory which suggests that opinion leaders not only influence but are influenced by the general public (opinion receivers).
Encoding	The procedure in a channel of communication whereby a thought or idea is translated into a message by the source.
Message	The combination of words and symbols transmitted to the audience through a channel of communication.
One-sided message	A message in which the firm mentions only the benefits of its product or service.
Two-sided message	A message in which a firm mentions both benefits and limitations of its product or service.
Comparative message	A promotion form which contrasts the firm's offering with those of competitors.
Massed promotion	Communication concentrated in peak periods, like holidays.
Distributed promotion	Communication efforts spread throughout the year.
Wearout rate	The period of time it takes for a message to lose its effectiveness.
Medium	The personal or nonpersonal channel in a channel of communication used to convey a message.
Decoding	The process in a channel of communication whereby the message sent by the source is interpreted by the audience.
Subliminal advertising	A controversial type of promotion that does not enable a consumer to consciously decode a message.
Audience	The object of the message in a channel of communication.
Feedback	The audience's response to a message in a channel of communication.
Noise	Interference at any stage along the channel of communication.
Hierarchy-of-effects model	Outlines the intermediate and long-term promotional objectives the firm should pursue: awareness,

knowledge, liking, preference, conviction, and purchase.

Primary demand
Consumer demand for a product category. Important when the product or service is little known.

Selective demand
Consumer demand for a particular brand or product.

Institutional advertising
Used to improve corporate image and not to sell products or services.

All-you-can-afford technique
A means of developing a promotional budget in which the firm first allocates funds for every element of marketing except promotion. Whatever funds are left over are placed in a promotion budget.

Incremental technique
A promotional budget method in which the company bases its new budget on previous expenditures. A percentage is either added to or subtracted from this year's budget in order to determine next year's.

Competitive parity technique
A method in which the company's promotional budget is raised or lowered according to the actions of competitors.

Percentage-of-sales technique
A promotional budget technique in which a company ties the promotion budget to sales revenue.

Objective-and-task technique
A promotional budget method in which the firm clearly outlines its promotional objectives and then establishes the appropriate budget.

S-curve effect
Occurs if the sales of a product rise sharply after it is introduced because of a heavy initial promotion effort (ads, coupons, samples, etc.), drop slightly as promotional support is reduced, and then rise again as positive word-of-mouth communication takes place.

Marginal return
The amount of sales each additional increment of promotion will generate.

Promotion mix
The overall and specific communication program of an organization, consisting of a combination of advertising, publicity, personal selling, and/or sales promotion.

Full disclosure
A consumer protection legal concept requiring that all data necessary for a consumer to make a safe and informed decision be provided.

Substantiation
A consumer protection legal concept that requires that a firm be able to prove all promotion claims it makes. This means thorough testing and evidence of performance are needed prior to making claims.

Cease-and-desist order
A form of consumer protection which legally requires a firm to discontinue deceptive practices and modify its promotion message.

Corrective advertising
A form of consumer protection which legally requires a firm to run new advertisements to correct the false impression made by previous ones.

Fine
A legal concept in consumer protection that levies a dollar penalty on a firm for a deceptive promotion or other illegal practices.

TRUE/FALSE

Circle the appropriate letter.

(T) F 1. Without sustained, positive word-of-mouth, it is difficult for a company to succeed in the long run.

✓ (T) F 2. Sales promotion involves advertising and publicity as well as personal selling.

T (F) 3. Frank Perdue is an example of a celebrity used as a source of communication.

✓ (T) F 4. Because they deal on a personal level, salespeople have strong credibility.

T (F) 5. In the two-step flow of communication, opinion leaders not only influence but are also influenced by the general public.

(T) F 6. At the encoding stage of communication, preliminary decisions are made regarding message content.

T (F) 7. Most communication involves two-sided messages.

T (F) 8. With symbolic messages, tangible product performance is stressed.

(T) F 9. Communication is concentrated in peak periods, like holidays, when massed promotion is used.

(T) F 10. Personal media work best with a concentrated target market.

(T) F 11. As symbolism increases, clarity of messages decreases.

T (F) 12. Noise facilitates feedback.

T (F) 13. At early stages of the hierarchy-of-effects model, selective demand should be sought.

T (F) 14. With the incremental technique, the promotion budget is raised or lowered according to the actions of competitors.

(T) F 15. The best of the methods for setting the promotion budget is the objective-and-task technique.

T (F) 16. Most companies use only one type of promotion.

(T) F 17. The content and timing of publicity cannot be controlled by a firm.

✓ (T) F 18. Substantiation requires that all data necessary for a consumer to make a safe and informed decision be provided.

✓ T (F) 19. In addition to government restrictions and self-regulation, the media place limits on promotion.

(T) F 20. Promotion is probably the most heavily criticized area of marketing.

COMPLETION

Fill in the missing word or words in the blanks provided.

[Promotion, word-of-mouth, pp. 433-434]

1. _____ enables a firm to establish an image, interact with channel members, and provide customer service. Important is _____ _____ _____ communication, in which people express their product-related opinions and experiences to one another.

[advertising, publicity, personal selling, sales promotion, p. 436]

2. Four basic types of promotion are _____, any paid form of impersonal presentation by an identified sponsor; _____, nonpersonal stimulation of demand by commercially-placed news not paid for by an identified sponsor; _____ _____, an oral presentation in a conversation for the purpose of making a sale; and _____ _____, involving marketing activities such as shows and demonstrations not in the ordinary promotion routine.

[channel of communication, p. 436]

3. A mechanism through which a source sends a message to an audience is a _____ _____ _____.

[company spokespeople, celebrities, actors playing roles, representative consumers, salespeople, p. 437]

4. Sources of communication include _____ _____, high-ranking employees in a firm; _____, used to gain audience attention and improve product awareness; _____ _____ _____, where emphasis is placed on presenting a message and not identifying personalities; _____ _____, who like a product and recommend it in advertisements; and _____ conversing with consumers.

[independent institutions, opinion leaders, p. 438]

5. Two other sources are _____ _____ reporting on a company but not controlled by it, and _____ _____ having face-to-face contact with potential customers.

[two-step flow of communication, multistep flow of communication, p. 438]

6. In the _____ _____ _____ _____ _____, the message travels from company to opinion leader to target market, whereas in the _____ _____ _____ _____ opinion leaders both influence and are influenced by the general public.

[encoding, decoding, pp. 438, 433]

7. Other components of the communication process are _____, translating a thought or idea into a message, and _____, translating the message.

[One-sided, two-sided, symbolism, comparative messages, p. 439]

8. _____ _____ messages mention only the benefits of a product or service, whereas _____ _____ messages stress benefits and limitations; firms may use _____, relating safety, social acceptance, or sexual appeal to the purchase of a product, or _____ _____, contrasting a firm's offerings with those of competitors.

[mass promotion, distributed promotion, p. 441]

9. With _____ _____ , communication is concentrated at peak periods, whereas with _____ _____ communication is spread throughout the year.

[medium, audience, feedback, noise, pp. 442-445]

10. The _____ is the personal or nonpersonal channel used to convey a message to an _____ , which is its target, in the hope of attaining _____ , in terms of a purchase or attitude change, unless _____ or interference occurs at a stage of the channel.

[hierarchy-of-effects, primary demand, selective demand, institutional advertising, pp. 445-446]

11. The _____ _____ _____ model outlines intermediate and long-term promotional objectives as the firm moves from seeking _____ _____ for a product category to _____ _____ for a particular brand of a product to _____ _____ to enhance the company's image.

[all-you-can-afford, incremental, competitive-parity, percentage-of-sales, objective-and-task, pp. 448-450]

12. Five methods for setting the total promotion budget are the _____ _____ _____ _____ technique, where the firm allocates money left over after other marketing components are funded; the _____ technique, where the company bases its new budget on previous expentures; the _____ _____ technique, where the budget is raised or lowered according to the actions of competitors; the _____ _____ _____ technique, which ties the budget to sales revenue; and the _____ _____ _____ technique, which outlines promotional goals, determines what will be needed, and establishes the appropriate budget accordingly.

[S-curve effect, marginal return, p. 450]

13. While a promotion budget is being developed, a firm should consider the _____ _____ _____ , where sales of a product rise sharply after a heavy promotional effort, dip slightly when that effort is reduced, and rise again as positive word-of-mouth communication takes place; and _____ _____ , the amount of sales each increment of promotion will generate.

[promotion mix, p. 450]

14. The _____ _____ is the overall and specific communication program of the firm, consisting of a combination of advertising, publicity, personal selling, and sales promotion.

[full disclosure, substantiation, cease, desist, corrective advertising, fines, pp. 453-454]

15. Four ways in which the legal environment protects consumers and and competitors against deceptive promotion are _____ _____ , requiring provision of all data necessary for consumers to make safe and informed decisions; _____ , mandating the firm to prove all claims the firm makes; _____ and _____ orders, necessitating discontinuance

of deceptive practices and modification of promotional messages; _____ _____ , requiring the running of new advertisements to right false impressions left by previous ones; and _____ , dollar penalties levied for deceptive promotion.

DEFINITIONS

Match the terms and concepts with the appropriate definitions. Each term or concept may only be used once; there are more terms and concepts than definitions.

Column A	*Column B*
a. advertising	____ 1. The period of time it takes for a message to lose its effectiveness.
b. all-you-can-afford technique	
c. audience	____ 2. The amount of sales each additional increment of promotion will generate.
d. cease-and-desist order	____ 3. The process in a channel of communication whereby the message sent by the source is interpreted by the audience.
e. channel of communication	
f. comparative message	
g. competitive parity technique	____ 4. Interference at any stage along a channel of communication.
h. corrective advertising	____ 5. A consumer protection legal concept requiring that all data necessary for a consumer to make a safe and informed decision be provided.
i. decoding	
j. distributed promotion	
k. encoding	____ 6. The object of the message in a channel of communication.
l. feedback	____ 7. Consumer demand for a particular brand or product.
m. fine	
n. full disclosure	____ 8. An oral presentation in a conversation with one or more prospective buyers for the purpose of making a sale.
o. hierarchy-of-effects model	
p. incremental technique	____ 9. Any paid form of nonpersonal presentation and promotion of ideas, goods, and services by an identified sponsor.
q. institutional advertising	
r. marginal return	____ 10. Theory stating that a message goes from the company to opinion leaders and then to the target market.
s. massed promotion	
t. medium	
u. message	____ 11. Communication concentrated in peak periods, like holidays.
v. multistep flow of communication	____ 12. A controversial type of promotion that does not enable a consumer to consciously decode a message.
w. noise	
x. objective-and-task technique	____ 13. A message in which the firm mentions only the benefits of its product or service.

y. one-sided message

z. percentage-of-sales technique

aa. personal selling

bb. primary demand

cc. promotion

dd. promotion mix

ee. promotion planning

ff. publicity

gg. S-curve effect

hh. sales promotion

ii. selective demand

jj. source of communication

kk. subliminal advertising

ll. substantiation

mm. two-sided message

nn. two-step flow of communication

oo. wearout rate

pp. word-of-mouth communication

____ 14. Used to improve corporate image and not to sell products or services.

____ 15. Outlines the intermediate and long-term promotional objectives the firm should pursue: awareness, knowledge, liking, preference, conviction, and purchase.

MULTIPLE CHOICE

Place the letter of the answer you think best in the blank provided.

 1. Consumers tend to question the objectivity and fairness of
   a. company spokespersons.
   b. celebrities.
   c. actors playing roles.
   d. salespeople.

 2. Consumers Union and Consumers' Research are examples of
   a. opinion leaders.
   b. representative consumers.
   c. independent institutions.
   d. company spokespersons.

 3. A firm wanting to stress the prestige of its product would *not* emphasize
   a. low price.
   b. exclusive ownership.
   c. special features.
   d. status.

_b_

4. Most messages to consumers are
   a. reminders.
   b. one sided.
   c. comparative.
   d. two sided.

_c_

5. Messages using symbolism do *not* typically emphasize
   a. social acceptance.
   b. sexual appeal.
   c. tangible performance.
   d. safety.

_a_

6. The Highway and Traffic Safety Commission found that consumers
   a. respond favorably to strong fear appeals.
   b. do not respond at all to fear appeals.
   c. are antagonized by fear appeals.
   d. respond favorably to moderate fear appeals.

_a_

7. The manner in which the content of a message is presented does *not* necessarily have to be
   a. desirable.
   b. exclusive.
   c. believable.
   d. one sided.

_a_

8. In comparison with personal media, nonpersonal media
   a. are inflexible.
   b. work best with a concentrated target market.
   c. are dynamic.
   d. involve high per customer costs.

_b_

9. In a 1983 survey of the American public, over half of those questioned felt that
   a. newspapers are most important regarding major purchases.
   b. advertising is not generally honest.
   c. the overall quality of advertising is good.
   d. personal communication is crucial for day-to-day shopping.

_b_

10. Which of the following is *not* a technique for monitoring or obtaining feedback?
    a. Monadic test
    b. Objective and task
    c. Unaided recall
    d. Comparison test

_d_

11. Which of the following is an example of noise?
    a. A telephone call asking you to buy a product
    b. A long-winded sales presentation of a product
    c. A celebrity promoting a product on a television commercial
    d. A conversation between two consumers during a sales presentation

12. The first objective in the hierarchy-of-effects model is consumer
    a. knowledge.
    b. awareness.
    c. liking.
    d. preference.

13. Institutional advertising focuses on
    a. demand for a product category.
    b. corporate image.
    c. demand for a particular brand.
    d. social acceptance.

 C

14. The weakest of the alternative techniques for formulating a promotion budget is the
    a. incremental approach.
    b. objective-and-task approach.
    c. all-you-can-afford approach.
    d. percentage-of-sales approach.

15. A major drawback of the competitive-parity technique is
    a. complexity in setting goals.
    b. the firm may not be similar to its competitors.
    c. difficulty of evaluating success or failure.
    d. overemphasis on "gut feelings."

16. Which of the following is associated with an S-curve effect?
    a. Sales rise when a product is introduced because of heavy promotion.
    b. Sales drop when positive word-of-mouth communication occurs.
    c. Promotional support is sustained at a constant level.
    d. Promotional support is increased when sales drop after product introduction.

17. Which of the following statements about the types of promotion is true?
    a. Sales promotion stimulates long-run sales.
    b. Without publicity, initial interest caused by ads would be wasted.
    c. Personal selling is time-consuming and has high per-customer costs.
    d. The content and timing of advertisements cannot be controlled by a firm.

18. The focus for a nonprofit firm should be on
    a. personal selling.
    b. publicity.
    c. advertisements.
    d. sales promotion.

C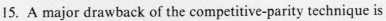

19. When diet products note that they include saccharin, they are conforming to the legal requirement of
    a. substantiation.
    b. corrective advertising.
    c. full disclosure.
    d. cease-and-desist orders.

20. An example of corrective advertising is
    a. Listerine's disclaimer that it is not a cold remedy.
    b. Sears' agreement not to use bait-and-switch practices.
    c. Alka-Seltzer's mentioning that it contains aspirin.
    d. STP's payment of a large sum to the government.

DISCUSSION QUESTIONS

1. What is the value of promotion?

2. What is the role of opinion leaders in the two-step flow of communications? In the multistep flow?

3. What advice would you give a travel agency about the timing of its messages?

4. Can you think of some ways in which noise can be reduced in a communications channel?

5. Which technique for setting a promotion budget and promotion mix would you recommend for a small firm? Why?

6. How does the legal environment protect consumers and competitors from deceptive promotion?

7. What are the most common criticisms of promotion and how do marketers respond to them?

EXERCISES

15-1.   In the United States, the recliner chair industry generates annual sales of about $1 billion. La-Z-Boy Chair Co. is by far the leader in this industry, with a market share of 27 per cent. As the marketing manager of a regional manufacturer intending to expand nationally, you are currently engaged in preparing the firm's first comprehensive promotion plan. The company's goal is to increase annual sales from $15 million to $30 million within two years. At present, the firm advertises in newspapers and magazines, runs an annual sales promotion event, and has a sales force of six calling on its retail accounts. The total promotion budget (including the sales force) is about $750,000.

An analysis of La-Z-Boy's promotion efforts indicates the following:[1]

- Alex Karras and his wife Susan Clark, stars of the "Webster" television series, have been featured in television and newspaper ads throughout the country.
- The promotion budget has increased dramatically in recent years to maintain and increase La-Z-Boy's market share.
- The major selling periods have been Christmas and Father's Day. To balance sales better throughout the year, La-Z-Boy has been expanding its promotion activities during September and March. Said the firm's director of advertising, "There used to be two sharp peaks in recliner sales: Father's Day and Christmas. This campaign is aimed at smoothing out sales more evenly throughout the year."
- Its theme is "La-Z-Boy. Because easy chairs lead tough lives."

---

[1] Scott Hume, "La-Z-Boy Ads Reach for Spread-Out Sales," *Advertising Age* (June 7, 1984), p. 37.

Questions

1.   How important is word-of-mouth communication for recliner chairs? Explain your answer.

2. Should your company follow La-Z-Boy and feature a celebrity in advertising? What are the pros and cons of this strategy?

3. Should your firm use comparative advertising? Why or why not?

4. Do you think La-Z-Boy will be successful in its efforts to balance sales throughout the year? Explain your answer.

15-2.   A trash-compactor manufacturer is concerned about the low proportion of consumer households that have purchased any type or brand of trash compactor. Its own trash compactor retails for between $300 and $400, is only fifteen inches wide, can be built-in or freestanding, and compacts the trash that would fill three twenty-gallon cans into one neat bag. Its trash compactor is also equipped with a deodorizing system and a safety mechanism to prevent accidental operation.

According to the manufacturer, trash compactors are commonly purchased as part of a comprehensive luxury kitchen renovation. Therefore, the influence of an architect or kitchen-renovating firm is extremely important. The manufacturer feels that key prospects are people who have lived in their current homes for seven to ten years; at that time they often can afford a kitchen renovation. Furthermore, because of high interest rates (relative to seven to ten years ago), many homeowners plan to renovate their existing homes rather than move.

The trash compactor industry has several important obstacles to overcome. First, many consumers are uncomfortable having a week's accumulation of trash in their kitchen. Second, many homeowners do not believe a trash compactor is a necessary appliance. Third, even though it is only fifteen inches wide, the compactor takes away valuable kitchen cabinet space. Fourth, homeowners with small children are often worried about its safety. A typical compactor generates 2,300 pounds of pressure during its thirty-second cycle.

Questions

1.   How could the trash compactor manufacturer use advertising, publicity, personal selling, and sales promotion?

2. What basic messages must be communicated to consumers? Distinguish between appeals to primary and selective demand in your answers.

3. How should the promotion effort aimed at kitchen-renovating firms differ from that geared to final consumers?

4. Should humor be used in a promotional campaign for trash compactors? What are some advantages and disadvantages of such an approach?

15-3.   Select current television advertisements involving a company spokesperson, a celebrity, an actor playing a role, and a representative consumer. Evaluate each.

15-4.   Develop an overall promotional plan to market a new film by Steven Spielberg. What are the unique considerations involved in promoting a movie?

ANSWERS

True/False

1. T, p. 433	11. T, p. 443
2. F, p. 436	12. F, pp. 444-445
3. F, p. 437	13. F, pp. 445-446
4. F, p. 438	14. F, pp. 448-449
5. F, p. 438	15. T, pp. 449-450
6. T, p. 438	16. F, p. 450
7. F, p. 439	17. T, p. 450
8. F, pp. 439-440	18. F, p. 453
9. T, p. 441	19. T, p. 454
10. T, p. 442	20. T, p. 455

Multiple Choice

1. d, p. 438	11. d, p. 445
2. c, p. 438	12. b, pp. 445-446
3. a, pp. 438-439	13. b, p. 446
4. b, p. 439	14. c, p. 448
5. c, p. 440	15. b, p. 449
6. d, p. 440	16. a, p. 450
7. d, p. 440	17. c, p. 450
8. a, p. 442	18. b, p. 450
9. c, p. 443	19. c, p. 453
10. b, pp. 444-445	20. a, p. 454

Definitions

1. oo	9. a
2. r	10. nn
3. i	11. s
4. w	12. kk
5. n	13. y
6. c	14. q
7. ii	15. o
8. aa	

Discussion Questions

1. pp. 433-434
2. p. 438
3. pp. 441-442
4. p. 445
5. pp. 448-452
6. pp. 452-454
7. p. 455

16 Advertising and Publicity

CHAPTER OBJECTIVES

1. To examine the scope, importance, and characteristics of advertising
2. To study the elements in an advertising plan: objectives, responsibility, budget, themes, media, advertisements, timing, cooperative efforts, and evaluation of success or failure
3. To examine the scope, importance, and characteristics of publicity
4. To study the elements in a publicity plan: objectives, responsibility, types, media, messages, timing, and evaluation of success or failure

CHAPTER OVERVIEW

Advertising and publicity are the two forms of mass communication available to a firm. Advertising expenditures exceed $85 billion annually through such media as newspapers, magazines, farm publications, television, radio, direct mail, business papers, and outdoor.

The advantages of advertising are appeal to a large and geographically dispersed audience, low per-customer costs, availability of a broad variety of media, control over all aspects of a message, surrounding editorial content, and how it complements personal selling. Disadvantages are inflexibility of messages, high total expenditures for some media, wasted viewers or readers, low audience involvement and high throwaway rates, limited information provided, and difficulty in obtaining audience feedback.

An advertising plan has nine steps: (1) setting objectives, (2) assigning responsibility, (3) establishing a budget, (4) developing themes, (5) selecting media, (6) creating advertisements, (7) timing advertisements, (8) considering cooperative efforts, and (9) evaluating success or failure.

Firms seek to obtain favorable publicity and avoid or minimize negative publicity. Competition is intense for placing publicity releases. The advantages of publicity are no costs for message time and content, high level of credibility, audience attentiveness, and mass audience. The disadvantages are lack of control by the firm and the difficulty of planning in advance. Public relations is mass and personal communication aimed at company image. It uses advertising, publicity, and personal contact.

A publicity plan has seven steps: (1) setting objectives, (2) assigning responsibility, (3) outlining types of publicity, (4) selecting media, (5) creating publicity messages, (6) timing publicity messages, and (7) evaluating success or failure.

KEY TERMS AND CONCEPTS

Advertising agency	An outside company that usually works with a firm in the development of its advertising plan including themes, media selection, copywriting, and other tasks.
Advertising themes	The overall appeals for a campaign. Themes can be product or service, consumer, or nonconsumer and nonproduct/service-related.
Advertising costs	Can be measured in terms of total media costs or per reader or viewer. Costs are expressed on a per thousand audience basis, except newspapers which use a cost per million base.
Waste	The portion of a medium's audience that is not in the firm's target market.
Reach	Refers to the number of viewers or readers in the audience. For television and radio, reach is the total number of people viewing or listening to a program. For print media, reach equals circulation plus passalong rate.
Frequency	How often a medium can be used.
Message permanence	Refers to the number of exposures one advertisement generates and how long it remains with the audience.
Persuasive impact	Involves the number of advertisements that are contained in a single program, issue, etc. of a medium.
Lead time	The time required by the medium for placing an advertisement.
Cooperative advertising plan	Allows expenses to be shared by channel members. It can be vertical or horizontal.
Public relations	Mass and personal communications that are image-directed.
Publicity types	Consist of news publicity, business feature articles, service feature articles, finance releases, product releases, pictorial releases, background editorial material, and emergency publicity.

TRUE/FALSE

Circle the appropriate letter.

T   F   1. Newspapers' share of advertising declined substantially since 1960.

T   F   2. Overall, advertising as a percentage of sales is quite low.

T   F   3. Standardized products with large markets and small average purchases often receive substantial advertising.

T   F   4. When editorial content surrounds an advertisement, readership or viewing declines.

T   F   5. Feedback on advertising is difficult to obtain and usually is not immediately available.

T   F   6. Diversified firms always use in-house advertising departments for each of their product lines.

T   F   7. The 15 per cent rate charged by advertising agencies for basic functions is mandatory.

T   F   8. Firms that maintain advertising during a recession generally do better than those who do not.

T   F   9. A consumer appeal advertising theme centers on the items and their attributes.

T   F   10. Since many media appeal to mass audiences, waste is a significant factor in advertising.

T   F   11. The pass-along rate for daily newspapers is much higher than for magazines.

T   F   12. Telephone directories have low frequency and long lead time.

T   F   13. Television requires a long lead time because the number of advertisements carried is limited.

T   F   14. Distributed advertising is used mostly by specialty manufacturers and retailers.

T   F   15. Public relations are mass- and personal communication that are demand directed.

T   F   16. There are no costs for publicity.

T   F   17. People are more likely to pay attention to publicity than to advertisements.

T   F   18. The objectives of publicity are the same as those of advertising.

T   F   19. Service feature articles deal with new products and product improvements.

T   F   20. The company can usually anticipate the timing of publicity.

COMPLETION

Fill in the missing word or words in the blanks provided.

[Advertising, publicity, p. 462]

1. _____ is the paid, nonpersonal presentation and promotion of ideas, goods, or services by an identified sponsor, whereas _____ is the nonpaid, nonpersonal presentation and promotion of ideas, goods, or services by an independent source.

[newspapers, television, pp. 463-464]

2. The leading two media in terms of advertising expenditures are _____ and _____ .

[standardized, large, small, p. 464]

3. It has been found that _____ products with _____ markets and _____ average purchases receive substantial advertising.

[geographically dispersed, low, control, standardized, inflexible, feedback, p. 466]

4. Among the positive aspects of advertising are the attraction of a large _____ _____ market, _____ per customer costs, and firm _____ over all aspects of advertising; on the negative side, because advertising messages are _____ , they are _____ , which makes it difficult to adapt to consumer needs and differences, and _____ is hard to obtain.

[setting objectives, assigning responsibility, establishing a budget, developing themes, pp. 467-468]

5. The first four steps in the development of an advertising plan are _____ _____ , to guide the entire advertising plan; _____ _____ , either in-house or through an outside agency; _____ _____ _____ , to delineate available funds; and _____ _____ , to set the overall appeals for the campaign.

[selecting media, creating ads, timing ads, considering cooperative efforts, evaluating success or failure, pp. 467-468]

6. The last five steps in the development of an advertising plan are _____ _____ , deciding who will carry the message; _____ _____ , deciding on message content, symbols, and variations; _____ _____ , deciding when to place the advertisements; _____ _____ _____ , deciding whether to share costs with other channel members; and _____ _____ _____ _____ , analyzing the effectiveness of the plan.

[waste, reach, circulation, passalong rate, pp. 471-472]

7. In choosing media, a firm should think about _____ , the portion of the audience that is not in the firm's target market; and _____ , which refers to the total number of people exposed to an advertisement, composed of _____ , the number of copies sold and distributed, and _____ _____ , the number of times each copy is placed with another reader.

[frequency, message permanence, persuasive impact, pp. 472-473]

8. In selecting media, a firm must consider _____ , how often a medium can be used; _____ _____ , the number of exposures an advertisement generates and how long it remains with the audience; and _____ _____ , the ability of a medium to stimulate consumers.

[clutter, lead time, p. 473]

9. In picking media, a firm must also take into account _____ , which involves the number of advertisements that are contained in a single program or issue of a medium; and _____ _____ , the period required by the medium for placing an advertisement.

[Distributed, massed, p. 478]

10. _____ advertising maintains company and brand recognition, balances sales, and increases sales in nonpeak periods, whereas _____ advertising concentrates on peak periods, maximizes returns, and generates short-run enthusiasm.

[vertical cooperative-advertising, horizontal cooperative-advertising, p. 478]

11. In a _____ _____ _____ agreement, channel members at different stages share costs, whereas in a _____ _____ _____ agreement, two or more channel members at the same stage share costs.

[Public relations, p. 482]

12. _____ _____ are mass and personal communications that are image directed.

[costs, credibility, attention, control, timing, placement, coverage, pp. 483-484]

13. With publicity, there are no _____ for message time and space, the _____ of messages is high, and people are more likely to pay _____ to news reports than to clearly identified advertisements. Yet the firm has little _____ over messages, their _____ , their _____ , or their _____ by a given medium.

[setting objectives, assigning responsibility, outlining types, selecting media, creating, timing, evaluating success or failure, p. 485]

14. Seven steps in developing a publicity plan are _____ _____ , which may be image or demand oriented; _____ _____ to an advertisement agency, public relations firm, or in-house department; _____ _____ of publicity, whether pictorial releases or production releases, for example; _____ _____ in which to place the message; _____ publicity messages, for example message content or production schedules; _____ publicity messages in terms of ongoing publicity or emergencies; and _____ _____ _____ _____ , to assess plan effectiveness.

[news publicity, business feature, service feature, finance releases, product releases, pictorial releases, background editorial, emergency publicity, pp. 486-487]

15. Of the forms publicity may take, _____ _____ deals with events of national or local interest; _____ _____ articles are detailed stories about a company or its offerings; _____ _____ articles are lighter stories focusing on personal care, household items, and recipes; _____ _____ are stories aimed at business sections of newspapers and magazines; _____ _____ deal with the introduction of goods and with their improvements; _____ _____ are illustrations supplied to media; _____ _____ material offers extra information for writers and editors; and _____ _____ provides special releases on disasters or other serious problems.

DEFINITIONS

Match the terms and concepts with the appropriate definitions. Each term or concept may only be used once; there are more terms and concepts than definitions.

Column A

a. advertising agency

b. advertising costs

c. advertising themes

d. clutter

e. cooperative advertising plan

f. frequency

g. lead time

h. message permanence

i. persuasive impact

j. public relations

k. publicity types

l. reach

Column B

____ 1. Refers to the number of exposures one advertisement generates and how long it remains with the audience.

____ 2. Allows expenses to be shared by channel members. It can be vertical or horizontal.

____ 3. Mass and personal communications that are image directed.

____ 4. How often a medium can be used.

____ 5. Refers to the number of viewers or readers in the audience.

____ 6. The ability of a medium to stimulate consumers.

____ 7. The period required by the medium for placing advertisements.

____ 8. The portion of a medium's audience that is not in the firm's target market.

____ 9. Can be measured in terms of total media or per reader or viewer.

____ 10. The overall appeals for a campaign.

MULTIPLE CHOICE

Place the letter of the answer you think best in the blank provided.

 1. Which of the following is common to both advertising and publicity?
   a. Paid presentation
   b. Nonpersonal presentation
   c. Source control of presentation
   d. Known sponsorship of presentation

 2. Which of the following statements about the scope and importance of advertising over the past twenty years is true?
   a. The importance of farm publications and outdoor advertising has increased steadily.
   b. Advertising expenditures on direct mail have declined steadily.
   c. Newspapers' share of expenditures have declined steadily.
   d. Television has become the leading medium in terms of expenditures.

C _b_ 3. Companies are most likely to advertise if
   a. products are custom made.
   b. their market shares are high.
   c. average purchases are small.
   d. there is limited production capacity.

_d_ 4. When editorial content surrounds an advertisement, the
   a. reading or viewing audience is decreased.
   b. company's image is diminished.
   c. product's image appears unfavorably.
   d. proper mood for the advertisement is created.

_g_ 5. The mass media
   a. rely on standardized, inflexible messages.
   b. cover small geographic areas.
   c. provide easily obtained feedback on advertisements.
   d. offer advertising containing much information.

_d_ 6. The first step in developing an advertising plan is
   a. assigning responsibility.
   b. establishing a budget.
   c. developing themes.
   d. setting objectives.

_c_ 7. Waste
   a. is comprised of circulation and pass-along rates.
   b. refers to the number of exposures a message generates.
   c. is the portion of the audience not in a firm's target market.
   d. refers to how often a medium can be used.

_a_ 8. Which of the following usually have the lowest frequency?
   a. Magazines
   b. Newspapers
   c. Radio
   d. Television

_b_ 9. The highest persuasive impact is found in
   a. telephone directories.
   b. television.
   c. outdoor advertisements.
   d. newspapers.

_d_ 10. The shortest lead time is generally required by
   a. television.
   b. magazines.
   c. telephone directories.
   d. newspapers.

_d_ 11. To create an advertisement, first a firm must
   a. outline a production schedule.
   b. determine how many variations of the basic message to have.
   c. decide where to locate the advertisement.
   d. determine message content.

_C_

12. Distributed advertising
    a. maximizes returns.
    b. generates short-run enthusiasm.
    c. balances sales.
    d. concentrates messages at peak periods.

_d_

13. According to PACT, a good advertising copy testing system
    a. will not necessarily yield similar results when repeated.
    b. ignores repetitious advertising.
    c. relies on a single measurement method.
    d. carefully specifies audience sampling.

_D_

14. Public relations can be distinguished from advertising and publicity because it alone
    a. is demand directed.
    b. involves personal communications.
    c. prepares paid messages.
    d. places news stories.

C   _d_

15. Which statement about the costs of publicity is *not* true?
    a. There are no costs for message time.
    b. There are costs for a publicity department.
    c. There are no costs in preparing news releases.
    d. There are no costs for space.

_C_

16. In comparison with advertising, publicity
    a. has lower credibility.
    b. receives less audience attention.
    c. is viewed as more objective.
    d. reaches a narrower audience.

_A_

17. When they use publicity, firms must realize that they
    a. cannot control coverage.
    b. can control timing.
    c. can control placement.
    d. cannot control news releases.

_C_

18. Which one of the following steps in developing an advertising plan is *missing* from the development of a publicity plan?
    a. Assigning responsibility
    b. Selecting media
    c. Timing placements
    d. Developing themes

     _a_

19. Lighter stories focusing on personal care, household items, and recipes are examples of
    a. background editorial material.
    b. news releases.
    c. product releases.
    d. service feature articles.

20. Business feature articles are
    a. detailed stories about the company or its offerings.
    b. stories dealing with finance found in business sections of newspapers and magazines.
    c. concerned with new products and product improvements.
    d. extra information provided to media writers and editors.

DISCUSSION QUESTIONS

1. You have recently become the author of a novel. Which medium would you prefer your publisher to place ads in for you? Why?

2. Evaluate the positive and negative characteristics of advertising.

3. How will message permanence, persuasive impact, and lead time affect the choice of media?

4. What kinds of decisions are involved in creating advertisements and timing their placement?

5. Why should publicity be considered complementary to advertising and not a substitute for it?

6. Enumerate the different forms publicity may take. Which forms would be most suitable for a company that has just replaced its corporate leadership? Why?

7. Explain why Coleco's use of publicity for its Cabbage Patch Kids dolls was so successful.

Student's Name _____ **Class/Section** _____ **Instructor** _____

EXERCISES

16-1.   Although U.S. firms annually spend over $85 billion on advertising, this amounts to only about 1 to 3 per cent of sales for most companies. Smaller firms have special needs when advertising, since their audiences are usually geographically concentrated and their advertising budgets generally preclude the use of television. Table 1 shows the advertising practices of a variety of small companies.

Table 1
Advertising as Practiced by Selected Small Businesses

Type of Business	Average Ad Budget (% of Sales)	Favorite Media	Other Media	Special Considerations	Promotional Opportunities
Apparel Stores	2.5-3.0%	Weekly or sub-urban newspapers; direct mail.	Radio;Yellow Pages; exterior signs.	Cooperative advertising available from manufacturers.	Fashion shows for community organizations or charities.
Auto Supply Stores	0.5-2.0%	Local newspapers; Yellow Pages.	Point-of-purchase displays; exterior signs.	Cooperative advertising available from manufacturers.	For specialty stores, direct mail is a popular medium.
Bars and Cocktail Lounges	1.0-2.0%	Yellow Pages; local newspapers (entertainment section).	Tourist publications; radio; specialties; exterior signs.	Manufacturers do all product advertising.	Unusual drinks at "happy hour" rates; hosting postevent parties.
Bookstores	1.5-1.7%	Newspapers; shoppers; Yellow Pages; local magazines.	Radio; exterior signs.	Cooperative advertising available from publisher.	Autograph parties.
Coin-Op Laundries	0.6-2.0%	Yellow Pages; handbills distrib-uted in area; local newspapers.	Direct mail; exterior signs.		Coupons in newspaper ads for "free trial."
General Job Printing	0.4-1.0%	Yellow Pages; trade journals.	Local newspapers; direct mail; exterior signs.		Samples of work can be used as promotional tools.
Gift Stores	1.5-2.5%	Weekly news-papers; Yellow Pages.	Radio; direct mail; consumer magazines; exterior signs.		Open houses; in-store demon-strations of products such as cookware.
Hairgrooming/ Beauty Salons	2.5-3.0%	Yellow Pages.	Newspapers; name credits for styles in feature articles; exterior signs.	Word-of-mouth advertising is very important to a salon's success.	Styling for com-munity fashion shows; conducting free beauty clinics and demon-strations.
Health Food Stores	1.1-2.8%	Local newspapers; shoppers; college newspapers.	Direct mail; point-of-purchase displays; exterior signs.		Educational displays and services.
Restaurants	0.8-3.0%	Newspapers; radio; Yellow Pages; transit; outdoor.	Local entertain-ment guides or tourist publi-cations; theater programs; TV for chain or franchise restaurants; exterior signs.	Word-of-mouth advertising is relied upon heavily by inde-pendently owned restaurants.	"Free" advertising in critics' columns; specialties; birthday cakes or parties for customers.

Source: Reprinted with permission from Bank of America, NT&SA, "Advertising Small Business," *Small Business Reporter* Copyright 1976, 1978, 1981, 1982, p. 19. Figures compiled in California.

Questions

1.   Describe at least five conclusions you reach from examining Table 1.

2.   How would you expect the advertising practices of an apparel store chain to differ from those of an independent apparel store?

3.   Select one of the types of businesses listed in Table 1 and interview the manager of a local company regarding his/her average advertising budget, favorite media, other media, special considerations, and promotional opportunities. How does this company compare with the typical practices of that type of business, as shown in Table 1?

4.   Which practices noted in Table 1 are forms of publicity? Why?

16-2.   A manufacturer of inexpensive women's jewelry (necklaces, bracelets, earrings, etc.) plans to spend $400,000 this year on a combination of half-page and full-page color ads in general-interest women's magazines. Among the magazines it is considering are *Cosmopolitan, Family Circle, Good Housekeeping, Ladies' Home Journal,* and *Woman's Day.*

The firm has specified these guidelines for its advertising:

- The number of consumers reached per $1,000 of advertising expenditures is a key criterion in the selection of magazines.
- Some repetition of the same advertisements in magazines is necessary to provide message reinforcement.
- A minimum ad size of half a page is required.
- In evaluating magazines, single-copy circulation should be treated separately from subscription circulation.
- No more than twelve pages of ads should be placed in any one magazine during the year.

Table 1 outlines important data relating to each of the magazines under consideration.

Table 1
Characteristics of Selected Magazines

Characteristics	Cosmopolitan	Family Circle	Good Housekeeping	Ladies' Home Journal	Woman's Day
Cost of 1 pg. 4-color ad- 1 insertion	$32,525	$78,400[1]	$69,245	$54,000	$73,000[2]
Cost of 1/2 pg. 4-color ad- 1 insertion	$19,435	$47,125	$41,540	$31,300	$43,500
Quantity discount schedule:					
6 pages per year	5%	7%	10%	10%	7%
12 pages per year	10%	10%	14%	12%	10%
Total paid circulation- per issue	3,038,400	7,193,079	5,393,087	5,252,444	7,025,290
Total subscription circulation per issue	234,822	147,117	3,401,317	4,280,705	54,217
Total single-copy circulation per issue	2,803,578	7,045,962	1,991,770	971,739	6,971,073

[1] Based on October-December issue

[2] Based on October-November rates

Source: Data from *Standard Rate & Data Service Consumer Magazine Agri-Media Rates and Data* (April 27, 1984), various pages.

Questions

1. Comment on the guidelines set by the firm.

2. Which of the magazines cited in this exercise should the firm use? Why? Refer to Table 1 in your answer.

3. What other magazine information would be useful before making a decision to advertise?

4. How could this jewelry manufacturer generate publicity?

16-3.   Develop a cooperative advertising plan for retailers handling your company's line of ballpoint pens. Make sure this plan reflects the dealer's past concerns that cooperative advertisements need to focus on the retailer as well as on the product. Also make sure the plan reflects seasonality, financial terms, responsibility for preparing advertising copy, and media selection.

16-4.   How would you handle publicity regarding the recall of a significant new product of your company? How would you use public relations?

ANSWERS

True/False

1. T, p. 464	11. F, p. 472
2. T, pp. 464-465	12. T, pp. 472-473
3. T, p. 464	13. T, pp. 473-474
4. F, p. 466	14. F, p. 478
5. T, p. 466	15. F, p. 482
6. F, p. 469	16. F, p. 483
7. F, p. 469	17. T, p. 483
8. T, p. 469	18. T, p. 486
9. F, p. 470	19. F, p. 486
10. T, p. 471	20. F, p. 488

Multiple Choice

1. b, p. 462	11. d, p. 475
2. c, pp. 463-464	12. c, p. 478
3. c, p. 464	13. d, p. 479
4. d, p. 466	14. b, p. 482
5. a, p. 466	15. c, p. 483
6. d, p. 467	16. c, p. 483
7. c, p. 471	17. a, pp. 483-484
8. a, p. 472	18. d, p. 485
9. b, p. 473	19. d, p. 486
10. d, pp. 473, 475	20. a, p. 486

Definitions

1. h	6. i
2. e	7. g
3. j	8. m
4. f	9. b
5. l	10. c

Discussion Questions

1. pp. 471-475
2. pp. 466-467
3. pp. 472-473
4. pp. 475-478
5. pp. 482-485
6. pp. 486-487
7. pp. 488-489

17 Personal Selling and Sales Promotion

CHAPTER OBJECTIVES

1. To examine the scope, importance, and characteristics of personal selling
2. To study the elements in a personal selling plan: objectives, responsibility, budget, type(s) of sales positions, sales techniques, sales tasks, and implementation
3. To examine the scope, importance, and characteristics of sales promotion
4. To study the elements in a sales promotion plan: objectives, responsibility, overall plan, types of sales promotion, coordination, and evaluation of success or failure

CHAPTER OVERVIEW

Almost seven million people are employed in personal-selling occupations. This number understates the value of personal selling, because every contact between a company representative and a customer involves some amount of personal selling. Selling costs as a percentage of sales fall between 1.6 and 16.9 per cent. The average cost of one sales call can be as high as $200.

Personal selling establishes a buyer-seller dyad (the two-way flow of communication between both parties), offers flexibility and adaptability, results in little waste in terms of audience, clinches sales, and provides immediate feedback. However, personal selling can handle only a limited number of customers, has high costs per customer, is ineffective for creating consumer awareness, and has a poor image for some consumers.

A personal-selling plan involves (1) setting objectives, (2) assigning responsibility, (3) establishing a budget, (4) determining the type(s) of sales positions, (5) selecting a sales technique, (6) outlining sales tasks, and (7) applying the plan.

Sales promotion encompasses all forms of promotion not defined as advertising, publicity, and personal selling. Sales promotion has annual expenditures of over $70 billion. The growth of sales promotion is the result of greater firm and consumer acceptance, better management, quick payoffs, competition, economic conditions, and demands by channel members.

Sales promotion helps attract customer traffic and loyalty, provides value to consumers and is sometimes retained by them, increases impulse purchases, creates excitement, is keyed to customer patronage, and improves channel-member cooperation. On the other hand, sales promotion may hurt the firm's image, encourage consumers to wait for promotions before making purchases, and shift the focus away from product or service attributes. Sales promotion cannot replace other forms of promotion.

A sales promotion plan includes (1) setting objectives, (2) assigning responsibility, (3) outlining the overall plan, (4) selecting types of sales promotion, (5) coordinating the plan, and (6) evaluating success or failure. Types of sales promotion include trade shows, training, allowances, free merchandise, and cooperative promotions for channel members and coupons, refunds, samples, stamps, and gifts for final consumers.

KEY TERMS AND CONCEPTS

Buyer-seller dyad	Two-way flow of communication between buyer and seller.
Sales-expense budget	Allocates expenditures among salespeople, products, customers, and geographic areas for a given period of time.
Order taker	Type of salesperson who processes routine orders and reorders. The order taker usually handles products or services that are presold.
Order getter	Type of salesperson who is involved with generating customer leads, providing information, persuading customers, and closing sales.
Missionary salesperson	Type of sales support person used to distribute information about new products or services. This person does not sell but describes the attributes of the new item, answers questions, and leaves written data.
Sales engineer	Accompanies an order-getter when a highly technical or complex item is being sold. This salesperson explains product specifications, alternatives, and long-range uses.
Service salesperson	Usually interacts with customers after sales are completed. Delivery, installation, or other follow-up tasks are undertaken.
Canned sales presentation	A memorized, repetitive sales presentation given to all customers interested in a particular item. This approach does not adapt to customer needs or traits but presumes that a general presentation will appeal to all customers.
Need-satisfaction approach	A sales presentation method based on the principle that each customer has different characteristics and wants. The sales presentation is adapted to each customer.

Selling process	Involves prospecting for customer leads, approaching customers, determining customer wants, giving a sales presentation, answering questions, closing the sale, and following up.
Prospecting	The stage in a sales process which generates a list of customer leads. It is common with outside selling. Prospecting can be blind or lead in orientation.
Approaching customers	The stage in the selling process that consists of the preapproach and greeting.
Sales presentation	Stage in the selling process that includes a description of the product or service, its benefits, available options and models, price, associated services (such as delivery and warranty), and a demonstration (if necessary).
Closing the sale	The stage in the sales process that involves getting the customer to agree to a purchase. The salesperson must be sure that no major questions remain before attempting to close a sale.
Sales management	The planning, analysis, and control of the personal sales function. It covers employee selection, training, territory allocation, compensation, and supervision.
Straight-salary plan	A sales compensation plan that pays a salesperson a flat fee per week, month, or year.
Straight-commission plan	A sales compensation plan that ties a salesperson's earnings directly to sales or profits.
Combination compensation plan	A sales compensation plan that combines salary and commission plans to provide control, flexibility, and employee incentives.
Sales promotion orientation	Refers to the focus of sales promotion towards channel members or final consumers.
Sales promotion conditions	The requirements channel members or final consumers must meet to be eligible for a sales promotion.

TRUE/FALSE

Circle the appropriate letter.

T   F   1. The costs of personal selling are much higher than those of advertising for most companies.

T   F   2. In personal selling there is a passive interaction between buyer and seller.

T   F   3. The buyer-seller dyad is not possible in advertising.

T   F   4. There is less waste with most forms of selling than with advertising.

T   F   5. The major goal of personal selling usually is persuasion.

T	F	6. Whereas the order taker expands company sales, the order getter is necessary to maintain sales.
T	F	7. The canned sales presentation technique is flexible and reflects a marketing orientation.
T	F	8. The need-satisfaction approach to sales works best with inexpensive, routine items.
T	F	9. With blind prospecting, a small percentage of the people contacted will be interested in a firm's offering.
T	F	10. In the case of major purchases, the salesperson's responsibilities terminate when the sale is closed.
T	F	11. Personality is the only attribute of importance to be considered when choosing salespeople.
T	F	12. Buyer-seller similarities are most important for high financial purchases.
T	F	13. Order takers are usually paid on a straight commission basis.
T	F	14. Salespeople go through career cycles similar to those of products.
T	F	15. Coupon redemption rates are relatively high.
T	F	16. As competition increases, sales promotion normally decreases.
T	F	17. The image of the firm may be lessened if it continuously runs special deals.
T	F	18. Sales promotion objectives are almost always image-oriented.
T	F	19. Usually, trading stamps are used to increase store traffic, and coupons are used to maintain loyalty.
T	F	20. The success of such promotions as calendars, pens, and special events is fairly straightforward to measure and evaluate because the promotions are closely linked to performance or sales.

COMPLETION

Fill in the missing word or words in the blanks provided.

[Personal selling, p. 494]

1. _____ _____ is that part of promotion involving an oral presentation in a conversation with one or more prospective buyers for the purpose of making a sale.

[buyer-seller dyad, p. 497]

2. A two-way flow of communication between salespeople and consumers is termed a _____ _____ _____ .

[demand, image, persuasion, pp. 498, 500]

3. Personal selling objectives are either _____ or _____ oriented, while the major goal is _____ .

[sales-expense budget, p. 500]

4. A _____ _____ _____ is usually based on a sales forecast and makes allocations among salespeople, products, customers, and geographic areas for a given time period.

[order taker, order getter, p. 502]

5. An _____ _____ processes routine orders and reorders, whereas an _____ _____ generates customer leads.

[missionary, sales engineer, service, p. 503]

6. Support personnel include a _____ salesperson, used to distribute information about new products or services; a _____ _____ salesperson, used to explain product specifications; and a _____ salesperson, used for installation and other follow-up tasks.

[canned sales, need-satisfaction, pp. 503-504]

7. Two basic techniques for selling are the _____ _____ presentation and the _____ _____ approach.

[selling process, sales presentation, closing, pp. 504-506]

8. The _____ _____ involves prospecting for customers, approaching customers, determining customer wants, giving a _____ _____ , answering questions, _____ the sale, and following up.

[prospecting, blind prospecting, lead prospecting, p. 504]

9. Generating a list of customer leads is termed _____; relying on telephone directories or other general listings of potential customers is called _____ _____ ; and depending on past customers or referrals is known as _____ _____ .

[preapproach, greeting, p. 504]

10. Customers are approached in two stages: _____ and _____ .

[nonselling, p. 507]

11. Setting up displays, pricing merchandise, and checking on competitor strategies are examples of _____ tasks.

[Sales management, p. 507]

12. _____ _____ is the planning, analysis, and control of the personal sales function.

[straight-salary, straight-commission, combination, p. 509]

13. Three sales compensation formats are _____ _____ , _____ _____ , or a _____ plan.

[Sales promotion, p. 510]

14. _____ _____ consists of the marketing activities other than advertising, publicity, or personal selling, that stimulate consumer purchases and dealer effectiveness.

[Conditions of sales promotion, p. 515]

15. _____ _____ _____ _____ are the stipulations channel members or final customers must meet to be eligible for a sales promotion.

DEFINITIONS

Match the terms and concepts with the appropriate definitions. Each term or concept may only be used once; there are more terms and concepts than definitions.

Column A	*Column B*
a. approaching customers	____ 1. Usually interacts with customers after sales are completed.

b. buyer-seller dyad

c. canned sales presentation

d. closing the sale

e. combination compensation plan

f. missionary salesperson

g. need-satisfaction approach

h. order getter

i. order taker

j. prospecting

k. sales engineer

l. sales-expense budget

m. sales management

n. sales presentation

o. sales promotion conditions

p. sales promotion orientation

q. selling process

r. service salesperson

s. straight-commission plan

t. straight-salary plan

____ 2. Two-way flow of communication between buyer and seller.

____ 3. A sales compensation plan that pays a salesperson a flat fee per week, month, or year.

____ 4. A memorized, repetitive sales presentation given to all customers interested in a particular item.

____ 5. The requirements channel members or final consumers must meet to be eligible for a sales promotion.

____ 6. The stage in a sales process which generates a list of customer leads.

____ 7. Type of sales support person used to distribute information about new products or services.

____ 8. Type of salesperson who processes routine orders and reorders.

____ 9. The stage in the sales process that involves getting the customer to agree to a purchase.

____ 10. The planning, analysis, and control of the personal sales function.

____ 11. Refers to the focus of sales promotion towards channel members or final consumers.

____ 12. The stage in the selling process that consists of the preapproach and greeting.

____ 13. Accompanies an order getter when highly technical or complex items are being sold.

____ 14. A sales presentation method based on the principle that each customer has different characteristics and wants.

____ 15. A sales compensation plan that ties a salesperson's earnings directly to sales or profits.

MULTIPLE CHOICE

Place the letter of the answer you think best in the blank provided.

__b__ 1. Which of the following functions is usually associated with the role of professional sales personnel?
   a. Receipt of payments
   b. Generation of customer accounts
   c. Procurement of stock from inventory
   d. Routine recommendations of the best brand in a product category

2. In comparison with advertising, personal selling
   a. is more passive.
   b. has less waste.
   c. passes along less information.
   d. costs less per customer.

3. Which of the following statements about the drawbacks of personal selling is *false*?
   a. Only a limited number of consumers can be accommodated at a given time.
   b. It is an ineffective tool for generating consumer awareness about a product or service.
   c. Feedback is more difficult to ascertain than with advertising.
   d. It has a poor image in the eyes of a number of consumers.

4. The major goal for personal selling is
   a. information.
   b. reminding.
   c. image.
   d. persuasion.

5. The last stage in developing a personal selling plan is
   a. selecting a sales technique.
   b. outlining sales tasks.
   c. applying the plan.
   d. determining types of sales positions.

6. Sales-expense budgets tend to be larger when
   a. customers are geographically concentrated.
   b. products are basically simple.
   c. few calls are made per salesperson.
   d. the firm deals in specialized products.

7. Both order takers and order getters typically
   a. restock merchandise.
   b. close sales.
   c. generate customer leads.
   d. receive low compensation.

8. Which of the following is *not* generally a function of support personnel?
   a. Making sales
   b. Distributing information
   c. Explaining product uses
   d. Installing equipment

9. In contrast with the need-satisfaction approach to sales, the canned sales presentation
   a. is more flexible.
   b. has a nonmarketing orientation.
   c. consists of spontaneous questions and answers.
   d. is the more popular technique.

10. The need-satisfaction approach works best with items that are
    a. inexpensive.
    b. heavily advertised.
    c. complex.
    d. relatively presold.

11. The first stage in the actual selling process involves
    a. determining customer wants.
    b. approaching customers.
    c. giving a sales presentation.
    d. prospecting for leads.

12. Sending a direct-mail piece to all people residing in a given area and waiting for replies is an example of
    a. blind prospecting.
    b. a sales presentation.
    c. lead prospecting.
    d. greeting customers.

13. Which of the following is *not* a nonselling task performed by salespeople?
    a. Setting up displays
    b. Writing up orders
    c. Pricing merchandise
    d. Checking competitors' strategies

14. Which of the following statements about the selection of sales personnel is *false?*
    a. It is preferable to match salespeople and customers on the basis of racial background.
    b. It is important to select employees on the basis of a number of attributes.
    c. It is desirable to match the traits of salespeople to the requirements of the product being sold.
    d. It is sound to select sellers whose backgrounds differ from buyers' when high financial purchases are at stake.

15. The allocation of a salesperson to a specific territory does *not* depend on
    a. his or her ability.
    b. the buyer-seller dyad.
    c. travel time.
    d. the competition.

16. Which of the following statements about sales promotion is true?
    a. Supermarkets use promotional displays most frequently for trash bags and headache remedies.
    b. Consumers have become more price conscious and less interested in trading stamps.
    c. Although few households use coupons, redemption rates are high.
    d. There are less than 500 nationally advertised sweepstakes each year.

17. Sales promotion may have an adverse effect on
    a. impulse purchasing.
    b. brand loyalty.
    c. new-product introduction.
    d. firm image.

_____ 18. In contrast to a sales manager, the sales promotion responsibility of an advertising manager would focus on
   a. trade shows.
   b. contests.
   c. special events.
   d. trade allowances.

_____ 19. An example of the conditions of sales promotion is a
   a. direct-mail solicitation.
   b. Thanksgiving theme.
   c. purchase of three bars of soap to get one free.
   d. a free sample of a new deodorant.

_____ 20. In a sales-promotion budget, the most money is allocated for
   a. direct mail.
   b. trade shows and exhibits.
   c. premiums, incentives, and specialties.
   d. business meetings and conventions.

DISCUSSION QUESTIONS

1. Why do you think the costs of personal selling are much higher than advertising for most companies?

2. Define the buyer-seller dyad. How might it affect the selection of sales personnel?

3. Compare personal selling and advertising in terms of waste, flexibility, and consumer awareness, as well as feedback.

4. Why is the need-satisfaction approach to selling considered a higher-level method than the canned sales presentation?

5. Trace the steps involved in the selling process and describe how supervision can affect the way in which they are performed.

6. Why do sales promotions generate consumer enthusiasm in the short run and yet have an adverse affect on the company in the long run?

7. Develop a sales promotion plan for an erasable ink pen, listing objectives, media, and several possible types of promotion.

EXERCISES

17-1.   Every year, *Sales & Marketing Management* magazine publishes a survey of selling costs. Some highlights of the 1980 study[1] follow.

- In 1972, sales expenses (meals, lodging, and auto rental) for a typical week in the field came to $250.45. In 1983, these expenses equalled $681.45: meals, $154.00; lodging, $254.50; and auto rental, $272.95.
- Between 1980 and 1983, meal costs increased 17.6 per cent, lodging costs increased 38.9 per cent, and auto rental costs increased by 1.1 per cent.
- The 1983 median cost per call differed by type of salesperson. For example, median cost per call: $76.35 for account representatives, $105.50 for sales engineers, $79.30 for industrial products salespersons, and $56.00 for service salespersons.
- Median daily dining costs in fifteen major cities varied widely, from a low of $75.90 in Boston to a high of $124.00 in Washington, D.C.
- During the year, account representatives located in metropolitan areas made an average number of 950 sales calls; in more dispersed areas or where longer sales calls were needed, the average number of calls was 475.

---

[1] "1984 Survey of Selling Costs," *Sales & Marketing Management* (February 20, 1984), pp. 13-14 ff.

Questions

1.   Interpret the marketing significance of the data presented in this exercise.

2. What can companies do to maximize the performance of their field sales forces?

3. What criteria should companies use to determine which customer accounts to call on and which to bypass (or handle by telephone)?

4. Interview an outside salesperson regarding his/her expenses. Be sure to ask the person whether or not the expense account is viewed as a fringe benefit, a business tool, or a combination of both. What conclusions do you reach?

17-2.   Jackson Hardware is one of the largest producers of hardware products in the U.S. Its products are sold exclusively in hardware stores, home-products stores, and outlets for professionals (such as builders, plumbers, etc.) through a national sales force of 100. Bill Jones is the company's top salesperson, consistently earning between $60,000 and $80,000 per year. While Bill has been relatively happy with Jackson Hardware, after twelve years with the company he has some points of dispute:

- Whenever he exceeds his sales quota by over 20 per cent, his new quota for the following year is set at 30 per cent above last year's performance. Bill feels that the new quota deprives him of additional income (Bill receives a higher commission rate on sales above quota). His sales manager feels that his original quotas are often set at too low a level.

- In recent years, the size of Bill's sales territory has been cut. Several profitable accounts were assigned to newer salespersons. Bill was upset, because he has developed these accounts. The reduction in territory size also limited his sales potential. His sales manager feels that Bill was no longer able to cover his entire territory properly; some accounts were virtually ignored.

- Bill is upset about the limits put on his entertainment budget. Jackson Hardware no longer compensates salespeople for lunches above $15 per person or for dinners above $20 per person, based on its accountant's recommendation. Bill is concerned about this. A lunch or dinner with one of his suburban customers is commonly less than half the cost of a comparable meal in a major city. Should larger accounts (and those located in major cities) be treated more poorly because of their location? Bill also feels that this policy may encourage unethical behavior as salespeople increase the number of people reported to be entertained on their expense records.

Table 1 contains some relevant data on Bill Jones' performance for the most recent five-year period.

Table 1
Bill Jones, Selected Performance Measures

	Territory Quota	Net Sales[1]	Entertainment Expenses	Total Income for Jones[2]
1980	$2,000,000	$2,500,000	$12,000	$67,500
1981	3,250,000	2,675,000	14,000	60,125
1982	3,250,000	3,477,500	17,000	76,713
1983	4,500,000	3,700,000	22,000	75,500
1984	4,500,000	4,440,000	33,000	86,600

[1] Total sales less returns

[2] Total income equals $20,000 salary plus 1.5 per cent of sales up to quota, and an additional 2 per cent on all sales above quota. There is no penalty for not reaching the quota.

Questions

1. Evaluate Table 1.

2. Evaluate Bill's and the company's positions on their points of dispute. Develop an equitable policy to resolve these areas of disagreement.

3. What should Bill do if Jackson Hardware refuses to change its policies with respect to his sales quota, territory size, and entertainment reimbursement?

4. Would Bill be a good candidate for a sales manager's position? There is currently an uncovered region in the Midwest (Bill services a Southeastern territory). Explain your answer.

17-3.   Compare the selling process that would be used by salespersons who cold canvass with that used by salespersons who work in retail stores.

17-4.   Candy brands vigorously battle for consumer attention and store displays in attractive locations (e.g., near cash registers). Develop consumer-oriented and retailer-oriented sales promotions that could be used for Snickers and Hershey chocolate candy.

ANSWERS

True/False

1. T, p. 495	11. F, p. 507
2. F, p. 497	12. T, p. 507
3. T, p. 497	13. F, p. 509
4. T, p. 497	14. T, p. 510
5. T, p. 499	15. F, p. 510
6. F, pp. 502-503	16. F, p. 512
7. F, p. 503	17. T, p. 513
8. F, p. 504	18. F, p. 513
9. T, p. 504	19. F, p. 512
10. F, pp. 505-506	20. F, p. 516

Multiple Choice

1. b, p. 494	11. d, pp. 504, 506
2. b, p. 497	12. a, p. 504
3. c, p. 498	13. b, p. 507
4. d, p. 499	14. d, p. 507
5. c, p. 499	15. c, p. 508
6. c, p. 501	16. b, pp. 510-512
7. b, pp. 502-503	17. d, p. 513
8. a, p. 503	18. b, pp. 514-515
9. b, pp. 503-504	19. c, p. 515
10. c, p. 504	20. d, p. 516

Definitions

1. r	9. d
2. b	10. m
3. t	11. p
4. c	12. a
5. o	13. k
6. j	14. g
7. f	15. s
8. i	

Discussion Questions

1. pp. 494-495
2. p. 497
3. pp. 497-498
4. pp. 503-505
5. pp. 504, 506
6. pp. 512-513
7. pp. 513-516

Part Five Review Quiz

DEFINITIONS

Define the following terms and concepts in your own words and then check your answers with the Key Terms and Concepts sections of the Study Guide, Chapters 15-17.

promotion
all-you-can-afford technique
S-curve effect
waste
publicity types
selling process
sales promotion orientation

SEQUENCES

For each of the following questions, arrange the events in chronological order by writing the numbers in the blanks provided, indicating the first in each series by 1.

1.   The Communication Process
       _____ audience
       _____ source
       _____ message
       _____ encoding
       _____ feedback
       _____ medium
       _____ decoding

2. Hierarchy-of-Effects Model
   _____ purchase
   _____ awareness
   _____ liking
   _____ knowledge
   _____ conviction
   _____ preference

3. Developing an Advertising Plan
   _____ considering cooperative efforts
   _____ developing themes
   _____ assigning responsibility
   _____ evaluating success or failure
   _____ establishing a budget
   _____ selecting media
   _____ setting objectives
   _____ timing advertisements
   _____ creating advertisements

4. Creating an Advertisement
   _____ determining how many variations of the basic message to utilize
   _____ determining message content
   _____ outlining a production schedule
   _____ locating an ad in a broadcast program or in a print medium

5. Developing a Publicity Plan
   _____ selecting media
   _____ setting objectives
   _____ timing publicity messages
   _____ assigning responsibility
   _____ outlining types of publicity
   _____ evaluating success or failure
   _____ creating publicity messages

6. Developing a Personal Selling Plan
   _____ outlining sales tasks
   _____ assigning responsibility
   _____ selecting a sales technique
   _____ determining types of sales positions
   _____ setting objectives
   _____ establishing a budget
   _____ applying the plan

7. The Selling Process
   _____ customer wants
   _____ follow up
   _____ sales presentation
   _____ prospecting
   _____ answering questions
   _____ approaching customers
   _____ closing the sale

SENTENCES

In each sentence, circle the word or phrase that is most appropriate.

1. For products that have a solid level of consumer awareness, the promotional thrust is on [persuasion/reinforcement].

2. A [company spokesperson/celebrity] is used in communication to gain the attention of the audience and improve product awareness.

3. [One/Two]-sided messages mention the benefits of company offerings.

4. Nonpersonal media provide a [large/small] audience and [high/low] per customer costs; they are [flexible/inflexible] and work best with a [concentrated/dispersed] target market.

5. In [aided/unaided] recall, feedback is obtained through the use of multiple-choice questions.

6. Institutional advertising is used to promote the company's [product/image].

7. When a product is new, the marginal return is [high/low], and after a product becomes established, each additional increment of promotion will have [more/less] impact on sales.

8. Since 1980, expenditures for direct mail have [risen/fallen] significantly.

9. Standardized products with [large/small] markets and [large/small] average purchase amounts receive substantial advertising.

10. In selecting advertising themes, the company may choose a [consumer/service] appeal which centers on attributes and characteristics rather than benefits.

11. [Clutter/Reach] refers to the number of advertisements that are contained in a single program or issue.

12. [Distributed/Mass] advertising maintains company and brand recognition in nonpeak periods.

13. Public relations is [image/demand]-directed.

14. [Business/Service] feature articles focus on the company and its offerings.

15. Personal selling involves [passive/dynamic] interaction between buyer and seller, [more/less] waste, and [immediate/remote] feedback.

16. An order [getter/taker] is involved with generating customer leads.

17.   [Blind/Lead] prospecting relies on telephone directories to generate potential customers.

18.   Setting up displays, pricing merchandise, and writing up information sheets are considered [nonselling/selling] tasks.

19.   Sales promotion objectives are almost always [demand/image]-oriented.

20.   [Coupons/Trading stamps] are used to increase store traffic.

ANSWERS

Sequences

1. 6,1,3,2,7,4,5, p. 436
2. 6,1,3,2,5,4, p. 446
3. 8,4,2,9,3,5,1,7,6, p. 468
4. 3,1,2,4, p. 475
5. 4,1,6,2,3,7,5, p. 485
6. 6,2,5,4,1,3,7, p. 499
7. 3,7,4,1,5,2,6, p. 506

Sentences

1. persuasion, p. 433
2. celebrity, p. 437
3. One, p. 439
4. large, low, inflexible, dispersed, p. 442
5. aided, p. 444
6. image, p. 446
7. high, less, p. 450
8. risen, p. 464
9. large, small, p. 464
10. service, p. 470
11. Clutter, p. 473
12. Distributed, p. 478
13. image, p. 482
14. Business, pp. 486-487
15. dynamic, less, immediate, p. 497
16. getter, p. 502
17. Blind, p. 504
18. nonselling, p. 507
19. demand, p. 513
20. Coupons, p. 515

Part
Six

Price Planning

18 An Overview of Price Planning

CHAPTER OBJECTIVES

1. To define price and price-planning terms
2. To demonstrate the importance of price and its relationship to other marketing variables
3. To differentiate between price and nonprice competition
4. To examine the factors affecting pricing decisions: consumers, government, channel members, competition, and costs

CHAPTER OVERVIEW

A price represents the value of a product or service for both the seller and the buyer. Price planning is systematic decision making relating to all aspects of pricing by a company; it involves tangible and intangible factors and can refer to the nonmonetary exchange of goods and services. A price contains all the terms of a purchase. Exchange does not take place unless both the buyer and seller agree that a price represents an equitable value. Price also balances supply and demand. The increased importance of price is the result of cost rises, consumer awareness, product shortages, deregulation, and foreign competition.

Under price competition, sellers influence demand primarily through changes in price levels. With nonprice competition, sellers minimize price and emphasize other marketing characteristics such as image, packaging, and features.

Several factors affect a firm's pricing decisions: consumers, government, channel members, competition, and costs. The law of demand states that consumers usually purchase more units at a low price than at a high price. Price elasticity of demand explains the sensitivity of buyers to price changes in terms of the quantities they purchase. Elastic demand occurs if relatively small changes in price result in large changes in quantity demanded; inelastic demand results if price changes have little impact on quantity demanded; and unitary demand occurs if price changes offset quantity changes. Demand is influenced by the availability of substitutes and urgency of need. Consumers can be divided into economical, personalizing, ethical, and apathetic market segments.

Government is active in a broad variety of pricing areas. Price fixing, both horizontal and vertical, is subject to severe restrictions. The Robinson-Patman Act bans most forms of price discrimination to channel members that are not justified by costs. A number of states have unfair-sales acts (minimum price laws) to protect small firms against predatory pricing. Unit pricing requires specified retailers to post prices in terms of quantity. The Federal Trade Commission has a series of guidelines for price advertising.

Each channel member seeks a major role in setting prices in order to generate sales, obtain adequate profit margins, sustain a suitable image, ensure repeat purchases, and meet its own goals. Manufacturers exert control through exclusive distribution, preticketing, opening their own outlets, offering goods on consignment, providing adequate margins, and having strong brands. Wholesalers and retailers exert control by making large purchases, linking sales support to margins, refusing to carry items, stocking competitive brands, and developing their own brands. Manufacturers need to consider channel member profit margins, price guarantees, special deals, and the ramifications of price increases.

A market-controlled price environment has a high level of competition, similar products and services, and little control over price by individual firms. A company-controlled price environment has a moderate level of competition, well-differentiated products and services, and strong control over price by individual firms. In a government-controlled price environment, the government sets prices. Some competitive actions may result in price wars, in which firms try to undercut each other's prices.

The costs of raw materials, supplies, labor, advertising, transportation, and other items affect prices. During the past decade, costs have risen significantly in many areas. This has caused companies to pass along increases to consumers, modify products and services, and abandon some offerings. Cost declines can benefit marketing strategies by improving the firm's ability to plan prices.

KEY TERMS AND CONCEPTS

Price	Represents the value of a product or service for both the seller and the buyer.
Price planning	The systematic decision making pertaining to all aspects of pricing by the organization.
Price competition	Demand influenced primarily through changes in price levels.
Nonprice competition	Reduces the role of price as a factor in consumer demand. This is accomplished by the creation of a distinctive product or service as expressed through promotion, packaging, delivery, customer service, availability, and other factors.
Law of demand	A theory which states that consumers usually purchase more units at a low price than at a high price.
Elasticity of demand	Defines the sensitivity of buyers to price changes in terms of the quantities they will purchase. Price elasticity is computed by dividing the percentage change in quantity demanded by the percentage change in price charged.

Elastic demand	Occurs if relatively small changes in price result in large changes in the quantity demanded.
Inelastic demand	Occurs when price changes have little impact on quantity demanded.
Unitary demand	Exists if changes in price are exactly offset by changes in quantity demanded so that total sales revenue remains constant.
Subjective price	The consumer's perception of a price as high or low.
Horizontal price fixing	Agreements among manufacturers, among wholesalers, or among retailers to set prices. Such agreements are illegal according to the Sherman Antitrust Act and the Federal Trade Commission Act, regardless of how "reasonable" the prices are.
Vertical price fixing	Occurs when manufacturers or wholesalers control the retail prices of their products or services. This practice is sometimes illegal.
Robinson-Patman Act	Prohibits manufacturers and wholesalers from price discrimination in dealing with different channel members purchasing products of "like quality," if the effect of such discrimination is to injure competition.
Unfair-sales acts (Minimum price laws)	Legislation in several states preventing retailers from selling merchandise for less than the cost of the product plus a fixed percentage that covers overhead and costs.
Predatory pricing	An illegal practice in which large companies cut prices on products in selected geographic areas below their cost with the intention of eliminating small, local competitors.
Loss leader	An item priced below cost that is restricted by unfair-sales acts in many states. Retailers use loss leaders, typically well-known and heavily advertised brands, to draw customer traffic into a store.
Unit pricing	Prices expressed per unit of measure as well as by total value. Enables consumers to compare price per quantity for competing brands and for various sizes of the same brand.
Bait-and-swith advertising	An illegal procedure whereby a retailer lures customers into a store by advertising items at exceptionally low prices and then telling customers that the items are out of stock or are of inferior quality. The retailer has no intention of selling the advertised items.
Selling against the brand	Retailers stocking manufacturers' brands and placing high prices on them in order to aid in selling private-label goods.
Price guarantee	A manufacturer's assurance to wholesalers or retailers that the prices they pay are the lowest available. Any discount given to competitors will also be given to the original purchaser.

Market-controlled price environment   Characterized by a high level of competition, similar products and services, and little control over price by individual companies.

Company-controlled price environment   Characterized by a moderate level of competition, well-differentiated products and services, and strong control over price by individual firms.

Government-controlled price environment   Characterized by prices set or directed by the government.

Price war   Situation in which various firms continually try to undercut each other's prices.

TRUE/FALSE

Circle the appropriate letter.

T   F   1. A price can refer to nonmonetary exchanges of goods and services.

T   F   2. If there is an excess of demand over supply, prices are usually reduced by sellers.

T   F   3. Price is present in every marketing transaction.

T   F   4. Of all the controllable marketing variables, a pricing strategy is the easiest for a competitor to duplicate.

T   F   5. For the most part, price decisions are independent of elements external to the firm.

T   F   6. Elastic demand occurs if price changes have little impact on the quantity of goods or services demanded.

T   F   7. When consumers believe there are many similar products or services from which to choose, or if there is no urgency to make a purchase, demand is inelastic.

T   F   8. Recent research confirms that all consumers use price as the dominant purchase determinant.

T   F   9. Consumers consider actual price more important than subjective price.

T   F   10. In order to avoid price-fixing charges, companies must be careful not to rotate low bids on contracts.

T   F   11. The Miller-Tydings Act prohibits price discrimination among channel-member purchasers if the effects of such discrimination are to injure competition.

T   F   12. Manufacturers and wholesalers can control retail prices through consignment selling.

T   F   13. The Robinson-Patman Act enables firms to strictly set and enforce retail prices if they desire.

T   F   14. At the federal level, predatory pricing is banned by the Sherman and Clayton Acts.

T   F   15. Because consumers normally benefit from loss leaders, unfair-sales acts are rarely enforced.

T   F   16. Recent research shows that unit pricing remains ineffective.

T   F   17. Prices are viewed as deceptive if sales are continued beyond defined time periods.

T   F   18. Selling against the brand often increases sales of private brands.

T   F   19. With price guarantees, discounts that manufacturers give to new retailer-customers are denied to original retailer-customers.

T   F   20. A company-controlled price environment is characterized by a high level of competition and similar products or services.

COMPLETION

Fill in the missing word or words in the blanks provided.

[price, price planning, p. 532]

1. A _____ represents the value of a product or service and is a mechanism for allocating goods and services. Systematic decision making by the organization pertaining to all aspects of that value is called _____ _____ .

[tangible, intangible, monetary, nonmonetary, p. 532]

2. The value of a product or service to organizational or final customers may involve both _____ and _____ factors and may refer to both _____ and _____ exchanges of goods and services.

[price competition, nonprice competition, pp. 535-536]

3. With _____ _____ , sellers influence demand primarily through changes in price levels, whereas _____ _____ minimizes price as a factor in consumer demand.

[law of demand, price elasticity of demand, p. 539]

4. The _____ _____ _____ states that consumers usually purchase more units at a low price than at a high price; the _____ _____ _____ _____ defines the sensitivity of buyers to price changes in terms of the quantities they will purchase.

[Elastic demand, inelastic demand, unitary demand, p. 540]

5. _____ _____ occurs if relatively small changes in price result in large changes in the quantity demanded; _____ _____ takes place if price changes have little impact on the quantity demanded; and _____ _____ exists if the percentage changes in price and quantity are equal so that total sales revenue remains constant.

[economical, personalizing, ethical, apathetic, p. 542]

6. Consumers can be divided into four categories, depending on their shopping orientation: the _____ shopper, interested in value and sensitive to prices; the _____ shopper, emphasizing product or service images and personal service; the _____ shopper, willing to sacrifice

low prices and wide assortments in order to patronize a smaller firm; and the _____ shopper, whose main concern is convenience.

[subjective, p. 543]

7. A consumer's perception of price is known as the _____ price.

[Horizontal price fixing, vertical price fixing, pp. 543-544]

8. _____ _____ _____ results from agreements among manufacturers, wholesalers, or retailers to set prices at a given stage in the channel of distribution, whereas _____ _____ _____ occurs when manufacturers or wholesalers are able to control the retail prices of their products or services.

[Robinson-Patman, price discrimination, predatory pricing, pp. 545-546]

9. The _____ _____ Act prohibits _____ _____ , so that competing channel members receive proportionately equal terms and conditions of sale; the Sherman and Clayton Acts bar _____ _____ where large firms attempt to drive small firms out of business by setting extremely low prices.

[Unit pricing, p. 546]

10. _____ _____ enables consumers to compare price and quantity for competing brands and for various sizes of the same brand.

[Federal Trade Commission, p. 547]

11. The _____ _____ _____ and various trade associations, such as the Better Business Bureau, have developed guidelines for price advertising.

[Bait-and-switch, p. 547]

12. _____ _____ _____ advertising is an illegal procedure retailers use to lure customers into stores by offering items at exceptionally low prices and telling them that the items are out of stock or of inferior quality.

[selling against the brand, p. 548]

13. Retailers may engage in _____ _____ _____ _____ , whereby they stock merchandise, place high prices on it, and then sell other brands for lower prices.

[price guarantee, p. 548]

14. Under a _____ _____ , manufacturers assure wholesalers or retailers that the prices they pay are the lowest available.

[market controlled, company controlled, government controlled, price wars, pp. 549-550]

15. The competitive environment in which a firm operates may be _____ _____ , characterized by a high level of competition and similar products or services; _____ _____ , having a moderate level of competition and well-differentiated products; or _____ _____ , where prices are set by government. Competition may lead to _____ _____ whereby various firms continually try to undercut each other's prices.

DEFINITIONS

Match the terms and concepts with the appropriate definitions. Each term or concept may only be used once; there are more terms and concepts than definitions.

Column A

a. bait-and-switch advertising

b. company-controlled price environment

c. elastic demand

d. elasticity of demand

e. government-controlled price environment

f. horizontal price fixing

g. inelastic demand

h. law of demand

i. loss leader

j. market-controlled price environment

k. nonprice competition

l. predatory pricing

m. price

n. price competition

o. price guarantee

p. price planning

q. price war

r. Robinson-Patman Act

s. selling against the brand

t. subjective price

u. unfair-sales acts

v. unit pricing

w. unitary demand

x. vertical price fixing

Column B

___ 1. Occurs when price changes have little impact on the quantity demanded.

___ 2. An item priced below cost that is restricted by unfair-sales acts in many states.

___ 3. The consumer's perception of a price as high or low.

___ 4. Demand influenced primarily through changes in price levels.

___ 5. Characterized by a moderate level of competition, well-differentiated products and services, and strong control over price by individual firms.

___ 6. Retailers stocking manufacturers' brands and placing high prices on them in order to aid in selling private-label goods.

___ 7. Represents the value of a product or service for both the seller and the buyer.

___ 8. Agreements among manufacturers, among wholesalers, or among retailers to set prices.

___ 9. Situation in which various firms continually try to undercut each other's prices.

___ 10. Exists if changes in prices are exactly offset by changes in quantity demanded so that total sales revenue remains constant.

___ 11. An illegal practice in which large companies cut prices on products in selected geographic areas below their cost with the intention of eliminating small, local competitors.

___ 12. A manufacturer's assurance to wholesalers or retailers that the prices they pay are the lowest available.

___ 13. Legislation in several states preventing retailers from selling merchandise for less than the cost of the product plus a fixed percentage that covers overhead and costs.

___ 14. Occurs if a relatively small change in price results in large changes in the quantity demanded.

___ 15. Characterized by prices set or directed by the government.

MULTIPLE CHOICE

Place the letter of the answer you think best in the blank provided.

_____ 1. The one element found in every marketing transaction is
   a. a product.
   b. price.
   c. delivery.
   d. promotion.

_____ 2. The law of demand
   a. defines the sensitivity of buyers to price changes.
   b. concerns nonprice competition.
   c. involves government regulation of price.
   d. relates purchase units to price.

_____ 3. If price elasticity is greater than one, demand can be characterized as
   a. inelastic.
   b. unitary.
   c. elastic.
   d. nonexistent.

_____ 4. Unitary demand exists when
   a. small changes in price result in large changes in demand.
   b. price changes have little impact on demand.
   c. there are no available substitutes for the product or service.
   d. total sales revenue remains constant.

_____ 5. Which of the following does *not* generate inelastic demand?
   a. Product uniqueness
   b. Brand loyalty
   c. Emergency conditions
   d. Existence of substitute products

_____ 6. The type of consumer *most* prone to the price elasticity of demand is the
   a. personalizing shopper.
   b. economical shopper.
   c. ethical shopper.
   d. apathetic shopper.

_____ 7. The category of shopper most concerned with convenience is the
   a. personalizing shopper.
   b. economical shopper.
   c. ethical shopper.
   d. apathetic shopper.

_____ 8. Recent research confirms that many consumers
   a. use price as the dominant purchase determinant.
   b. regard actual price as more important than subjective price.
   c. may be more concerned with convenience than price.
   d. allow price consciousness to override their brand preferences.

_d_ 9. Horizontal price fixing has been outlawed by the
   a. Sherman Act.
   b. Robinson-Patman Act.
   c. Miller-Tydings Act.
   d. McGuire Act.

_d_ 10. To avoid price-fixing charges, companies should *not*
   a. preprint prices on products.
   b. sell by consignment.
   c. suggest realistic retail list prices.
   d. discuss prices at trade association meetings.

_c_ 11. When manufacturers or wholesalers are able to control the retail prices of their products or services, they are engaged in
   a. horizontal price fixing.
   b. price discrimination.
   c. vertical price fixing.
   d. unit pricing.

_a_ 12. Fair trade practices refer to
   a. vertical price fixing.
   b. price controls.
   c. price discrimination.
   d. unfair-sales acts.

_b_ 13. It is now illegal for manufacturers or wholesalers to control retail prices through
   a. consignment sales.
   b. resale price maintenance.
   c. establishment of customary prices.
   d. careful screening of retailers.

_d_ 14. The Robinson-Patman Act places legal restrictions on
   a. price fixing.
   b. minimum pricing.
   c. price advertising.
   d. price discrimination.

_c_ 15. Unfair-sales acts are most often used to bar
   a. loss leaders.
   b. unit pricing.
   c. predatory pricing.
   d. bait-and-switch advertising.

_b_ 16. Which of the following enables consumers to compare price per quantity for competing brands?
   a. Predatory pricing
   b. Unit pricing
   c. Price wars
   d. Price competition

17. Under Federal Trade Commission advertising guidelines, a firm can
    a. continue to offer low prices beyond defined sales periods.
    b. make bargain offers without disclosing terms.
    c. claim a price is lower than its competitors' prices without verification.
    d. imply a price reduction if the original price was recently and regularly offered to the public.

18. Selling against the brand is a technique that
    a. is preferred by manufacturers.
    b. allows wholesalers to strengthen their control over prices.
    c. encourages sales of private brands.
    d. is disliked by retailers.

19. Price guarantees
    a. bar entry into established channels of distribution.
    b. help wholesalers and retailers maintain inventory value and profit.
    c. usually grant discounts to purchasers who are not competitors.
    d. encourage passing price increases along to consumers.

20. In a market-controlled price environment, one finds
    a. a high level of competition.
    b. well-differentiated products.
    c. public utilities, buses, and taxis.
    d. strong control over prices by individual firms.

DISCUSSION QUESTIONS

1. Explain how pricing can refer to nonmonetary as well as monetary exchanges of goods and services.

2. Differentiate among elastic, inelastic, and unitary demand.

3. Discuss the statement "Not all consumers are equally price conscious."

4. What measures can a company take to avoid charges of price fixing?

5. How are consumers protected from predatory pricing?

6. Describe some of the restrictions the Federal Trade Commission has placed on price advertising.

7. Which price-controlled environment would be *most* attractive to discounters? Why?

EXERCISES

18-1.   A movie theater has developed a demand schedule that shows the relationship between ticket prices and demand. The demand schedule (presented in Table 1) assumes that (a) the movie is a moderate attraction, (b) consumers are attending a Saturday evening performance, and (c) another neighborhood theater is not featuring a blockbuster movie.

Table 1
A Movie Theater's Demand Schedule for a
Saturday Evening Performance

Ticket Price (Per Adult)	Demand (Number of Adults Buying Tickets)
$2.00	600
2.50	500
3.00	450
3.50	375
4.00	300
4.50	200
5.00	70

Note: The theater capacity is 450 persons.

Questions

1.   Compute the price elasticities for the movie theater, based on Table 1.

2. What price should the theater charge? Explain your answer.

3. The theater nets 70 cents of each dollar spent on candy, popcorn, or soda. The average purchase per customer is 75 cents. Given this information, would your answer to the previous question change? Why or why not?

4. What technique could a movie theater use to establish a demand schedule? Describe the limitations of this technique.

18-2.   Between 1980 and 1983, the prices of all U.S. commodities rose by 13 per cent while prescription drug prices rose by 37 per cent. As one government official noted, "Drug costs have been rising faster than before and faster than most other medical costs." Because of the price rises, a barrage of criticism has been directed at the pharmaceutical industry. For example, some critics suggest[1] that:

- Price increases are really being used to offset lower international profits, higher marketing costs and slower growth in the U.S., sales difficulties during the recession (when people visited doctors less often), and tighter Medicaid provisions.
- Few new drugs have recently been introduced. Therefore, "What some are doing is salvaging profits through price increases instead of by expanding business."
- "In terms of their actual costs—labor, supplies, etc.—there's no real excuse for the current activity."
- The prices for some essential drugs have risen much too fast. During 1983 alone, cancer therapy drug prices rose by 24 per cent.
- "The danger is that they'll bring on regulation" by the government.

Industry officials respond[2] that:

- The sharp prices are temporary.
- Since 1971, drug prices have risen less than overall consumer prices.
- Petrochemicals, key ingredients in many drugs, are much more costly to pharmaceutical firms.
- Research and development costs are very high. The development of a single new drug may cost $50 million to $70 million, compared with $24 million in 1972.
- The prices for specific drugs may be unrelated to their costs. Drugs are priced to assure a cash flow, to provide the kind of return needed to support new research, and to attract capital and talent.

---

[1] Michael Waldholz, "Prices of Prescription Drugs Soar After Years of Moderate Increases," *Wall Street Journal* (May 25, 1984), p. 31.

[2] Ibid.

Questions

1. Comment on this statement: "The public often judges profits from products used to keep people healthy and alive more harshly than profits from other consumer goods like cars and toasters."

2. Evaluate the two positions on drug pricing stated in this exercise.

3. Some observers believe that pharmaceutical companies are setting high prices on popular branded prescription drugs that will lose their patent protection within the next few years. These drugs will then be available in generic form from competitors. Assess this practice.

4. Should all or some of the prices for prescription drugs be controlled by the federal government? Explain your answer.

18-3.   Create both a price and a nonprice strategy for an automated car wash targeted at final consumers. Which strategy should be chosen? Why?

18-4.   Develop a checklist for a firm by which it can measure its compliance with government regulations pertaining to prices.

ANSWERS

True/False

1. T, p. 532
2. F, p. 533
3. T, p. 534
4. T, p. 537
5. F, p. 538
6. F, p. 540
7. F, p. 540
8. F, pp. 542-543
9. F, p. 543
10. T, p. 543
11. F, p. 545
12. T, pp. 544-545
13. F, p. 545
14. T, p. 546
15. T, p. 546
16. F, pp. 546-547
17. T, p. 547
18. T, p. 548
19. F, p. 548
20. F, pp. 549-550

Multiple Choice

1. b, p. 534
2. d, p. 539
3. c, p. 540
4. d, p. 540
5. d, p. 542
6. b, p. 542
7. d, p. 542
8. c, pp. 542-543
9. a, p. 543
10. d, p. 544
11. c, pp. 544-545
12. a, p. 544
13. b, pp. 544-545
14. d, p. 545
15. c, pp. 545-546
16. b, p. 546
17. d, p. 547
18. c, p. 548
19. b, p. 548
20. a, p. 549

Definitions

1. g
2. i
3. t
4. n
5. j
6. s
7. m
8. f
9. q
10. v
11. l
12. o
13. u
14. c
15. e

Discussion Questions

1. p. 532
2. p. 540
3. pp. 542-543
4. p. 544
5. pp. 545-546
6. pp. 547-548
7. pp. 549-550

19

Developing a Pricing Strategy

CHAPTER OBJECTIVES

1. To study the overall process of developing a pricing strategy
2. To analyze sales-based, profit-based, and status-quo-based pricing objectives
3. To examine the aspects of a broad price policy, including the multistage approach, and to consider the alternative pricing techniques
4. To show how a pricing strategy can be implemented
5. To present the major ways that prices can be adjusted

CHAPTER OVERVIEW

Developing a pricing strategy consists of objectives, broad policy, strategy, implementation, and adjustments. Pricing objectives may be sales-, profit-, or status quo-based. Sales objectives center on growth or market share. A penetration price is a low price intended to capture the mass market. Profit objectives center on profit maximization, satisfactory profits, optimizing return on investment, or early cash recovery. Profit can be expressed in per unit or total dollar terms. A skimming price is a high price intended to capture the market segment less concerned with price than quality or status. A firm may use a skimming and then a penetration pricing strategy. Status quo objectives are geared toward avoiding declines in business and minimizing the impact of outside parties. Objectives may be combined.

A broad price policy integrates pricing decisions with the firm's target market, image, and marketing mix. Within its broad price policy, the company determines whether it is price- or nonprice-oriented. A popular technique for planning a broad policy is the multistage approach to pricing.

A price strategy may be cost-, demand-, or competition-based. With cost-based pricing, prices are computed by adding desired profits to the costs of production and selling. In demand-based pricing, final prices are based on consumer research. The firm works backward to determine the costs it can afford to incur and still sell an item at the price sought by consumers. Under competition-based pricing, prices are set below, at, or higher than those of competitors. All three approaches should be integrated when establishing a price strategy.

Implementing a price strategy involves a variety of separate but interlocking specific decisions. Customary pricing exists when a channel member maintains prices for an extended period of time. With variable pricing the marketer alters prices to coincide with fluctuations in costs or consumer demand. With a one-price policy, all consumers making a purchase under similar conditions pay the same price. Flexible pricing allows the marketer to vary prices based on the consumer's ability to negotiate or the buying power of a large customer.

An odd-pricing strategy is used when final selling prices are set at levels below even-dollar values. The price-quality association states that consumers believe there is a correlation between price and quality. With prestige pricing, it is assumed that consumers do not buy products or services at prices that are considered too low. They set price floors as well as price ceilings. Under leader pricing, key items are sold at less than their usual profit margins in order to increase consumer traffic.

Multiple-unit pricing is a practice in which a company offers final consumers discounts for buying in quantity. Price lining is the sale of merchandise at a range of prices, with each price representing a distinct level of quality. Geographic pricing outlines the responsibility for transportation charges. Terms are the provisions of price agreements, including discounts, timing of payments, and credit arrangements.

After a price strategy is implemented, it usually requires regular fine tuning to reflect cost, competition, or demand changes. Prices can be adjusted by changing list prices, including escalator clauses and surcharges in contracts, marking prices up or down, and offering direct manufacturer rebates.

KEY TERMS AND CONCEPTS

Sales-based objective

A pricing objective which orients a firm's pricing strategy toward high sales volume or expanding sales relative to competitors.

Penetration price

A low price intended to capture the mass market for a product or service.

Profit-based objective

A pricing objective which orients a firm's pricing strategy toward some type of profit goal: profit maximization, return on investment, and/or early recovery of cash.

Skimming price

A high price intended to attract the market segment that is more concerned with product quality, uniqueness, or status than price.

Status quo-based objective

A pricing objective which orients a firm's pricing strategy toward stability or continuing a favorable climate for operations.

Broad price policy

Coordinates pricing decisions with the firm's target market, image, and marketing mix. It generates a coordinated series of actions, a consistent image, and a strategy that incorporates short- and long-term goals.

Multistage approach to pricing	A popular technique for developing a broad price policy. Divides price planning into six successive steps, with each placing constraints on the next step.
Cost-based price strategy	Sets prices by computing merchandise, service, and overhead costs, and then adding the desired profit to these figures. Demand is not analyzed.
Price floor	The lowest acceptable price the firm can charge and attain its profit goal.
Demand-based price strategy	Prices set after researching consumer desires and ascertaining the range of prices acceptable to the target market.
Price ceiling	The maximum amount customers will pay for a given product or service.
Competition-based price strategy	Prices set in accordance with competitors. Prices may be below the market, at the market, or above the market.
Customary pricing	Occurs when a channel member sets product or service prices and seeks to maintain them for an extended period.
Variable pricing	Prices modified to coincide with fluctuations in costs or consumer demand. The same product or service may be priced at two or more levels based on the customer's ability to pay, service location, or time.
One-price policy	The same price charged to all customers who seek to purchase a product or service under similar conditions.
Flexible pricing	Allows the marketer to adjust prices based on the consumer's ability to negotiate or the buying power of a large customer.
Odd-pricing strategy	Used when final selling prices are set at levels below even dollar values, such as 49¢, $4.95, and $199.
Price-quality association	Concept stating that consumers believe high prices mean high quality and low prices mean low quality.
Prestige pricing	Assumes that consumers do not buy products or services at prices that are considered too low.
Psychological pricing	Assumes consumers are perceptually sensitive to certain prices. Departures from these prices in either direction result in decreases in demand. Customary, odd, and prestige pricing are all forms of psychological pricing.
Leader pricing	Advertising and selling key items in the product assortment at less than their usual profit margins. The objective of leader pricing is to increase store traffic or to gain greater consumer interest in an overall product line.
Multiple-unit pricing	A practice by which a company offers final consumers discounts for buying in quantity in order to increase sales volume.

Price lining	Involves the sale of merchandise at a range of prices, with each individual price representing a distinct level of quality.
Geographic pricing	Outlines the responsibility for transportation charges. The basic forms of geographic pricing are FOB (free on board), uniform delivered price, zone pricing, and base-point pricing.
FOB mill (factory) pricing	A form of geographic pricing in which the buyer selects the transportation form and pays all freight charges. The delivered price to the buyer depends on the freight charges.
Uniform delivered pricing	A form of geographic pricing in which all buyers pay the same delivered price for the same quantity of goods, regardless of their location. The seller pays for shipping.
Zone pricing	A form of geographic pricing which provides for a uniform delivered price to all buyers within a geographic zone. In a multiple-zone system, delivered prices vary by zone.
Base-point pricing	A form of geographic pricing in which firms in an industry establish basing points from which costs of shipping are computed. The delivered price to a buyer reflects the cost of transporting goods from the basing point nearest to the buyer, regardless of the actual site of supply.
Terms	The provisions of price agreements, including discounts, timing of payments, and credit arrangements.
Discount	A reduction from the final selling price that is available to channel members and final consumers for performing certain functions, paying in cash, buying large quantities, purchasing in off-seasons, or enhancing promotions.
Open credit account	A credit purchase in which a buyer receives a monthly bill for goods bought during the preceding month. The account must be paid in full each month.
Revolving credit account	A credit purchase in which the buyer agrees to make minimum payments during an extended period of time and pays interest on outstanding purchases.
List price	A regularly quoted price provided to customers. It is preprinted on price tags, in catalogs, and in dealer purchase orders.
Escalator clause	A form of price adjustment that allows a firm to contractually raise the price of an item to reflect higher costs in the item's essential ingredients without changing printed list prices.
Surcharge	A form of price adjustment in which across-the-board price increases are published to supplement list prices. Frequently used with catalogs because of their simplicity; an insert is distributed with the catalog.

Additional markup	Used to raise regular retail prices because demand is unexpectedly high or costs are rising.
Markdown	Reduction from the original price of an item to meet lower prices of competitors, counteract overstocking of merchandise, delete an assortment of odds and ends, and increase customer traffic.
Rebate	A form of price adjustment in which a cash refund is given directly from the manufacturer to the consumer in order to stimulate consumption.

TRUE/FALSE

Circle the appropriate letter.

T   F   1. With sales-based objectives, a firm is interested in securing an early recovery of cash.

T   F   2. A company can only pursue one pricing objective at a time.

T   F   3. Penetration pricing may discourage actual and potential competitors.

T   F   4. One profit-based objective is a return on investment.

T   F   5. High per unit profits usually rely on skimming pricing.

T   F   6. Status quo objectives require little or no effort on the part of the firm.

T   F   7. With a cost-based price strategy, demand is not analyzed.

T   F   8. Demand-based pricing is used by marketers who believe that price is a key factor in consumer decision making.

T   F   9. With items such as candy and gum, manufacturers tend to reduce package size or change ingredients rather than raise prices to reflect cost increases.

T   F   10. Throughout the United States, flexible pricing policies are the rule for most retailers.

T   F   11. Customary, odd, and prestige pricing are all forms of psychological pricing.

T   F   12. For a retailer the objective of leader pricing is to gain greater consumer interest in an overall product line.

T   F   13. Price lining is a strategy designed to enable a firm to clear out slow-moving merchandise.

T   F   14. Generally, geographic pricing is negotiated and does not depend on traditional industry practices.

T   F   15. Functional discounts compensate wholesalers and retailers for distribution tasks they perform.

T   F   16. In the chain method of discounting, cash, quantity, seasonal, and promotional discounts are deducted after the trade discount has been determined.

T	F	17. Terms of 4/16, net 20 means that a buyer receives a 25 per cent discount if the full bill is paid within twenty days after receipt of the merchandise.
T	F	18. With an open account, a buyer makes minimum payments and pays interest on the outstanding balance.
T	F	19. To tie prices to volatile costs, catalogs frequently use escalator clauses rather than surcharges because of their simplicity.
T	F	20. Manufacturer cash rebates to customers alter basic list prices and generate less enthusiasm than price cuts by retailers.

COMPLETION

Fill in the missing word or words in the blanks provided.

[sales-based, penetration price, p. 560]

1. A company with _____ _____ objectives seeks to expand its market share relative to competitors and frequently uses a _____ _____ to capture the mass market for a product or service.

[satisfactory-profit, return-on-investment, early-recovery-of-cash, p. 561]

2. A company pursuing profit-based goals may seek a _____ _____ objective to gain stable profits over a period of time; a _____ _____ _____ objective to relate profits to investment costs; or an _____ _____ _____ _____ objective to achieve high initial profits.

[per unit, total, p. 562]

3. Profit can be expressed in _____ _____ or _____ terms.

[skimming price, pp. 562-563]

4. A _____ _____ is used to attract the market segment most concerned with product quality, uniqueness, or status.

[status quo, p. 564]

5. A company with _____ _____ objectives is interested in stability, or in continuing a favorable climate for its operations.

[broad price, multistage, p. 564]

6. A _____ _____ policy integrates pricing decisions with a firm's target market, image, and marketing mix and often utilizes a _____ approach to pricing that has six successive steps.

[cost-based, demand-based, competition-based, pp. 565-566]

7. Price strategy may be _____ _____ , adding the desired profit to computed overhead costs; _____ _____ , researching consumer desires and price acceptability; or _____ _____ , setting prices according to what competitors do.

[price floor, price ceiling, p. 566]

8. A _____ _____ is the lowest price a firm can charge to attain its profit goals; a _____ _____ is the maximum amount consumers will pay.

[Customary, variable, pp. 566-568]

9. _____ pricing occurs when channel members set product or service prices and seek to maintain them over an extended period of time; _____ pricing occurs when prices are altered to coincide with fluctuations in costs or consumer demand.

[one-price, flexible, p. 568]

10. Under a _____ _____ policy, a firm charges the same price to all customers; under a _____ policy firms adjust prices according to the customer's ability to negotiate or their buying power.

[odd, prestige, price-quality association, p. 569]

11. Psychological pricing includes customary pricing; _____ pricing, when final selling prices are set below even dollar values; and _____ pricing, which assumes that consumers do not buy products at prices they consider low. The latter theory is drawn from the _____ _____ _____ , a concept stating that consumers think that prices connote quality.

[leader, multiple-unit, price lining, pp. 570-571]

12. Under _____ pricing, a firm sells key items in its product assortment at less than its usual profit margins; under _____ _____ pricing, the firm offers final consumers discounts for buying in quantity; and _____ _____ refers to the sale of merchandise at a range of prices corresponding to distinct levels of quality.

[Geographic, FOB mill pricing, uniform delivery pricing, zone pricing, base-point pricing, Terms, discounts, pp. 573-574]

13. _____ pricing outlines responsibility for transportation charges. Four commonly used forms are _____ _____ _____ , _____ _____ _____ , _____ _____ , and _____ _____ _____ . _____ are provisions of price agreements, including _____ , which are reductions from the final selling price that are available to channel members and final consumers for performing certain functions.

[open account, revolving account, p. 575]

14. Firms that allow credit purchases may use an _____ _____ , where the buyer receives a monthly bill that must be paid in full each month, or a _____ _____ , where the buyer makes minimum payments over an extended period and pays interest on outstanding balances.

[List, escalator clauses, surcharges, markups, p. 575]

15. _____ price may be modified because of changing economic conditions. To tie prices to volatile costs, firms may use _____ _____ , where selling prices are linked to the costs of a product's essential ingredients; _____ , where prices are altered by a given percentage; or additional _____ , which are amounts added to the regular retail price when demand is unexpectedly high or costs are rising.

DEFINITIONS

Match the terms and concepts with the appropriate definitions. Each term or concept may only be used once; there are more terms and concepts than definitions.

Column A	*Column B*
a. additional markup	___ 1. A low price intended to capture the mass market for a product or service.
b. base-point pricing	___ 2. A regularly quoted price provided to customers.
c. broad price policy	___ 3. Occurs when a channel member sets product or service prices and seeks to maintain them for an extended period.
d. competition-based price strategy	
e. cost-based price strategy	___ 4. Used when final selling prices are set at levels below even dollar values.
f. customary pricing	___ 5. The lowest acceptable price the firm can charge and attain its profit goal.
g. demand-based price strategy	
h. discounts	___ 6. Assumes consumers are perceptually sensitive to certain prices.
i. escalator clause	___ 7. A practice by which a company offers final consumers discounts for buying in quantity in order to increase sales volume.
j. flexible pricing	
k. FOB mill pricing	___ 8. Assumes that consumers do not buy products or services at prices that are considered too low.
l. geographic pricing	___ 9. A form of geographic pricing in which the buyer selects the transportation form and pays all freight charges.
m. leader pricing	
n. list price	
o. markdown	___ 10. A credit purchase in which a buyer receives a monthly bill for goods bought during the preceding month which must be paid in full each month.
p. multiple-unit pricing	
q. multistage approach to pricing	___ 11. Sets prices by computing merchandise, service, and overhead costs, and then adding the desired profit to these figures.
r. odd-pricing strategy	
s. one-price policy	___ 12. A high price intended to attract the market segment that is more concerned with product quality, uniqueness, or status than price.
t. open credit account	
u. penetration price	___ 13. The provisions of price agreements, including discounts, timing of payments, and credit arrangements.
v. prestige pricing	
w. price ceiling	___ 14. The same price charged to all customers who seek to purchase a product or service under similar conditions.
x. price floor	
y. price lining	___ 15. Prices modified to coincide with fluctuations in costs or consumer demand.
z. price-quality association	
aa. profit-based objective	
bb. psychological pricing	
cc. rebate	
dd. revolving credit	

ee. sales-based objective

ff. skimming price

gg. status quo-based objective

hh. surcharges

ii. terms

jj. uniform-delivered pricing

kk. variable pricing

ll. zone pricing

MULTIPLE CHOICE

Place the letter of the answer you think best in the blank provided.

_____ 1. Which of the following statements is *not* true?
a. Different firms in the same industry always have the same pricing strategies.
b. A company can pursue more than one pricing objective at the same time.
c. A pricing strategy must be consistent with overall company objectives.
d. A firm can set different long- and short-run objectives.

_____ 2. With sales-based objectives, the firm focuses on
a. optimizing the return on investment.
b. minimizing the effects of competitor actions.
c. maximizing market share.
d. maintaining good channel relations.

_____ 3. Companies with sales-based objectives frequently use
a. skimming prices.
b. penetration prices.
c. flexible prices.
d. prestige prices.

_____ 4. With profit-based objectives, the firm focuses on
a. stabilizing prices.
b. precluding unfair government actions.
c. reducing demands from suppliers.
d. securing an early recovery of cash.

_____ 5. Firms seeking stable profits over a period of time use
a. return-on-investment objectives.
b. early-recovery-of-cash objectives.
c. status quo-based objectives.
d. satisfactory-profit objectives.

_____ 6. High total profits usually involve
   a. penetration pricing.
   b. flexible pricing.
   c. skimming pricing.
   d. prestige pricing.

_____ 7. A skimming price is a proper strategy where
   a. competition is intense.
   b. there are economies of scale.
   c. funds are needed for further expansion.
   d. the market is sensitive to price.

_____ 8. The first step in a multistage approach to developing a broad price policy is
   a. examining brand image.
   b. identifying a target market.
   c. analyzing the marketing mix.
   d. determining a pricing strategy.

_____ 9. Price floors are frequently set in
   a. demand-based strategies.
   b. cost-based strategies.
   c. status quo-based strategies.
   d. competition-based strategies.

_____ 10. Price ceilings
   a. do not take demand into account.
   b. are the lowest acceptable prices firms can charge to gain their profit goals.
   c. depend on the availability of substitutes and the urgency of need.
   d. are the minimum amounts consumers will pay for products or services.

_____ 11. Under customary pricing, channel members
   a. alter prices to coincide with fluctuations in costs.
   b. adjust prices to levels of demand.
   c. offer discounts to those who buy in quantity.
   d. modify package size or change ingredients to reflect cost increases.

_____ 12. Flexible pricing
   a. is easy to administer.
   b. builds customer confidence.
   c. encourages bargaining.
   d. permits self-service.

_____ 13. Which of the following is _not_ a form of psychological pricing?
   a. Customary pricing
   b. Variable pricing
   c. Odd pricing
   d. Prestige pricing

_____ 14. Leader pricing is most often used with
   a. low-turnover products.
   b. high-quality products.
   c. infrequently purchased items.
   d. nationally branded items.

_____ 15. Which of the following is *not* a major reason for employing multiple-unit pricing?
    a. Total dollar sales are maintained.
    b. The firm can clear our slow-moving merchandise.
    c. Greater consumption is encouraged.
    d. Competitors' customers may be attracted.

_____ 16. Which of the following is *not* a constraint on price lining?
    a. Consumers may perceive gaps between prices as too large.
    b. Rising costs may make it hard for a firm to maintain the proper relationship among prices.
    c. Consumers have a wide assortment from which to select.
    d. Markdowns may disrupt the balance in a price line.

_____ 17. Geographic pricing does *not*
    a. cover delivery dates.
    b. affect all firms in an industry.
    c. depend on traditional industry practices.
    d. outline responsibility for transportation charges.

_____ 18. Which of the following is *not* a method of geographic pricing?
    a. Uniform delivered pricing
    b. Base-point pricing
    c. Zone pricing
    d. Multiple-unit pricing

_____ 19. Trade discounts
    a. relate to efficiencies from large-volume purchases.
    b. encourage advance orders.
    c. offer compensation for distribution tasks.
    d. reimburse channel members for promoting products.

_____ 20. In catalogs, to tie prices to rising costs, it is simplest to
    a. include escalator clauses.
    b. add on surcharges.
    c. increase markups.
    d. change list prices.

DISCUSSION QUESTIONS

1. List the components of a pricing strategy and explain why the construction of a pricing strategy is not a one-time occurrence.

2. Discuss the statement "It should not be inferred that status quo objectives require no effort on the part of the firm."

3. Describe the multistage approach to broad price policy.

4. Why should cost-, demand-, and competition-based pricing strategies be considered when establishing a pricing strategy?

5. Discuss the statement "Customary, odd, and prestige pricing are all forms of psychological pricing."

6. What factors must be taken into consideration in the timing of payments by channel members?

7. Compare and contrast escalator clauses and surcharges. When is it advisable to use these forms of price adjustment? Why?

EXERCISES

19-1.   When developing a pricing strategy, a firm must first consider whether the strategy is cost-based, demand-based, or competition-based. In a cost-based strategy, the marketer sets prices by computing merchandise, service, and overhead costs and then adding the desired profit to these figures. In a demand-based strategy, the marketer sets prices after researching consumer desires and ascertaining the range of prices acceptable to the target market. In a competition-based strategy, the marketer sets prices in accordance with competitors. Many companies combine elements of these three approaches.

The firm must also make a number of other decisions, regarding concepts such as flexible pricing, odd pricing, and leader pricing.

Questions

1.   Provide an example of cost-based, demand-based, and competition-based pricing.

2.　Why do antique shops usually engage in flexible pricing while antique departments in department stores utilize a one-price policy?

3.　Draw a demand curve for a firm using an odd-pricing strategy. Explain this curve.

4.　Distinguish among leader pricing, loss leaders, bait-and-switch advertising, and price lining. Give an example of each.

19-2.   Traditionally, textbook publishers provided college bookstores with a functional discount of 20 per cent below suggested list price. The discount was to cover store operating costs and a profit margin. However, many bookstore managers stated that increases in shipping charges (most publishers sent their books FOB from their warehouses), rent, heat, labor, and other factors drove their operating costs over 20 per cent of sales. Managers maintained that they were losing more money on texts each year.

In the face of this criticism, publishers proposed to sell their books on a "net" basis to bookstores. List prices would not appear on book jackets, in publishers' catalogs, or elsewhere. Bookstores would pay publishers' net prices and set their own selling prices. A director of marketing for a large publisher stated:

> We recognize the cost of doing business varies among college bookstores. We believe that each bookstore should set its own retail prices independently, without regard to a publisher's suggested price, but based upon its operating costs and the competitive situation which it faces.

The reaction to net pricing has been mixed. One bookstore manager said, "Net pricing is purely a cop-out. Most publishers don't want to increase the discount because they make high profits under the present arrangement." Another manager believed that stores would be able to "control their own destiny" under net pricing. According to a survey of bookstores with more than $3 million in yearly sales, 54 per cent preferred net pricing over a 20 per cent discount. However, only 17 per cent favored net pricing if bookstores were to be given 25 per cent discounts instead. The survey also found that operating expenses averaged 22.7 per cent of sales, more than the publishers' traditional 20 per cent discount.[1]

---

[1] "Some Publishers to Relax Pricing Rules for Textbooks," *Chronicle of Higher Education* (May 5, 1980), p. 10.

Questions

1.   Why would most bookstore managers choose larger discounts over net pricing?

2. Is net pricing a good or bad method for bookstores to follow? Explain your answer.

3. What are the pricing objectives of the average college bookstore?

4. Do textbooks follow a penetration or skimming-price strategy? Why?

19-3.   Visit both a new car dealer and a used car dealer. Select a car model at each and negotiate a price. What are the similarities and differences in pricing strategies between these two dealers?

19-4.   Interview five restaurant owners and ask how frequently they change prices. What conclusions can you reach?

ANSWERS

True/False

1. F, p. 560
2. F, p. 560
3. T, p. 560
4. T, pp. 561-562
5. T, pp. 562-563
6. F, p. 564
7. T, pp. 565-566
8. T, p. 566
9. T, p. 568
10. F, p. 568
11. T, p. 569
12. F, pp. 570-571
13. F, pp. 571-573
14. F, p. 573
15. T, p. 574
16. T, p. 574
17. F, pp. 574-575
18. F, p. 575
19. F, p. 575
20. F, p. 576

Multiple Choice

1. a, p. 560
2. c, pp. 559-560
3. b, pp. 561-562
4. d, p. 560
5. d, p. 564
6. a, p. 560
7. c, pp. 562-563
8. b, p. 564
9. b, p. 566
10. c, p. 566
11. d, pp. 566-567
12. c, p. 568
13. b, p. 569
14. d, pp. 570-571
15. a, p. 571
16. c, p. 573
17. a, p. 573
18. d, p. 573
19. c, p. 574
20. b, p. 575

Definitions

1. u
2. n
3. f
4. r
5. x
6. bb
7. p
8. v
9. k
10. t
11. c
12. ff
13. ii
14. s
15. kk

Discussion Questions

1. pp. 558-559
2. p. 564
3. p. 564
4. pp. 565-566
5. pp. 566-569
6. pp. 574-575
7. p. 575

20

Applications of Pricing Techniques

CHAPTER OBJECTIVES

1. To examine and evaluate various cost-, demand-, and competition-based pricing techniques
2. To present applications of cost-, demand-, and competition-based pricing techniques
3. To explain the mathematics of pricing techniques
4. To demonstrate why cost-, demand-, and competition-based pricing techniques must be integrated

CHAPTER OVERVIEW

With cost-based pricing, the firm computes merchandise, service, and overhead costs and then adds an amount to cover profit. Cost-based prices are relatively easy to implement, are founded on comparative certainty, and incorporate profitability. They also disregard market conditions, plant capacity, competitive prices, the product's phase in its life cycle, market share, and the consumer's ability to pay. Overhead costs may be difficult to allocate. When using cost-based techniques, it is necessary to understand several cost concepts, including fixed costs, variable costs, total costs, average costs, and marginal costs.

Cost-plus pricing is the simplest cost method. It adds costs and a desired profit rate to determine price. It is most effective when the manufacturer is able to control selling price. In markup pricing, the firm sets prices by determining the markup percentages needed to cover selling costs and profit and calculating per unit merchandise costs. Markup pricing is common among wholesalers and retailers. A variable markup policy allows a company to use different markups for distinct products or services. In target pricing, prices are set to provide a specified rate of return on investment for a standard volume of production. Standard volume is the level of production the firm anticipates achieving. When a firm has excess capacity, it may use price-floor pricing, in which prices are set to cover variable costs and contribute to overhead. Traditional break-even analysis determines the sales quantity at which total costs equal total revenues for a chosen price. It can be extended to include profit analysis.

For demand-based pricing, the company first determines the prices final consumers and channel members will pay, then figures the markups needed to cover selling expenses and profits, and finally derives the maximum merchandise costs that can be incurred. Prices are linked to consumer preferences, channel needs, and product image. Demand techniques require consumer research, are predicated on imprecise data, and sometimes are not keyed to profitability.

In demand-minus pricing, the firm works backward from final selling price to costs. Chain markup pricing extends demand-minus calculations from the retailer back to the manufacturer, and assures a proper final selling price and equitable markups throughout the channel. Modified break-even analysis combines traditional break-even analysis with an evaluation of demand at various levels of price. It helps select the price-quantity mix that optimizes profit. Price discrimination is a technique with which a firm sets two or more prices for a product or service in order to appeal to different market segments. Price discrimination may be based on customers, products, time, and/or place.

In competition-based pricing, the firm uses competitors' prices as its main guideposts. Prices may be below, at, or above the market. It is simple, provides equity for customers and companies, and minimizes price confrontations. A firm must determine whether it has the ability and the interest to be a price leader or price follower. Under competitive bidding, two or more companies independently submit prices in response to precise customer requests. The expected profit concept states that as the bid price increases, the profit to a firm increases, but the probability of the firm's winning the contract decreases.

Cost-, demand-, and competition-based pricing techniques should be combined so that all necessary factors are considered. Otherwise, critical decisions are likely to be overlooked.

KEY TERMS AND CONCEPTS

Cost-plus pricing	A form of cost-based pricing in which prices are computed by adding a predetermined profit to costs. It is the simplest form of cost-based pricing.
Markup pricing	A form of cost-based pricing in which the price is set by calculating per-unit merchandise costs and then determining the markup percentages that are needed to cover selling costs and profit.
Variable markup policy	A form of cost-based markup pricing whereby separate categories of goods and services receive different percentage markups. Variable markups recognize differences in personal selling efforts, customer service, alterations, and end-of-season markdown requirements.
Target pricing	A form of cost-based pricing in which prices are set to provide a specified rate of return on investment for a standard volume of production.
Traditional break-even analysis	Determines the sales quantity (in units or dollars) at which total costs equal total revenues at a given price.

Demand-minus (Demand-backward) pricing	A form of demand-based pricing whereby the firm ascertains the appropriate final selling price and works backward to compute costs.
Chain-markup pricing	A form of demand-based pricing in which final selling price is first determined, then markups for each channel member are examined, and the maximum acceptable costs to each member are computed. Chain-markup pricing extends demand-minus calculations from the retailer all the way back to the manufacturer.
Modified break-even analysis	Combines traditional break-even analysis with an evaluation of demand at various levels of price. Determines the price-quantity mix that maximizes profits.
Price discrimination	A form of demand-based pricing in which the firm sets two or more distinct prices for a product or service in order to appeal to different final consumer or organizational consumer market segments. Price discrimination may be customer-, product-, version-, time-, or place-based.
Price leadership	A form of competition-based pricing in which one firm is usually the first to announce price changes and the other companies in the industry follow.
Expected profit concept	A mathematical calculation applied to competitive bidding which states that as bid price increases, the profit to a firm increases, but the probability of its winning the contract decreases. The long-run average expected profit at each bid equals the company's profit times its probability of obtaining the contract at this bid amount.

TRUE/FALSE

Circle the appropriate letter.

T F 1. Most firms use demand-based pricing techniques.

T F 2. Cost-based prices consider market conditions and plant capacity.

T F 3. The simplest form of cost-based pricing is cost-plus pricing.

T F 4. Cost-plus pricing is most effective when price fluctuations have little influence on sales.

T F 5. Markup pricing is usually expressed in terms of cost.

T F 6. For target pricing to operate properly, the company must sell its entire standard volume at specified prices.

T F 7. Target pricing is used by capital-intensive firms and public utilities.

T F 8. Under target pricing, prices are keyed to demand.

T F 9. Price-floor pricing is often used when a firm has excess capacity.

T   F   10. Traditional break-even analysis does not consider demand.

T   F   11. Demand-based pricing is more precise and less subject to change than cost estimation.

T   F   12. In demand-minus pricing, the firm computes costs first and then ascertains the appropriate final selling price.

T   F   13. With chain-markup pricing, final selling price is determined after the maximum acceptable costs to each member are computed.

T   F   14. Under chain-markup pricing, channel members can set prices independently of one another.

T   F   15. Under modified break-even analysis, it is assumed that the same volume can be sold at any price.

T   F   16. Price discrimination depends on elasticity of demand.

T   F   17. Competition-based pricing requires calculation of per-unit costs.

T   F   18. Price leaders are firms that are respected by competitors and have significant market shares.

T   F   19. During the past several years, the role of the price leader has become substantially more important in many industries.

T   F   20. Under the expected profit concept, the company's potential profit cannot be determined.

COMPLETION

Fill in the missing word or words in the blanks provided.

[cost, demand, competition, p. 582]

1. Three techniques for setting prices are based on _____ , _____ , and _____ .

[cost-plus, p. 584]

2. Under _____ _____ pricing, prices are determined by adding a predetermined profit to costs.

[projected profit, units produced, p. 584]

3. To calculate it, total fixed costs are added to total variable costs and _____ _____ and divided by _____ _____ .

[markup, p. 586]

4. In _____ pricing, the firm sets prices by calculating per unit merchandise costs and then determining the amounts needed to cover selling costs and profits.

[variable markup policy, p. 587]

5. Under a _____ _____ _____ , separate categories of goods and services receive distinct prices in response to differences in selling costs among them.

[target pricing, standard volume of production, p. 588]

6. In _____ _____ , prices are set to provide a specified rate of return on investment for a _____ _____ _____ _____ , the level a firm anticipates achieving.

[investment, average
total costs, p. 588]

7. To compute it, _____ costs are multiplied by the target return on investment, and then divided by standard volume. To this amount, _____ _____ _____ are added.

[price-floor pricing,
capacity, p. 589]

8. When a company determines the lowest price at which it is economical to offer additional units for sale, it is using _____ _____ _____ , which is useful for plants that have excess _____ .

[Traditional break-even
analysis, p. 589]

9. _____ _____ _____ _____ examines the relationship among costs, revenues, and profits.

[Demand-minus, consumer
surveys, profits, costs,
p. 593]

10. _____ _____ pricing is used when a firm ascertains the appropriate final selling price and works backward to compute costs. It is comprised of three steps: determining the final selling price through _____ _____ and other research techniques, deriving a markup percentage from selling expenses and desired _____ , and finding maximum acceptable merchandise _____ .

[Chain-markup,
p. 594]

11. _____ _____ pricing extends demand-minus calculations from the retailer all the way back to the manufacturer.

[customer, product,
time, place, p. 596]

12. Four forms of price discrimination are based on _____ , _____ , _____ , and _____ .

[price leadership,
pp. 597-598]

13. Regarding _____ _____ , the firm must determine whether it has the ability to be an initiator of price changes.

[competitive bidding,
p. 599]

14. When two or more companies independently submit prices for specific products, projects, and/or services, _____ _____ takes place.

[expected profit concept,
increases, decreases,
pp. 599-600]

15. The _____ _____ _____ states that as the bid price increases, the profit to a firm _____ , but the probability of its winning the contract _____ .

DEFINITIONS

Match the terms and concepts with the appropriate definitions. Each term or concept may only be used once; there are more terms and concepts than definitions.

Column A

a. chain markup pricing

b. cost-plus pricing

c. demand-minus pricing

d. expected profit concept

Column B

___ 1. A form of cost-based pricing in which prices are set to provide a specified rate of return on investment for a standard volume of production.

___ 2. A form of cost-based pricing in which prices are computed by adding a predetermined profit to costs.

e. markup pricing

f. modified break-even analysis

g. price discrimination

h. price leadership

i. target pricing

j. traditional break-even analysis

k. variable markup policy

____ 3. A form of competition-based pricing in which one firm is usually the first to announce price changes and the other companies in the industry follow.

____ 4. A form of cost-based pricing in which the price is set by calculating per-unit merchandise costs and then determining the percentages that are needed to cover selling costs and profit.

____ 5. Determines the sales quantity (in units or dollars) at which total costs equal total revenues at a given price.

____ 6. Form of demand-based pricing whereby the firm ascertains the appropriate final selling price and works backward to compute costs.

____ 7. Refers to a mathematical calculation applied to competitive bidding which states that as bid price increases, the profit to a firm increases, but the probability of its winning the contract decreases.

____ 8. A form of demand-based pricing in which the firm sets two or more distinct prices for a product or service in order to appeal to different final consumer or organizational consumer market segments.

____ 9. A form of cost-based markup pricing whereby separate categories of goods and services receive different percentage markups.

____ 10. A form of demand-based pricing in which final selling price is first determined, then markups for each channel member are examined, and the maximum acceptable costs to each member are computed.

MULTIPLE CHOICE

Place the letter of the answer you think best in the blank provided.

_____ 1. In a classic study of pricing techniques it was found that most manufacturers of consumer and industrial products use
a. demand-based pricing.
b. cost-based pricing.
c. government-regulated pricing.
d. competitive pricing.

_____ 2. In comparison with demand- and competition-based pricing, cost-based pricing
a. is relatively easy to implement.
b. bases estimates on the product's phase in its life cycle.
c. is more responsive to market conditions.
d. is more marketing oriented.

_____ 3. The simplest form of cost-based pricing is
   a. target pricing.
   b. break-even analysis.
   c. markup pricing.
   d. cost-plus pricing.

_____ 4. Cost-plus pricing is most advantageous for firms
   a. facing rising costs.
   b. having excess capacity.
   c. seeking improved efficiency.
   d. confronting few price fluctuations.

_____ 5. Which of the following is _not_ a reason why markups are expressed in terms of selling price?
   a. Profit planning is aided.
   b. Retail sales price information is more available.
   c. Profitability statistics appear higher.
   d. Criticism over high profits is reduced.

_____ 6. Which of the following statements about a variable markup policy is _not_ true?
   a. It regards product investment as constant.
   b. It is a response to differences in selling effort.
   c. It recognizes that some items require extensive allowances.
   d. It reflects greater end-of-season markdowns for some items.

_____ 7. A limitation of target pricing is that
   a. it is not suitable for capital-intensive firms.
   b. prices are too dependent on demand.
   c. price reductions to handle overstocked merchandise are not planned for.
   d. standard volume of production may be exceeded.

_____ 8. When a firm has excess capacity, the most appropriate strategy to use is
   a. price leadership.
   b. price-floor pricing.
   c. competitive bidding.
   d. demand-based pricing.

_____ 9. Traditional break-even analysis
   a. considers demand.
   b. holds variable costs per unit constant.
   c. allows for changes in fixed costs.
   d. divides all costs into marginal, fixed, and variable.

_____ 10. Under demand-based pricing,
   a. highly competitive situations result in high prices.
   b. noncompetitive situations encourage low markups.
   c. research is needed on market segments.
   d. costs are adequately covered.

_____ 11. Which of the following is _not_ a demand-based pricing technique?
   a. Modified break-even analysis
   b. Price discrimination
   c. Chain markup pricing
   d. Traditional break-even analysis

_____ 12. With demand-minus pricing, the first step consists of deriving
    a. markup percentage.
    b. merchandise costs.
    c. final selling price.
    d. fixed costs.

_____ 13. Through chain-markup pricing
    a. price decisions are related to costs.
    b. channel members cannot set prices independently of one another.
    c. cost increases are borne by the manufacturer.
    d. new-product pricing research is fairly precise.

_____ 14. Which of the following is an example of demand-based pricing?
    a. Target pricing
    b. Markup pricing
    c. Modified break-even analysis
    d. Competitive bidding

_____ 15. When buying power is an important dimension of price discrimination, the price discrimination is based on
    a. time.
    b. product.
    c. customer.
    d. place.

_____ 16. Price differentials are greater than cost differentials under price discrimination, which is based on
    a. product.
    b. place.
    c. customer.
    d. time.

_____ 17. Competition-based pricing
    a. requires calculations of demand curves and costs per unit.
    b. leads to retaliations.
    c. assumes the ongoing price level is fair.
    d. helps absorb excess plant capacity.

_____ 18. A form of competition-based pricing is
    a. price discrimination.
    b. price leadership.
    c. price-floor pricing.
    d. chain-markup pricing.

_____ 19. Price leaders usually
    a. lack competitors' respect.
    b. confer with other firms before setting prices.
    c. have a limited market share.
    d. are well established within the industry.

_____ 20. The expected profit concept is a method of computing how
  a. cost-, demand-, and competition-based pricing can be combined.
  b. market share is affected by competitive bidding.
  c. the market price level is determined under competition-based pricing.
  d. bid price increases affect firm profit and contract awards.

MATHEMATICAL PROBLEMS

Enter the correct answers in the spaces provided.

_____ 1. A company selling vacuum cleaners has total fixed costs of $200,000 and total variable costs of $120,000. It desires a profit of $40,000 and expects production to be 1,000 units. Under cost-plus pricing, the firm would set a selling price of
  a. $320.
  b. $360.
  c. $520.
  d. $750.

_____ 2. A firm has merchandise costs of $20 and seeks a markup on the selling price of 40 per cent. Under markup pricing, the selling price would be
  a. $28.00.
  b. $28.57.
  c. $33.33.
  d. $50.00.

_____ 3. An automobile manufacturer has investment costs of $200 million and average total costs of $5,000. It desires a 15 per cent return on investment, with a standard volume of 10,000 units. Under target pricing, the selling price would be
  a. $ 8,000.
  b. $12,500.
  c. $14,500.
  d. $20,000.

_____ 4. If the manufacturer in problem 3 produced 10,000 units but could only sell 7,000 of them, what would its profits (loss) be? Do not consider investment costs in your calculation.
  a. $ 6,000,000
  b. $11,000,000
  c. $14,000,000
  d. $22,000,000

_____ 5. A guitar manufacturer has fixed costs of $100,000 and variable costs per unit of $18. Its selling price is $30. Compute its break-even point in units.
  a. 3,333
  b. 5,556
  c. 8,333
  d. 10,000

_____ 6. For the firm in problem 5, calculate its break-even point in dollars.
  a. $133,333
  b. $145,145
  c. $166,667
  d. $250,000

_____ 7. A retailer knows it can sell an electric train set for $40. It seeks a 40 per cent markup on selling price to cover selling costs and profit. What is the maximum the retailer will pay for the train set under demand-based pricing?
  a. $16
  b. $24
  c. $32
  d. $37

_____ 8. If the train set discussed in problem 7 also requires a 30 per cent markup by the wholesaler on its selling price and a 30 per cent markup by the manufacturer on its selling price, what are the maximum costs the manufacturer can incur when producing a set?
  a. $11.76
  b. $19.60
  c. $21.54
  d. $25.41

_____ 9. A firm makes one model of radio. Its fixed costs are $25,000 and variable costs per unit are $15. It sells 10,000 radios at $25 per radio. The firm has recently decided to introduce a second model in order to use price discrimination. This model's fixed costs will be zero, because it will share the facilities used by the first model. Its variable costs will be $25 per unit. The firm projects that 4,000 units of the second model will sell at $40 each. It also projects that the sales of the first model will drop to 8,000 units. How much will profits be increased by introduced the second model? (_Hint_: The profits in selling 10,000 units of one model are $75,000.)
  a. $ 40,000
  b. $ 60,000
  c. $ 80,000
  d. $115,000

_____ 10. In bidding for interior bus renovation contracts in various cities throughout the country, a manufacturer usually bid $25,000 per bus and estimated its costs at $22,000 per bus. It believed its probability of winning a bid was 40 per cent. Calculate the firm's average expected profit per contract if it bid on 10 contracts involving 40 buses each.

a. $ 30,000

b. $ 48,000

c. $ 75,000

d. $100,000

DISCUSSION QUESTIONS

1. Under what situations is cost-plus pricing an effective technique for pricing? What are the shortcomings of this method?

2. When is the use of a variable markup policy appropriate?

3. What are some of the limitations of traditional break-even analysis?

4. How does chain-markup pricing extend demand-minus pricing calculations? What are the advantages and disadvantages of these pricing methods?

5. Compare and contrast the four forms of price discrimination. Give two examples in which the forms can be combined.

6. What are the effects of price leadership?

7. Unless cost-, demand-, and competition-based pricing techniques are combined, critical decisions can be overlooked. Discuss this.

EXERCISES

20-1.   An appliance repair company sets its service-call prices by target pricing. Accordingly, the firm has assembled the data necessary to undertake target pricing. These data are shown in Table 1. Now, it is ready to determine the appropriate price for its service calls. The company has made a total investment of $40,000 and requires a 25 per cent return on investment. It expects to make 4,000 service calls during the next year. The service staff consists of the owner and one employee, both of whom repair appliances on a full-time basis.

Table 1
ABC Appliance Repair Company,
Total Service Call Costs
(Based on 4,000 Calls per Year)

Out-of-pocket costs	$40,000
(Salary for a repairperson, answering service, rent, electricity, advertising, and other operating costs)	
Value of owner's services	25,000
(As a manager, repairperson, and entrepreneur)	
Reserve funds	5,000
(Savings for replacement of trucks and office equipment)	
Total	$70,000

Questions

1.   Compute the target price for a service call based on the information provided.

2.   If the average total price for a service call plus the parts used in a repair equals $28, what will the firm earn/lose on a yearly basis if 4,000 calls per year are made?

3.   Compute a service-call price using the cost-plus pricing method. Assume all service-call costs are fixed. Compare your answer with that in Question 1.

4.   Calculate a break-even point in units, using the target price for a service call determined in Question 1. Assume all service-call costs are fixed. Explain your answer.

20-2.   A stationery manufacturer makes plain and monogrammed 5″ x 7″ note pads. It sells these pads to business customers through direct mail and to final consumers through a chain of wholesalers and retailers. By conducting marketing research, the company knows that business customers will pay $5.00 for five plain pads with 100 sheets each and $7.50 for five monogrammed pads with 100 sheets each. Final customers will pay $6.00 for the five plain pads and $10.00 for the five monogrammed pads.

The manufacturer seeks a 25 per cent markup on all sales. Wholesalers and retailers each require a 30 per cent markup for sales made to final consumers.

Questions

1.   What would be the maximum merchandise costs the manufacturer could incur in selling to business customers?

2. What would be the maximum merchandise costs the manufacturer, wholesalers, and retailers could incur in selling to final customers?

3. Which market segment enables the manufacturer to obtain the highest dollar mark-up, business customers or final customers? Explain this.

4. Currently, it costs the manufacturer $3.00 to make five plain pads and $5.00 to make five monogrammed pads. Business customers purchase 1,000 sets (five pads per set) of plain pads and 5,000 sets of monogrammed pads. Final customers buy 500 sets of plain pads and 3,000 sets of monogrammed pads. Since the plain pads account for relatively few sales, the manufacturer is considering dropping them and selling only monogrammed pads. By doing so, it expects that business customers will buy an additional 250 sets of monogrammed pads and final customers will buy an additional 200 sets of these pads. Should the plain pads be dropped? Explain your answer and show all work.

20-3.   Price discrimination can be customer-based, product-based, time-based, or place-based. Provide two actual examples of each form of price discrimination and explain the benefits to the firm.

20-4.   Call three different airlines (two traditional and one no-frills) and determine their fare structures between two cities. Be sure to determine how these fares vary by airline based on time of day, day of week, level of service (coach, business class, first-class), and travel restrictions. Explain the differences in rates.

ANSWERS

True/False

1. F, p. 582
2. F, p. 583
3. T, p. 584
4. T, p. 585
5. F, p. 585
6. T, pp. 588-589
7. T, p. 588
8. F, pp. 588-589
9. T, p. 589
10. T, p. 591
11. F, pp. 591-592
12. F, p. 593
13. F, p. 594
14. F, p. 594
15. F, p. 595
16. T, p. 596
17. F, p. 597
18. T, pp. 597-598
19. F, p. 598
20. F, pp. 599-600

Multiple Choice

1. d, p. 582
2. a, p. 583
3. d, p. 584
4. d, pp. 585-586
5. c, pp. 586-587
6. a, p. 587
7. c, pp. 588-589
8. b, p. 589
9. b, pp. 589-590
10. c, pp. 591-592
11. d, p. 593
12. c, p. 593
13. b, p. 594
14. c, p. 593
15. c, p. 596
16. a, p. 596
17. c, p. 597
18. b, p. 597
19. d, pp. 597-598
20. d, pp. 599-600

Definitions

1. i
2. b
3. h
4. e
5. j
6. c
7. d
8. g
9. k
10. a

Mathematical Problems

1. b, p. 584
2. c, p. 586
3. a, p. 588
4. a, p. 588
5. c, p. 590
6. d, p. 590
7. b, p. 593
8. a, p. 594
9. a, p. 595
10. b, p. 600

Discussion Questions

1. pp. 585-586
2. p. 587
3. p. 591
4. pp. 593-595
5. p. 596
6. pp. 597-598
7. pp. 600-601

Part Six Review Quiz

DEFINITIONS

Define the following terms and concepts in your own words and then check your answers with the Key Terms and Concepts sections of the Study Guide, Chapters 18-20.

nonprice competition
elasticity of demand
bait-and-switch advertising
skimming price
price lining
markup pricing
modified break-even analysis

SEQUENCES

For each of the following questions, arrange the events in chronological order by writing the numbers in the blanks provided, indicating the first in each series by 1.

1. Developing a Pricing Strategy
    _____ implementation of price strategy
    _____ broad price policy
    _____ price adjustments
    _____ objectives
    _____ price strategy

2. Multistage Approach to Pricing
   _____ examining brand image
   _____ outlining a broad price policy
   _____ arriving at a specific price
   _____ analyzing the other components of the marketing mix
   _____ identifying the target market
   _____ determining a pricing strategy

SENTENCES

In each sentence, circle the word or phrase that is most appropriate.

1. If there is an excess of supply over demand, prices are usually [increased/reduced] by the seller.

2. Over the past twenty years, pricing has become [more/less] important to marketing executives.

3. Sellers influence demand primarily through changes in price levels in [price/nonprice] competition.

4. With [inelastic/unitary] demand, changes in price are exactly offset by changes in quantity demanded so that total sales revenue remains constant.

5. The [apathetic/personalizing] shopper is primarily concerned with convenience.

6. The Robinson-Patman Act was enacted to protect [small/large] retailers from [unit pricing/price discrimination].

7. Selling against the brand is often done to [increase/decrease] sales of private brands, a practice [encouraged/discouraged] by manufacturers.

8. A pricing strategy is performing poorly when too [many/few] different price options are available.

9. High per-unit profits usually rely on [penetration/skimming] prices.

10. With [demand/competition]-based price strategy, the marketer sets prices after researching consumer desires and ascertaining the range of prices acceptable to the target market.

11. Items like candy, gum, and magazines are usually subject to [customary/variable] pricing.

12. [Flexible/One-price] policies to channel members are subject to Robinson-Patman Act restrictions.

13. [Leader/Prestige] pricing is an example of psychological pricing.

14. Price [lining/ceiling] refers to selling merchandise at a range of prices.

15. [Zone/Uniform delivered] pricing provides all buyers within a geographic zone with a uniform delivered price.

16. The simplest form of cost-based pricing is [cost-plus/markup] pricing.

17. Target pricing is most useful for firms with [high/low] capital investments.

18. [Traditional/Modified] break-even analysis is an example of demand-based pricing.

19. Front-row theater seat charges are an example of [product/place]-based price discrimination.

20. The expected profit concept states that as the bid price [increases/decreases], the probability of winning the contract decreases.

ANSWERS

Sequences

1. 4,2,5,1,3, p. 559
2. 2,4,6,3,1,5, p. 564

Sentences

1. reduced, p. 533
2. more, p. 534
3. price, p. 535
4. unitary, p. 540
5. apathetic, p. 542
6. small, price discrimination, p. 545
7. increase, discouraged, p. 548
8. many, pp. 558-559
9. skimming, pp. 562-563
10. demand, p. 566
11. customary, p. 568
12. Flexible, p. 568
13. Prestige, p. 569
14. lining, p. 571
15. Zone, p. 573
16. cost-plus, p. 584
17. high, p. 588
18. Modified, p. 595
19. place, p. 596
20. increases, p. 599

Part
Seven

**Expanding the
Scope of
Marketing**

21

International Marketing

CHAPTER OBJECTIVES

1. To define international and multinational marketing
2. To explain why international marketing has developed
3. To study the scope of international marketing
4. To explore the cultural, economic, political and legal, and technological environments facing international marketers
5. To analyze the stages in the development of an international marketing strategy: company organization, degree of standardization, and product, distribution, promotion, and price planning

CHAPTER OVERVIEW

International marketing involves the marketing of goods and services outside the organization's home country. Multinational marketing is a complex form of international marketing that engages an organization in marketing operations in many countries. For international companies to succeed in the 1980s, it is vital that they research and understand the similarities and differences among countries and adapt their strategies accordingly.

International marketing has developed for several reasons. Countries are interested in exchanging products with which they have comparative advantages for those with which they do not. Firms seek to minimize adverse economic conditions, attract growing markets, avoid intense domestic competition, extend the product life cycle, dispose of discontinued items, and utilize tax breaks.

The United States accounts for 10 per cent of the world's exports. Yet, more than 90 per cent of United States firms do not engage in international marketing. The United States also imports $270 billion in goods annually, causing a substantial trade deficit. Non-U.S. firms are rapidly increasing their role in international marketing.

International marketers work within several environments. The cultural environment includes the behavior standards, language, life-styles, and goals of a country's citizens. The economic environment incorporates a country's standard of living, GNP, stage of economic development, and stability of currency. The political and legal environment encompasses nationalism, trade restrictions, and trade agreements such as the European Community. The technological environment refers to a country's production and measurement systems. These environments create opportunities as well as problems and vary by country.

In the development of an international marketing strategy, the firm may emphasize exporting, engage in joint ventures, or directly own foreign subsidiaries. It may adopt a standardized, nonstandardized, or mixed approach to marketing.

Product planning would extend existing products into foreign markets, modify existing products to local needs, produce less sophisticated items for developing nations, or invent new products specifically for foreign markets. Distribution planning would investigate channel relationships and establish a formal network for direct sales or middlemen. In addition, physical distribution features would be analyzed and the proper modifications made. Promotion planning would stress standardized, mixed, or nonstandardized campaigns. Mixed strategies combine the best standardized and nonstandardized promotion tools. Price planning would outline whether prices should be standardized, the level at which prices are set, the currency in which prices are quoted, and terms of sale.

KEY TERMS AND CONCEPTS

International marketing	Involves the marketing of goods and services outside the organization's home country.
Multinational marketing	A complex form of international marketing that involves an organization engaged in marketing operations in many foreign countries.
Comparative advantage	Concept in international marketing which states that countries have different rates of productivity for different products. Countries can benefit by exchanging goods in which they have relative production advantages for those in which they have relative disadvantages.
Trade deficit	Occurs when the value of imports exceeds the value of exports.
Standard of living	The average quantity and quality of goods and services consumed in a country.
Gross National Product (GNP)	The total value of goods and services produced in a country each year.
Industrialized countries	Have high literacy, modern technology, and high per capita income.
Developing countries	Have rising educational levels and technology but a per capita income of about $1,500.
Less-developed countries	Have low literacy, limited technology, and per capita income generally less than $500.

Currency stability An economic factor that could affect sales and profits if a foreign country revalues its currency in relation to the company's home country.

Nationalism Refers to a country's efforts to become self-reliant and raise its status in the eyes of the world community. Frequently, nationalism leads to tight restrictions for foreign companies and fosters the development of domestic industry at their expense.

Government stability Refers to the consistency of political policies and the orderliness in installing leaders.

Tariff The most common form of trade restriction in which a tax is placed on imported goods by a foreign government.

Trade quota A form of trade restriction in which limits are set on the amount of goods that may be imported into a country.

Embargo A form of trade restriction that prohibits specified products from entering a country.

Local content law Requires foreign-based manufacturers to establish local plants and to use locally produced components. The goal of these laws is to promote domestic employment.

General Agreement on Tariffs and Trade (GATT) A multilateral agreement that allows every nation covered to obtain the best contract terms received by a single nation. GATT members agree to meet every two years and to negotiate for tariff reductions.

Most-favored nation principle Allows every nation covered by the General Agreement on Tariffs and Trade to obtain the best contract terms received by any single nation.

European Community (EC) Also known as the Common Market. The EC calls for no tariffs among members and a uniform tariff with nonmember nations. In addition, the agreement encourages common standards for food additives, labeling requirements, and package sizes, and a free flow of capital and labor.

Exporting A form of international marketing company organization in which a company reaches international markets by selling directly through its own sales force or indirectly through foreign merchants or agents. An exporting structure requires minimal investment in foreign facilities.

Joint venture A form of international marketing company organization in which a firm combines some aspect of its manufacturing or marketing efforts with those of a foreign company in order to share expertise, costs, and connections with important persons.

Direct ownership A form of international marketing company organization that involves the full undertaking and control of all international operations.

Pure standardized approach	An international marketing strategy in which a common marketing plan is used for all countries in which a firm operates.
Pure nonstandardized approach	An international marketing strategy that assumes that each market is different and requires a distinct market plan.
Mixed approach to international marketing	An international marketing strategy which combines standardized and nonstandardized efforts to enable a company to maximize production efficiencies, maintain a consistent image, exercise home-office control, and yet be sensitive and responsive to local needs.
Straight-extension strategy	An international product-planning strategy in which a company manufactures the same products for domestic and foreign sales.
Product-adaptation strategy	An international product-planning strategy in which domestic products are modified to meet foreign conditions, taste preferences, electrical requirements, water conditions, or legal requirements.
Backward invention	An international product strategy in which a firm appeals to developing countries by making products that are less complex than the ones it sells in its domestic market.
Forward invention	An international product strategy in which a company develops new products for its international markets.
Dumping	Selling a product in a foreign country at a price lower than that prevailing in the exporter's home country, below the cost of production, or both.

TRUE/FALSE

Circle the appropriate letter.

T   F   1. In terms of ownership and top management, large multinational corporations do not have a home country.

T   F   2. Large and small firms are guaranteed success today by exporting products that have sold well in the United States to foreign markets.

T   F   3. During the late 1970s and early 1980s, the economic climate in parts of Europe and Asia was better than that in the United States.

T   F   4. Services make up one third of American exports.

T   F   5. The United States is the world's largest importer.

T   F   6. Marketing principles can be applied in the same way to both domestic and foreign markets.

T   F   7. Per capita GNP figures can be misleading because they represent income distribution, not means.

T	F	8. The greatest marketing opportunities generally occur in industrialized countries.
T	F	9. Devaluation of its currency facilitates a nation's exports at reduced prices.
T	F	10. An international firm cannot protect itself against the adverse effects of nationalism.
T	F	11. The most common form of trade restriction is the quota.
T	F	12. General Agreement on Tariffs and Trade (GATT) members are not permitted to join regional trade associations or economic communities under any circumstances.
T	F	13. Joint ventures represent the lowest level of commitment to international marketing.
T	F	14. Both Coca-Cola and Pepsi-Cola license their products.
T	F	15. Exporting is the riskiest form of international marketing organization.
T	F	16. Under a pure standardized approach to international marketing plans, training of foreign personnel is reduced.
T	F	17. Backward invention is a product planning strategy most suitable for developing nations.
T	F	18. For companies marketing in different European countries, some degree of standardization of promotion is necessary.
T	F	19. Standardization of prices is more difficult if a firm operates within an economic community such as the Common Market.
T	F	20. If a firm sets prices on the basis of its own national currency, it assumes the risk of foreign currency revaluation.

COMPLETION

Fill in the missing word or words in the blanks provided.

[International marketing, multinational marketing, p. 615]

1. _____ _____ involves the marketing of goods and services outside the organization's home country; _____ _____ involves complex marketing operations in many foreign countries.

[comparative advantage, p. 616]

2. The concept of _____ _____ states that countries have different rates of productivity for different products due to resources, specialization, mechanization, or climate.

[exports, import, p. 618]

3. Services make up one third of total U.S. _____ while petroleum is a leading U.S. _____ .

[Culture, pp. 620-621]

4. _____ refers to a group of people sharing a distinctive heritage.

[standard of living, Gross National Product, p. 622]

5. Among the factors in the economic environment of interest to international marketers are the _____ _____ _____ , which refers to the

average quantity and quality of goods and services consumed in a country, and the _____ _____ _____ , which indicates the total value of goods and services produced in a country each year.

[industrialized, developing, less-developed, p. 624]

6. One way of classifying the economic growth of countries is to divide them into _____ countries with high literacy rates, modern technology, and per capita incomes of several thousand dollars; _____ countries, where education and technology are rising and where per capita income is about $1,500; and _____ _____ countries, where literacy is low, technology is limited, and per capita GNP is below $500.

[demand, currency, pp. 624-625]

7. By examining product ownership per thousand population, a marketer can obtain a good estimate of the current size of _____ ; and a marketer must also study _____ stability because sales and profits can be affected by foreign currency revaluation.

[nationalism, government stability, pp. 625-626]

8. In the political and legal environment, firms must be concerned with the effects of _____ , by which countries try to become self-reliant and raise their international standing; and _____ _____ , the consistency of politics and orderliness in installing leaders.

[tariffs, quotas, embargoes, local content laws, p. 626]

9. Three common trade restrictions are _____ in which taxes are placed on imported goods; _____ which set limits on the amount of goods that may be imported, including _____ , which disallow entry of specified products into a country; and _____ _____ _____ which require foreign-based manufacturers to use locally produced components.

[multilateral, most-favored nation, European Community, pp. 627-628]

10. GATT is a _____ agreement that reduces trade barriers through the _____ _____ _____ principle. This allows every nation covered by the agreement to obtain the best contract terms received by any single nation; however, it makes exceptions in the cases of regional trade associations and economic communities such as the _____ _____ .

[exporting, joint venture, direct ownership, pp. 630-631]

11. Three organizational formats in marketing abroad are _____ , where a company reaches international markets through direct or indirect selling; _____ _____ , where the firm agrees to combine some aspects of its manufacturing and marketing efforts with those of a foreign company; and _____ _____ , which involves the full undertaking and control of all international operations.

[licensing, contract manufacturing, management contracting, joint ownership, p. 631]

12. Four forms of joint venture enterprises are _____ , giving rights to a foreign firm in exchange for compensation; _____ _____ , having a foreign firm produce the firm's products locally; _____ _____ , acting as a consultant to a foreign firm; and _____ _____ , where the firm agrees to manufacture and market products in partnership with a foreign company.

[pure standardized, pure nonstandardized, mixed, pp. 632-633]

13. International marketing plans reflect either a _____ _____ approach with a common marketing plan for each country; a _____ _____ approach, where each market is treated differently; or a _____ approach, which combines the two.

[straight extension, product adaptation, backward invention, forward invention, pp. 634-635]

14. Four international product-planning strategies are _____ _____ , manufacturing the same products for foreign and domestic markets; _____ _____ , modifying domestic products for foreign markets; _____ _____ , making less complex products for foreign markets; and _____ _____ , developing new products for international markets.

[dump, p. 638]

15. In international pricing decisions, firms may choose to _____ , thereby selling products abroad at prices below production costs or lower than those prevailing in the home country.

DEFINITIONS

Match the terms and concepts with the appropriate definitions. Each term or concept may only be used once; there are more terms and concepts than definitions.

Column A

a. backward invention

b. comparative advantage

c. currency stability

d. developing countries

e. direct ownership

f. dumping

g. embargo

h. European Community

i. exporting

j. forward invention

k. General Agreement on Tariff and Trade

Column B

___ 1. Allows every nation covered by GATT to obtain the best contract terms received by any single nation.

___ 2. An international product strategy in which a firm appeals to developing countries by making products that are less complex than the ones it sells in its domestic market.

___ 3. A form of trade restriction that prohibits specified products from entering a country.

___ 4. A form of international marketing company organization in which a firm combines some aspects of its manufacturing or marketing efforts with those of a foreign company in order to share expertise, costs, and control of all international operations.

l. government stability

m. Gross National Product

n. industrialized countries

o. international marketing

p. joint venture

q. less-developed countries

r. local content law

s. mixed approach

t. most-favored nation principle

u. multinational marketing

v. nationalism

w. product-adaptation strategy

x. pure nonstandardized
   approach

y. pure standardized approach

z. standard of living

aa. straight-extension strategy

bb. tariff

cc. trade deficit

dd. trade quota

—— 5. Refers to a country's efforts to become self-reliant and raise its status in the eyes of the world community.

—— 6. An international marketing strategy in which a common marketing plan is used for all countries in which a firm operates.

—— 7. Concept in international marketing which states that countries have different rates of productivity for different products.

—— 8. A complex form of international marketing that involves an organization engaged in marketing operations in many foreign countries.

—— 9. Selling a product in a foreign country at a price lower than that prevailing in the exporter's home country, below the cost of production, or both.

—— 10. An international product strategy in which a company develops new products for its international markets.

—— 11. Occurs when the value of imports exceeds the value of exports.

—— 12. The total value of goods and services produced in a country each year.

—— 13. The average quantity and quality of goods and services consumed in a country.

—— 14. A form of international marketing company organization that involves the full undertaking and control of all international operations.

—— 15. An international marketing strategy that assumes that each market is different and requires a distinct marketing plan.

MULTIPLE CHOICE

Place the letter of the answer you think best in the blank provided.

—— 1. Companies are more likely to engage in international marketing when
   a. competition in the home country slackens.
   b. the home population base is stagnant.
   c. the home economy is growing.
   d. the home tax rates are lower.

—— 2. Which of the following statements about the scope of international marketing is *false*?
   a. Services make up one third of U.S. exports.
   b. Ninety-two per cent of American companies confine themselves to domestic markets.
   c. The United States is the world's largest importer.
   d. The United States had a positive trade balance of $43 billion in 1982.

_C_   3. Cultural awareness most clearly requires marketing research on
     a. the stability of currency.
     b. trade restrictions.
     c. hidden meanings.
     d. size of demand.

_C_   4. The Gross National Product
     a. refers to the average quantity and quality of goods and services consumed in a country.
     b. is difficult to calculate.
     c. does not take into account differences in living standards in different countries.
     d. gives the U.S. an index of 100 against which other countries are rated.

_a_   5. Developing societies have
     a. one third of the world's income.
     b. most of the world's population.
     c. widespread modern technology.
     d. low literacy rates.

_b_   6. Marketing opportunities in developing and less-developed countries show great promise because of
     a. the amount of discretionary income.
     b. an expanding population base.
     c. their standards of living.
     d. their currency stability.

_a_   7. Which of the following is _not_ a way in which an international firm can protect itself from the adverse effects of nationalism?
     a. Engaging in direct ownership
     b. Measuring domestic instability
     c. Taking in foreign partners
     d. Insuring itself

_a_   8. The most common form of trade restriction is the
     a. tariff.
     b. quota.
     c. most-favored-nation agreement.
     d. comparative advantage doctrine.

_b_   9. GATT
     a. bars regional trade associations.
     b. negotiates tariff reductions.
     c. discourages use of the most-favored-nation principle.
     d. encourages restrictive quotas.

_d_   10. The most important economic community is the
     a. Latin American Integration Association.
     b. Council for Mutual Economic Assistance.
     c. Asian Common Market.
     d. European Community.

_c_

11. Which of the following uses the metric system?
    a. Borneo
    b. United States
    c. Canada
    d. Liberia

b ✓ _a_

12. Which of the following is *not* a major organizational format for international marketing?
    a. Exporting
    b. Management contracting
    c. Joint venture
    d. Direct ownership

a ✓ _b_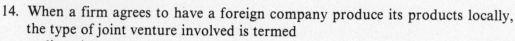

13. The lowest level of commitment to international marketing is
    a. exporting.
    b. licensing.
    c. contract manufacturing.
    d. direct ownership.

c ✓ _b_

14. When a firm agrees to have a foreign company produce its products locally, the type of joint venture involved is termed
    a. licensing.
    b. management contracting.
    c. contract manufacturing.
    d. joint ownership.

_d_

15. The riskiest form of organization for international marketing is
    a. joint venture.
    b. exporting.
    c. management contracting.
    d. direct ownership.

_d_

16. The pure-nonstandardized international marketing plan
    a. reduces training of foreign personnel.
    b. presents a uniform image.
    c. utilizes a common marketing plan.
    d. undertakes decentralized control.

b ✓ _d_

17. The international product planning strategy appropriate for gasoline formulation is
    a. backward invention.
    b. product adaptation.
    c. forward invention.
    d. straight extension.

_a_

18. The sale of nonelectric sewing machines to developing countries is an example of
    a. backward invention.
    b. product adaptation.
    c. forward invention.
    d. straight extension.

19. The lowest per capita advertising expenditures are found in
    a. Latin America.
    b. Asia.
    c. Europe.
    d. North America.

_C_   20. Dumping refers to selling goods abroad
    a. at high prices.
    b. with prices similar to those in the home market.
    c. to remove excess supply from the home market.
    d. so that cheap labor may be used.

DISCUSSION QUESTIONS

1. How may economic trends, demographic conditions, and domestic competition levels encourage the development of international marketing?

2. How do you account for the fact that the United States is one of the largest exporters in the world and yet it has a trade deficit?

3. How may a multinational company increase its cultural awareness? Why is it important that it do so?

4. Explain why per capita GNP figures may mislead international marketers. What other data might they substitute instead?

5. Which forms of organization for international marketing would be most susceptible to nationalism? Least? Why?

6. Why are more and more firms turning to a mixed approach to international marketing planning?

7. Why do firms engage in dumping? How may tariffs and quotas discourage this?

EXERCISES

21-1.   Many new goods and services fail in domestic markets because of excessive enthusiasm and poor timing, but the failure rate in international marketing is often due to cultural factors. For example, Household Finance, Beneficial Finance, Avco, and other United States finance companies began operations in Japan in 1977. These firms believed that extending consumer credit to the prosperous Japanese held great opportunity.[1]

The finance companies would be competing with *sarakins*, Japanese lenders who charged customers as much as 109.5 per cent a year for money and used high-pressure collection tactics. Japanese banks concentrated on making large loans to corporations. Credit-card balances had to be paid in full each month by automatic transfers from consumers' bank accounts. Although the average Japanese worker earned about as much as his or her American counterpart, financial obligations could include parental support, private school tuition for children, and mortgage payments.

Despite these factors, the growth anticipated by the American firms did not materialize, and they have since cut back on their plans. The estimated value of loans by American firms reached only $15 million by 1980. In comparison, *sarakin* firms loaned $328 million.

Apparently, the United States companies did not sufficiently understand the Japanese culture in respect to money handling. In Japan, women traditionally manage household finances, and husbands receive a daily allowance. The husbands do not want to ask their wives for more money, nor do they wish to answer the many questions posed by American finance companies.

When American firms required wives to sign credit applications, the blow to the Japanese male ego was tremendous. Many continued to borrow from *sarakins*, who required no paperwork or spouse's knowledge. Because *sarakins'* loans are secret, the United States firms had no way to determine who had outstanding debts and how large they were. Often Japanese customers used American loans to repay *sarakins*.

---

[1] Louis Kraar, "Our Small-Loan Companies Invade Japan," *Fortune* (September 22, 1980), pp. 146-148, 152, 156, and John Marcom, "Consumer Credit Expands in Japan," *Wall Street Journal* (March 3, 1981), p. 35.

Questions

1.   Cite at least three separate problems facing U.S. firms in the Japanese financial market.

2. How could the American companies have foreseen these cultural problems before entering the market?

21-2.   One approach to international marketing is to present a standardized effort in all markets. Another is to customize offerings for each market. Professor Theodore Levitt of Harvard asserts that well-managed firms will gravitate toward "globally standardized products that are advanced, functional, reliable—and low priced"; companies concentrating on "idiosyncratic consumer preferences have become befuddled and unable to take in the forest because of the trees." Examples of globally standardized products and services are Coca-Cola, Pepsi-Cola, McDonald's, rock music, Greek salad, Hollywood movies, Revlon, Sony, and Levi's.

According to Levitt, consumers in different world markets will purchase standardized products if they enable costs and prices to be lowered, and push quality and reliability higher—regardless of differences in national and regional tastes, needs, institutions, and preferences. This in large part explains the success of the Japanese and vindicates the mass-marketing concept behind the Model T. Customized offerings will not do well because costs and prices will rise, while quality and reliability fall—regardless of the firm's responsiveness to an individual market. Over-reliance on the marketing concept may lead to unintended negative results.[1]

However, many companies believe that some customization of marketing efforts by market is necessary[2]:

- General Foods found that Tang powdered orange drink had a name that Germans did not like and a taste that the British disliked. Now, "Seefrisch" is marketed in West Germany and a tarter-tasting Tang is carried in Great Britain.
- Unilever, the giant Anglo-Dutch food and detergent corporation, has discovered that relatively standard preferences exist for detergents and soaps but not for foods. Jif liquid soap sells well throughout Europe, but Unilever's margarine has different names and styles in every country.
- Acorn Computers, a British computer maker, emphasizes technical features in domestic ads and ease of use in German ads.

---

[1] Theodore Levitt, "The Globalization of Markets," *Harvard Business Review*, Vol. 61 (May-June 1983), pp. 92-102.

[2] George Anders, "Ad Agencies and Big Concerns Debate World Brands' Value," *Wall Street Journal* (June 14, 1984), p. 33.

Questions

1.   Discuss the pros and cons of standardized and nonstandardized international marketing efforts.

2. Under what circumstances should a standardized approach be followed? A non-standardized approach?

3. Comment on this statement, made by a former Gillette chief executive:

> More and more we're looking at things from a worldwide perspective. We're constructing new worldwide product lines with products generated both here and abroad. At the same time, our overseas companies sell separate product lines adapted to their own local markets. We take advantage of resources *wherever* they exist.

4. Buy a foreign-language magazine and examine the ads placed by American firms you recognize. Describe and evaluate two of these ads.

21-3.   Your health-food store plans to import a line of frozen croissants from Canada into the United States. The pastries are currently packaged three to a container, labelled in both French and English, and must be defrosted overnight prior to being placed in a preheated oven for twenty minutes at 400°F. Taste tests with 500 consumers in four major cities consistently rated the croissants equivalent to bakery quality. What criteria must be considered in a marketing strategy for the U.S.?

21-4.   Construct a short questionnaire dealing with the quality of American versus foreign products. Administer it to fellow students. What do you conclude? What do you recommend?

ANSWERS

True/False

1. F, p. 615
2. F, p. 615
3. T, p. 616
4. T, p. 618
5. T, p. 618
6. F, p. 620
7. F, pp. 623-624
8. T, p. 624
9. T, p. 625
10. F, p. 626
11. F, p. 626
12. F, p. 628
13. F, p. 630
14. T, p. 631
15. F, p. 632
16. T, p. 632
17. T, p. 634
18. T, p. 636
19. F, p. 638
20. F, pp. 638-639

Multiple Choice

1. b, pp. 616-617
2. d, p. 618
3. c, pp. 621-622
4. c, pp. 622-623
5. a, p. 624
6. b, p. 624
7. a, p. 626
8. a, p. 626
9. b, pp. 627-628
10. d, p. 628
11. c, p. 629
12. b, p. 630
13. a, p. 630
14. c, p. 631
15. d, pp. 631-632
16. d, p. 632
17. b, p. 634
18. a, pp. 633-634
19. b, p. 636
20. c, p. 638

Definitions

1. t
2. a
3. g
4. p
5. v
6. y
7. b
8. u
9. f
10. j
11. cc
12. m
13. z
14. e
15. x

Discussion Questions

1. pp. 616-617
2. pp. 618-620
3. pp. 621-622
4. pp. 622-625
5. pp. 630-632
6. p. 633
7. p. 638

22

Service and Nonprofit Marketing

CHAPTER OBJECTIVES

1. To differentiate between the marketing of services and products
2. To describe the characteristics of services, their role in the U.S. economy, special considerations for service marketers, and applications of service marketing
3. To distinguish between nonprofit and profit-oriented marketing
4. To discuss the characteristics of nonprofit marketing, its role in the U.S. economy, and applications of nonprofit marketing

CHAPTER OVERVIEW

Service marketing involves product rental, product alteration and repair, and personal services. In general, services are less tangible, more perishable, less separable from their provider, and more variable in quality than products that are sold. Service and product marketing may be interconnected.

Services can be categorized by market, degree of tangibility, skill of the service provider, goal of the service provider, degree of regulation, labor intensiveness, and amount of customer contact. An organization would be classified on the basis of a combination of these factors.

The United States is the leading service economy in the world, with two thirds of the American private labor force employed in services. United States families spend almost 50 per cent of their income on services. Twenty per cent of all industrial capital goods are leased.

Service firms have lagged behind manufacturing firms in the use of marketing because of technical emphasis, small size, less competition, the lack of a need for marketing, past prohibitions on advertising, and a dislike of marketing by some service professionals. Special considerations in service marketing are an inability to stockpile, lack of visibility of effort, difficulties in pricing and promotion, importance of customer relations, the cost/reliability mix, and peripheral services.

Nonprofit marketing is conducted by organizations that operate in the public interest or to foster a cause and do not seek financial profits. It may involve organizations, people, places, ideas, products, and services. Exchanges do not have to involve money, and objectives can be difficult to formulate. Benefits are often distributed unequally, and economically unfeasible market segments may be served. Two constituencies must be satisfied: clients and donors.

Nonprofit marketing can be classified on the basis of tangibility, organization structure, objectives, and constituency. In 1982, the U.S. government spent about $206 million for national advertising. Total advertising for nonprofit institutions is estimated at over $10 billion per year.

KEY TERMS AND CONCEPTS

Service marketing	Encompasses the rental of products, the alteration or repair of products owned by consumers, and personal services.
Intangibility of services	Inability of many services to be displayed, transported, stored, packaged, or inspected before buying.
Perishability of services	Occurs because unused capacity cannot be stored for future use or shifted from one time period to another for many services.
Inseparability of services	Inability of many services to be separated from the service provider. Customer contact is considered an integral part of the service experience.
Variability of service quality	Due to difficulty of diagnosing a problem (for repairs), the inability of the customer to verbalize his or her service needs, and the lack of standardization and mass production for most services.
Hidden service sector	Causes service data to be underestimated because many firms that perform services are classified as manufacturers.
Industrialization of services	Improves service efficiency by applying hard, soft, and hybrid technologies.
Hard technology	A way some services are industrialized by substituting machinery for people.
Soft technology	A way to industrialize services by substituting pre-planned systems such as prepackaged vacation tours for individual services.
Hybrid technology	A technique for industrializing services that combines hard and soft technologies such as computer-based truck routing and specialized low-priced auto repair facilities.
Peripheral service	A complementary service needed to supplement the basic service offering.
Nonprofit marketing	Conducted by organizations that operate in the public interest or to foster a cause and do not seek financial profits. Nonprofit marketing may involve organizations, people, places, and ideas as well as products and services.

Social marketing	The use of marketing to increase the acceptability of social ideas.
Client	The constituency for which a nonprofit organization offers membership, elected officials, locations, ideas, products, and services.
Donor	The constituency from which a nonprofit organization receives resources.

TRUE/FALSE

Circle the appropriate letter.

T   F   1. Service and nonprofit marketing are distinct and different from product- and profit-oriented marketing.

T   F   2. In service marketing, the product dominates the offering and services augment it.

T   F   3. In general, the more tangible the service, the more service marketing resembles product marketing.

T   F   4. Labor-intensive services can be performed by do-it-yourself consumers.

T   F   5. Service firms have typically lagged behind manufacturing firms in the development and use of marketing.

T   F   6. Services that are equipment-based and routine in nature usually rely on competitive pricing.

T   F   7. Much service promotion must rely on performance attrtibutes that can only be measured after a purchase is made.

T   F   8. The industrialization of services substitutes machinery and preplanned systems for more variable personal services.

T   F   9. Foreign car dealers are finding that more and more of their customers are demanding dealer servicing.

T   F   10. Legal marketing has inhibited the spread of legal clinics and prepaid services.

T   F   11. Usually, the prices charged by nonprofit organizations have no relationship to the cost or value of services.

T   F   12. Profit-oriented marketing is much more prone to promote ideas than is nonprofit marketing.

T   F   13. A successful nonprofit marketing campaign may lose money.

T   F   14. The benefits of nonprofit organizations are often distributed unevenly.

T   F   15. Whereas nonprofit organizations have one primary constituency, profit-oriented firms usually have two.

T   F   16. The largest advertiser in the country is the United States government.

T   F   17. Advertising estimates for nonprofit organizations include the costs of marketing research but neglect the value of volunteers.

T F   18. Since the Postal Service has become an independent agency, it has continued to report deficits.

T F   19. The expansion of marketing into higher education is limited to poor- or average-quality institutions.

T F   20. Demographic trends do not indicate automatic future increases in library patronage.

COMPLETION

Fill in the missing word or words in the blanks provided.

[Service marketing, p. 645]

1. _____ _____ encompasses the rental of products, the alteration or repair of products, and personal services.

[intangibility, perishability, inseparability, quality, pp. 645-646]

2. Four characteristics that distinguish services from products are _____, which means they cannot be displayed before buying; _____, which means they cannot be stored for future sale; _____ from the service provider; and variability in _____ .

[market, tangibility, professionals, nonprofessionals, p. 648]

3. When services are classified by _____ , they involve consumer or industrial segments; by _____ , they may involve rental goods or non-good services; and by service provider, they involve _____ or _____ .

[profit, nonprofit, regulation, labor intensity, customer contact, p. 648]

4. Services may also be classified by orientation toward _____ or _____ , involving the purposes of sales and exchanges; by the extent of _____ undertaken by the government; by _____ _____ , whether machine based or people based; and by the degree of _____ _____ , where technical and interpersonal skills may be important.

[hidden service factor, p. 649]

5. The _____ _____ _____ encompasses, for example, systems planning and preinstallation support by product-oriented firms and leads to underestimation of data on services.

[technical expertise, small, licensing, pp. 650-651]

6. Service organizations and professionals are less inclined to use marketing because they stress _____ _____ , are _____ in size, and may be bound by strict _____ provisions, which limit competition.

[stockpiled, mix, intangibility, interpersonal, pp. 652-653]

7. Service marketers must recognize that services cannot usually be _____ or stored, that only a small portion of the service _____ is visible to customers, that the _____ of services makes pricing and promotion difficult, and that the existence of close provider-consumer relationships makes _____ skills important.

[industrialization of services, hard technologies, soft technologies, hybrid technologies, p. 654]

8. To solve the problem of high costs and low reliability, one option is the ____ ____ ____ , whereby firms use ____ ____ , substituting machinery for people; ____ ____ , which substitute preplanned systems for individualized services; or ____ ____ , which combine the two.

[Peripheral services, p. 654]

9. ____ ____ are complementary and supplement the basic service offering.

[Nonprofit marketing, fund raising, p. 658]

10. ____ ____ is conducted by organizations that operate in the public interest or foster causes; they do not seek financial profits, but often rely on ____ ____ .

[social marketing, p. 660]

11. The promotion of ideas, such as recycling and highway safety, is referred to as ____ ____ .

[unevenly, clients, donors, p. 660]

12. The benefits of nonprofit organizations are often distributed ____ , and these organizations usually serve two constituencies: ____ and ____ .

[government, private, cooperative, p. 662]

13. Nonprofit organizations may have one of three alternative structures: ____ , ____ , or ____ .

[military recruitment, Postal Service, Amtrak, p. 664]

14. The largest advertising expenses of the U.S. government were for ____ ____ , the ____ ____ , and ____ .

[market research, volunteers, p. 665]

15. Estimates of nonprofit advertising do not include the costs of ____ ____ , the value of ____ (unpaid workers), or free advertising.

DEFINITIONS

Match the terms and concepts with the appropriate definitions. Each term or concept may only be used once; there are more terms and concepts than definitions.

Column A

a. client

b. donor

c. hard technology

d. hidden service sector

e. hybrid technology

f. industrialization of services

g. inseparability of services

h. intangibility of services

Column B

___ 1. Causes data to be underestimated because many firms that perform services are classified as manufacturers.

___ 2. Due to difficulty of diagnosing a problem (for repairs), the inability of the customer to verbalize his or her service needs, and the lack of standardization and mass production for most services.

___ 3. A way some services are industrialized by substituting machinery for people.

___ 4. A complementary service needed to supplement the basic service offering.

i. nonprofit marketing

j. peripheral service

k. perishability of services

l. service marketing

m. social marketing

n. soft technology

o. variability of service quality

_____ 5. The constituency from which a nonprofit organization receives resources.

_____ 6. Encompasses the rental of products, the alteration or repair of products owned by consumers, and personal services.

_____ 7. A way to industrialize services by substituting preplanned systems for individual services.

_____ 8. Inability of many services to be displayed, transported, stored, packaged, or inspected before buying.

_____ 9. Conducted by organizations that operate in the public interest or to foster a cause and do not seek financial profits.

_____ 10. Occurs because unused capacity cannot be stored for future use or shifted from one time period to another for many services.

_____ 11. The constituency for which a nonprofit organization offers membership, elected officials, locations, ideas, products, and services.

MULTIPLE CHOICE

Place the letter of the answer you think best in the blank provided.

 1. Which of the following is *not* encompassed by the term service marketing?
a. Product rentals
b. Fund raising
c. Product repairs
d. Personal services

 2. When the service operator can only describe the benefits that can be derived from the service experience, the service is said to
a. be perishable.
b. have quality variations.
c. be intangible.
d. be inseparable from the provider.

 3. When services are classified by their labor intensity, they are based on
a. rental goods and nongoods services.
b. professionals and nonprofessionals.
c. profit and nonprofit orientations.
d. machinery or people.

a

4. When services are classified by their degree of customer contact, they are based on
   a. technical or interpersonal skill training.
   b. professionals or nonprofessionals.
   c. machinery or people.
   d. final consumers or industrial consumers.

c

5. Which of the following is *not* a major component of American consumer service spending?
   a. Housing
   b. Medical care
   c. Leisure activities
   d. Household operations

d

6. Which of the following is *not* part of the hidden service sector?
   a. Systems planning
   b. Repair
   c. Preinstallation support
   d. Product sales

c

7. Many service organizations and professionals do *not* use marketing because
   a. their associations prohibit it.
   b. they de-emphasize technical expertise.
   c. demand for these services is already high.
   d. their customers would reject it.

b

8. Which of the following is *not* true for service marketers?
   a. Services cannot be stockpiled.
   b. Much of the service mix is visible.
   c. Intangibility makes pricing and promotion difficult.
   d. Service provider-consumer relationships are close.

9. To overcome high costs and low reliability, many firms involved in services rely on
   a. social marketing.
   b. peripheral services.
   c. industrialization of services.
   d. hidden service sectors.

c

10. Hard technologies
    a. are applicable to medical and legal services.
    b. supplement basic service offerings.
    c. substitute machinery for people.
    d. replace individual services with preplanned packages.

a

11. An example of a soft technology is the
    a. prepackaged vacation tour.
    b. electronic credit authorization system.
    c. muffler repair shop.
    d. parking service at a hotel.

_b_

12. Peripheral services
    a. combine hard and soft technologies.
    b. create and sustain competitive advantages.
    c. have low costs and high reliability.
    d. offer preplanned, standardized services.

_b_

13. Which of the following is *not* a result of the Supreme Court decision that attorneys can advertise their fee structures?
    a. The spread of legal clinics
    b. The decline of legal marketing
    c. The growth of prepaid legal services
    d. The availability of services to new consumer groups

_d_

14. Which of the following is *not* an aspect of nonprofit marketing?
    a. Fostering a cause
    b. Operating in the public interest
    c. Spreading social ideas
    d. Relating pricing to costs

_d_

15. Nonprofit organizations often
    a. do not conduct exchanges.
    b. charge prices related to the value of services.
    c. do not involve products or services.
    d. serve uneconomical market segments.

_a_

16. Social marketing involves the use of marketing to
    a. increase the acceptability of ideas.
    b. find new energy sources.
    c. reduce imports.
    d. reduce interest rates.

_b_

17. In contrast to profit-oriented marketing, nonprofit marketing
    a. is less prone to promote ideas.
    b. generates revenues through daily exchanges.
    c. has more accountability.
    d. distributes benefits unevenly.

_c_

18. An example of a private nonprofit organization is
    a. the Postal Service.
    b. Yankee Stadium.
    c. the American Cancer Society.
    d. the New York Public Library.

_d_

19. College and university marketing
    a. ignores traditional students.
    b. is confined to average-quality institutions.
    c. is on the decline.
    d. actively seeks adults.

_c_

20. Which of the following is becoming more marketing-oriented and turning facilities into multimedia or community center operations?
    a. The U.S. Postal Service
    b. Colleges and universities
    c. Public libraries
    d. The Red Cross

DISCUSSION QUESTIONS

1. Explain five ways in which services can be classified.

2. Describe the scope of services in the American economy and explain why the data may be underestimated.

3. How might service organizations and professionals be encouraged to expand their marketing efforts?

4. Outline possible marketing strategies for services that cannot be stockpiled and where only a small portion of the service mix is visible to consumers.

5. Describe the impact of the 1977 Supreme Court decision overturning bans on legal service advertising.

6. Compare and contrast profit and nonprofit marketing.

7. How does the need to service two distinct constituencies affect nonprofit organizations?

EXERCISES

22-1.   Beth Alexander is a recent graduate of a Southwestern law school who has decided to establish her own practice. As a recent graduate, she is especially concerned about never having completed a course in basic marketing and not having a feel for how to set up and maintain a successful practice.

Beth's first reflections about marketing relate to three issues. First, in the late 1970s the Supreme Court removed American Bar Association prohibitions regarding advertising by its members. Thus, attorneys are now able to use mass media and advertise their fees, specialties, and educational background and experience. Second, a number of discount legal services have become extremely successful. Many are in shopping center locations, have low fee structures, and are open long hours. Third, these legal firms have raised price consciousness among clients and expanded the number of people seeking legal services, through their advertising and reduced fees.

Among the questions Beth must resolve regarding her law practice are the following:

- Would advertising cheapen her firm's image?
- If advertising is used, what media should be chosen? What should messages communicate?
- If Beth does not advertise, how can she build a client base?
- Should a price list of services be published to give clients greater confidence in Beth's fairness? If a price list is published, how should a typical situation be handled?
- Should Beth specialize or be a generalist?
- What target market should be sought?
- Should a costly office-building location near a courthouse or a site in a residential neighborhood with good pedestrian traffic be chosen? Would a shopping center location be best?

Questions

1.   What other questions should Beth resolve before establishing her law practice?

2.   Develop a marketing plan for Beth based upon the questions she has raised and those you have added.

3.   Visit one law firm located in a shopping center and another in an office building. From a marketing perspective, contrast the two.

4.   Why do many professionals not actively engage in marketing analysis or other marketing activities?

22-2.   Sandy University is a private, nonprofit university located in the Northeast, approximately a one-hour car drive from New York City. This location gives the university (and its students and faculty) access to New York's excellent cultural attractions as well as access to many major corporations and trade associations. Sandy University is also situated within a ten-minute drive of several beaches, parks, and other recreational facilities.

A significant concern of the school involves the stagnant or declining population in the region that surrounds it. For example, the fifteen-mile area surrounding the university consists almost entirely of one-family homes built twenty or more years ago. Overall population forecasts for this area predict a 3 per cent drop over the next five years. More worrisome to the university is the fact that the population in the area is aging and fewer young adults are available to attend Sandy University and other colleges and universities. According to Sandy University's president, "They're closing down elementary schools in our county right now. I'm afraid that in five to ten years they'll be closing down some universities."

To ensure its long-run viability, the university has developed a marketing strategy that seeks to increase the geographic area from which it draws students, to improve the quality of the school's programs and facilities, and to provide educational opportunities for the large number of office workers that are employed near to the school.

- In the past, Sandy University drew 90 per cent of its students from within a fifteen-mile radius of the school. Currently, 70 per cent of the students are from this area. In five years, the university plans to have less than 50 per cent of its students from the local community. This will broaden its base and lessen the impact of the area's population decline.

- Like his predecessor, Sandy University's present president has embarked on a program to increase the school's academic quality and visibility. Admission standards have been raised, new faculty hired, and library and computer facilities strengthened. Student facilities (e.g., dormitories, dining rooms, recreational facilities) have been upgraded substantially. The university has also hosted several important conferences and art exhibitions.

- The university is promoting its credit and noncredit courses and programs to employees at five large office building complexes within three miles of campus. It is estimated that 200 or more of these employees can be drawn to the university each year.

Questions

1.   What changes will the university face when more than half of its students are drawn from outside the local community?

2. Quality is a largely intangible attribute when applied to a college or university. Develop a campaign to effectively illustrate the quality of Sandy University. Include at least five differential advantages for the university.

3. What should be the emphasis of Sandy University's efforts to attract nearby office workers? How will these efforts be different from those used to attract out-of-town high school seniors to enter as freshmen?

4. Sandy University is a private institution. How would its marketing strategy vary if it was a public institution?

22-3.   An accounting firm has decided to compete with H & R Block and open a national chain of tax preparation centers. On what basis will the new company be able to compete with Block? What problems may it encounter? Why would a consumer select the new firm?

22-4.   Develop a marketing campaign that would encourage more people to undergo annual physical examinations.

ANSWERS

True/False

1. T, p. 645
2. F, p. 646
3. T, p. 647
4. T, p. 647
5. T, p. 650
6. F, p. 653
7. T, p. 653
8. T, p. 654
9. F, p. 657
10. F, pp. 657-658

11. T, p. 659
12. F, p. 660
13. T, p. 660
14. T, p. 660
15. F, p. 661
16. F, p. 664
17. F, p. 665
18. F, p. 666
19. F, pp. 666-667
20. T, pp. 667-668

Multiple Choice

1. b, p. 645
2. c, pp. 645-646
3. d, pp. 647-648
4. a, pp. 648-649
5. c, p. 649
6. d, p. 649
7. c, pp. 650-651
8. b, p. 653
9. c, p. 654
10. c, p. 654

11. a, p. 654
12. b, p. 654
13. b, pp. 657-658
14. d, p. 658
15. d, pp. 660-661
16. a, p. 660
17. d, p. 660
18. c, p. 662
19. d, pp. 666-667
20. c, pp. 666-667

Definitions

1. d
2. o
3. c
4. j
5. b
6. l

7. n
8. h
9. i
10. k
11. a

Discussion Questions

1. pp. 647-649
2. pp. 649-650
3. pp. 650-653
4. pp. 652-654
5. pp. 657-658
6. pp. 659-661
7. pp. 661, 664

23 Marketing and Society

CHAPTER OBJECTIVES

1. To provide an overview of marketing and society
2. To study social responsibility and consider its benefits and costs
3. To define consumerism and examine the consumer bill of rights
4. To discuss the responses of manufacturers, retailers, and trade associations to consumerism
5. To explore the future of consumerism

CHAPTER OVERVIEW

Marketing interacts with the society it serves. It can have both positive and negative effects on such areas as the quality of life and consumer expectations.

Social responsibility involves business actions based on a sense of moral obligation. The socioecological view of marketing considers all stages of a product's life from raw materials to junkpile and includes the interests of consumers and nonconsumers.

To stem the depletion of natural resources, cooperative efforts among business, stockholders, government, employees, the general public, consumers, and others are needed. In response to excessive littering and abandoned cars, several states have enacted legislation. Various environmental pollutants such as fluorocarbon propellants and certain pesticides have also been removed from the market. Product obsolescence is a heavily criticized practice that encourages material wearout, style changes, and functional product changes.

Ethical behavior, based on honest and proper conduct, can be divided into two categories: process-related and product-related. Ethical considerations include the consequences of actions, consumer happiness, honesty, fairness, concern for all people, and spin-off effects. Social responsibility has many benefits as well as a number of costs; the two need to be balanced.

Consumerism deals with the relationship of marketing and its consumers. It is defined as a social force within the environment designed to aid and protect the consumer by exerting legal, moral, and economic pressure on business. Consumerism has progressed through three eras: early 1900s, 1930s to 1950s, and 1960s to the present. The latter era has been the most important and began with President John F. Kennedy's announcement of a consumer bill of rights. The Federal Trade Commission is the major federal agency responsible for consumer protection.

The right to be informed includes protection against fraudulent, deceitful, or grossly misleading information, advertising, labeling, pricing, packaging, or other practices. Consumer education involves teaching consumers to use their financial resources wisely. The right to safety arises from the large numbers of people who are injured, disabled, or killed in accidents. The Consumer Product Safety Commission has the power to order product recalls or modifications. The right to choose stipulates that consumers have several products and brands from which to choose. The right to be heard is the consumer's right to a voice in business and government decision making. A number of consumer groups and government agencies provide this voice.

Many individual companies and trade associations are reacting positively to consumer issues. This group grows each year. A smaller number of organizations intentionally or unintentionally pursue unfair, misleading, or dangerous practices. There are remedies to correct these actions.

Consumerism is now in a period of maturity. The 1980s are witnessing less activism as a result of self-regulation, the past accomplishments of consumerism, the increased conservatism in the U.S., and the importance of other issues.

KEY TERMS AND CONCEPTS

Social responsibility	The possession of a corporate conscience or a response to social problems based on a sense of moral obligation.
Socioecological view of marketing	Examines all the stages of a product's life span from raw materials to junkpile. The socioecological view incorporates the interests of all consumers who are influenced by the use of a product or service.
Planned obsolescence	A practice which encourages short-run material wear-out, style changes, and functional product changes.
Ethical behavior	Based on honest and proper conduct.
Process-related ethical issue	Involves the unethical use of a marketing strategy or tactic.
Product-related ethical issue	Involves the ethical appropriateness of marketing a certain product.
Consumerism	A social force within the environment designed to aid and protect the consumer by exerting legal, moral, and economic pressure on business.
Consumer Bill of Rights	Stated by President Kennedy in 1962: information, safety, choice in product selection, and a voice in decision making.

Warranty	An assurance given to consumers that a product will meet certain performance standards.
Consumer education	A learning process whereby the consumer acquires the skills and knowledge to use his or her financial resources wisely in the marketplace.
Consumer Product Safety Commission (CPSC)	The major federal agency responsible for product safety. It has jurisdiction over more than 11,000 products.
Product recall	The primary enforcement tool of the Consumer Product Safety Commission.
Class-action suit	A suit filed on behalf of many affected consumers.
Item price removal	Practice whereby prices are marked only on store shelves or aisle signs and not on individual items.

TRUE/FALSE

Circle the appropriate letter.

T   F   1. Bruskin and Nielsen's studies showed that at least one third of all Americans feel cheated in the purchases they make.

T   F   2. Most disgruntled customers take time to write offending companies.

T   F   3. The socioecological view of marketing requires consumers to act responsibly.

T   F   4. Since World War II, the consumption of packaging materials has increased several times faster than the population.

T   F   5. The use of fluorocarbon propellants has been banned by the federal government.

T   F   6. According to estimates by the Environmental Protection Agency, about half of the dangerous wastes produced in the United States are disposed of adequately.

T   F   7. With functional planned obsolescence, the manufacturer makes some minor changes to clearly differentiate this year's model from last year's.

T   F   8. Product-related ethical issues involve the unethical use of marketing strategy or tactics.

T   F   9. The general public rates the honesty and ethics of business executives as high.

T   F   10. The second era of consumerism focused on business protection against unfair practices.

T   F   11. Ralph Nader's *Unsafe at Any Speed* heralded the first era of consumerism.

T   F   12. Cooling-off laws give consumers time to reconsider and cancel purchases from direct-to-home salespeople.

T   F   13. Many studies show that those who need it most benefit most from consumer information programs.

T   F   14. More than twenty million people are hurt yearly in nonautomotive product-related incidents.

T   F   15. The Consumer Product Safety Commission has jurisdiction over firearms and pesticides.

T   F   16. The primary enforcement tool used by the Consumer Product Safety Commission is product recall.

T   F   17. Under breach of warranty, the seller is liable for falsities leading to consumer misuse of products.

T   F   18. To give consumers more choice, franchising laws have been tightened.

T   F   19. Retailers and consumer groups agree on item price removal.

T   F   20. The largest and broadest business-operated trade association involved with consumer issues is the Better Business Bureau.

COMPLETION

Fill in the missing word or words in the blanks provided.

[Social responsibility, socioecological view of marketing, pp. 676-677]

1. _____ _____ is the "possession of a 'corporate conscience' or a response to social problems based on a sense of moral obligation," while the _____ _____ _____ _____ includes all stages of a product's life span, from raw materials to junkpile, and incorporates the interests of all consumers who are influenced by the use of a product or service.

[Packaging, p. 677]

2. _____ materials absorb large amounts of natural resources; their consumption has increased many times faster than the population.

[No-deposit, landscape, p. 679]

3. _____ _____ beverage containers and abandoned automobiles are examples of items that mar the _____ .

[fluorocarbon propellants, pesticides, industrial wastes, pp. 680-681]

4. Dangerous pollutants include _____ _____ which were used in most spray cans until the late 1970s; _____ , some of which were contaminated with dioxin; and _____ _____ produced by chemical plants as well as rubber and plastics manufacturers.

[material, style, functional, pp. 681-682]

5. Three forms of planned obsolescence are _____ , where components break or wear out prematurely; _____ , where minor changes differentiate this year's model from last year's; and _____ , where new product features are introduced to generate consumer dissatisfaction with a currently owned product.

[Process, product, p. 682]

6. _____ -related ethical issues involve misuse of market strategies and tactics, whereas _____ -related ethical issues involve the appropriateness of marketing certain products.

[Consumerism, unfair practices, p. 689]

7. _____ involves exerting legal, moral, and economic pressure on business to protect customers; it has evolved through three eras, during the first of which emphasis was placed on business protection against _____ _____ .

[informed, safety, choice, decision making, p. 689]

8. President Kennedy's announcement of a consumer bill of rights included the right to be _____ in product selection, product _____ , a _____ in product selection, and a voice in _____ _____ .

[cooling-off, unit-pricing, warranties, pp. 690-691]

9. Regulations related to information include _____ _____ laws, allowing consumers to reconsider and cancel, if they desire, purchase commitments made in their homes with direct-to-home salespeople; _____ _____ legislation, aimed at enabling consumers to compare prices for products of different sizes or brands; and _____ , which assure consumers that products will meet certain performance standards.

[Consumer education, p. 691]

10. _____ _____ teaches consumers the skills and knowledge for using their financial resources wisely in the marketplace.

[Consumer Product Safety Commission, product recall, pp. 692-693]

11. The _____ _____ _____ _____ is the major agency responsible for product safety; it uses _____ _____ as its primary enforcement tool.

[negligence, breach of warranty, strict liability, misrepresentation, p. 695]

12. Consumers can sue manufacturers on the basis of _____ , if they can prove that carelessness on the part of the seller resulted in injury; _____ _____ _____ , where the seller is responsible for failures to abide by expressed or implied warranties; _____ _____ , where the manufacturer is liable when an article placed on the market is proven to have a defect causing injury; or _____ , where the seller is liable for falsities leading to consumer misuse of the product.

[*Consumer Reports*, p. 699]

13. _____ _____ , which provides monthly evaluations of a wide variety of products and services for its readers, objected to its ratings being used in advertisements.

[Better Business Bureau, p. 702]

14. The largest and broadest business-operated trade association is the _____ _____ _____ .

[consumerism, pp. 702-703]

15. In the future, _____ will become more passive because of the current level of self-regulation, past successes, a relatively conservative Congress, and the importance of other issues.

DEFINITIONS

Match the terms and concepts with the appropriate definitions. Each term or concept may only be used once; there are more terms and concepts than definitions.

Column A

a. class-action suit

b. consumer bill of rights

c. consumer education

d. Consumer Product Safety Commission

e. consumerism

f. ethical behavior

g. item price removal

h. planned obsolescence

i. process-related ethical issue

j. product recall

k. product-related ethical issue

l. social responsibility

m. socioeconomic views of marketing

n. warranty

Column B

____ 1. A practice whereby prices are marked only on store shelves or aisle signs and not on individual items.

____ 2. A practice which encourages short-run material wearout, style changes, and functional product changes.

____ 3. The possession of a corporate conscience or a response to a social problem based on a sense of moral obligation.

____ 4. A suit filed on behalf of many affected consumers.

____ 5. An assurance given to consumers that a product will meet certain performance standards.

____ 6. Involves the unethical use of a marketing strategy or tactic.

____ 7. A social force within the environment designed to aid and protect the consumer by exerting legal, moral, and economic pressure on business.

____ 8. Involves the ethical appropriateness of marketing a certain product.

____ 9. The primary enforcement tool of the Consumer Product Safety Commission.

____ 10. A learning process whereby the consumer acquires the skills and knowledge to use his or her financial resources wisely in the marketplace.

____ 11. Stated by President Kennedy in 1962: information, safety, choice in product selection, and a voice in decision making.

____ 12. Based on honest and proper conduct.

MULTIPLE CHOICE

Place the letter of the answer you think best in the blank provided.

 ____ 1. Which of the following products or services no longer offers a dilemma to the socially responsible marketer?
  a. Crash diets
  b. Cigarettes
  c. Aerosol spray cans with fluorocarbons
  d. High-heeled shoes

_a_   2. Depletion of natural resources requires business to
   a. change styles less frequently.
   b. offer fewer trade-in allowances.
   c. produce more disposable products.
   d. give products more packaging.

_d_   3. A practice that encourages short-run material wearout, style changes, and functional product changes is
   a. a class-action suit.
   b. item price removal.
   c. product recall.
   d. planned obsolescence.

_C_   4. An example of a product-related ethical issue is
   a. bait-and-switch advertising.
   b. price fixing.
   c. cigarette manufacturing.
   d. bribing purchase agents.

_a_   5. The controversy over the introduction of auto air bags illustrates the benefits and costs associated with
   a. social responsibility.
   b. planned obsolescence.
   c. product recall.
   d. class-action suits.

_b_   6. During the second era of consumerism,
   a. emphasis was on business protection against unfair practices.
   b. issues were initiated but seldom resolved.
   c. a consumer bill of rights was announced.
   d. a federal consumer protection agency was created.

_c_   7. The book discussing marketing's contribution to environmental deterioration was titled
   a. *Hidden Persuaders.*
   b. *Unsafe at Any Speed.*
   c. *Silent Spring.*
   d. *American Way of Death.*

_b_   8. Cooling-off laws relate to consumer
   a. choice in product selection.
   b. information.
   c. safety.
   d. voice in decision making.

_c_   9. Which of the following does *not* directly aid consumers in product selection?
   a. Unit-pricing
   b. *Consumer Reports* ratings
   c. Cooling-off laws
   d. Warranties

10. Consumers who need it most
    a. use product information in their decision making.
    b. use product information infrequently.
    c. demand more product information.
    d. use product information to complain to manufacturers.

11. The Consumer Product Safety Commission does not have jurisdiction over
    a. aerosol spray cans.
    b. bicycles.
    c. electrical wiring.
    d. pesticides.

12. The primary enforcement tool of the Consumer Product Safety Commission is
    a. fines.
    b. imprisonment.
    c. product recall.
    d. purchase-price refunds.

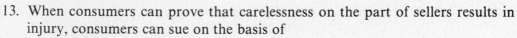

13. When consumers can prove that carelessness on the part of sellers results in injury, consumers can sue on the basis of
    a. negligence.
    b. misrepresentation.
    c. breach of warranty.
    d. strict liability.

14. Under misrepresentation,
    a. consumers must prove that the seller's carelessness resulted in injury.
    b. sellers are responsible for failures to abide by expressed or implied warranties.
    c. manufacturers are liable when an article placed on the market is proven to have a defect that causes injury.
    d. sellers are liable for falsities leading to consumer misuse of products.

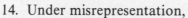

15. When an article placed on the market is proven to have a defect that causes injury, the manufacturer can be sued on grounds of
    a. negligence.
    b. misrepresentation.
    c. breach of warranty.
    d. strict liability.

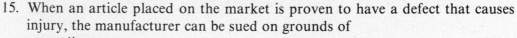

16. Which of the following is *not* available to consumers in their quest to be heard?
    a. A federal consumer agency
    b. Consumer groups
    c. Industry specialists
    d. A directory of federal agencies regulating business

17. Businesses today
    a. ignore consumerism.
    b. are developing their own programs to deal with consumer issues.
    c. reject consumerism as a passing fad.
    d. are less likely to use voluntary recalls for defective products.

18. Where consumers and retailers disagree most is over
    a. item price removal.
    b. product recalls.
    c. warranties.
    d. unit-pricing.

19. The largest and broadest business-operated trade association involved with consumer issues is the
    a. National Retail Merchants Association.
    b. Better Business Bureau.
    c. Association of Home Appliance Manufacturers.
    d. Bank Marketing Association.

C

20. Which of the following is *not* a reason why consumerism may be expected to become more passive in the 1980s and 1990s?
    a. The importance of other issues
    b. Past consumer successes
    c. Congressional liberalism
    d. More voluntary product recalls

DISCUSSION QUESTIONS

1. How does packaging pose a dilemma for socially responsible marketers? What can they do?

2. What are some of the important ethical issues for marketers?

3. Describe some of the events of the 1960s that contributed to today's consumerism.

4. What kinds of information are available to consumers or are now being considered by government agencies to assist consumers in making their product choices? Do you think this information will be used? Why? Why not?

5. How can marketing play a role in consumer education?

6. "Responsibility for product safety on the federal level is divided among too many agencies." Discuss.

7. Why do you think there is no overall federal consumer affairs agency?

EXERCISES

23-1.   The quality and speed of automobile repairs have been and continue to be a prime source of consumer complaints. Many American consumers have experienced faulty repairs, costly repairs, delays in receiving satisfactory service, breakdowns shortly after warranties have expired, uncooperative service managers, etc. Since cars are so expensive to own and operate, and involve personal safety, consumers are more concerned about inadequate service than they are with less costly and less risky products and services. In addition, the reputation of the U.S. auto industry has not been aided by the high number of product recalls and its slowness in embracing consumer arbitration panels.

Today, consumer complaints about autos are being handled in two different ways, through voluntary arbitration panels and via "lemon" laws in several states. While the industry only began extensive use of arbitration panels in the late 1970s, it is vigorously pursuing this option now and lobbying against state legislation.[1]

All of the auto makers are affiliated with some type of arbitration system, which enables a consumer to receive an open hearing about a dispute that cannot be settled at a local car dealer or district office. On the basis of arbitration, the consumer can receive a new car, free repairs, or no compensation at all. In general, arbitration awards are binding on the company but not consumers—who retain their right to sue.

The basic plans are as follows:

- General Motors—affiliated with the Better Business Bureau, permits complaints on cars less than five years old; arbitrator agreed upon by both GM and consumer.
- Ford—will hear any complaint; panel picked by Ford contains two dealers and three consumer representatives.
- Chrysler—mediates warranty complaints; panel picked by Chrysler but company proponents cannot vote.
- Automotive Consumer Action Program (AUTOCAP)—sponsored by the National Automobile Dealers Association, used by American Motors and most foreign firms; panels recommended to firms have half consumer advocates.

However, legislatures in a number of states have enacted lemon (repair-replace) laws to further increase auto makers' accountability, clarify consumer rights to redress, and outline binding procedures for automobile complaints. In general, these laws protect consumers against unsatisfactory, lengthy, and/or excessively costly repairs. In the case of some laws, gross violations automatically result in a new car for the consumer. For example, the Connecticut law states that a new car must be repaired within four separate visits to a repair shop or within thirty days in the shop, or a new car must be provided.

---

[1] "Detroit's Tonic for Lemon Buyers," *Business Week* (April 4, 1983), pp. 54-55; and William M. Bulkeley, "'Lemon Laws' Gaining Popularity Despite Auto Makers' Opposition," *Wall Street Journal* (July 12, 1983), p. 41.

Questions

1. Compare the arbitration panels used by the various auto manufacturers.

2. Are lemon laws necessary? Explain your answer.

3. Why have consumer complaints about cars gotten so out of hand?

4. Should manufacturers advocate the licensing of auto mechanics? Explain your answer.

23-2.   A dishwasher manufacturer has just determined that approximately 20,000 of the 100,000 Model A portable units that it sold last year were assembled incorrectly in the factory. As a result, users of these units may receive an electrical shock if their dishwashers are not properly rewired.

While the company plans a recall of the 10,000 unsold Model A portable units remaining with its retailers, it is unsure how to correct the problem for those units already in use. From past experience, the firm realizes that:

- Only one quarter of purchasers typically respond to the firm's warranty questionnaire, which is used to set up a file of customer names and addresses.
- It does not know which of the 27,000 consumers completing warranty information for the Model A portable unit bought defective units.
- Many consumers would not bother to have a repairperson visit their homes and have the units rewired, even if they were contacted.
- A repair program would cost about $200,000 to implement, including advertising, mailing, and service expenditures.
- Its image will be adversely affected.

The firm has identified several options from which it can choose: (1) do nothing further and close out the file, (2) have repair personnel correct the problem on regular service calls (this would affect about 1,000 units per year), (3) send letters to consumers who have filled out warranty information and request that they call a toll-free number to set up repairs, (4) telephone consumers who have filled out warranty information and set up repair appointments, or (5) advertise in newspapers in areas where Model A units have been sold and have appropriate signs posted in retail stores that carry the model.

Questions

1.   What are the pros and cons of each alternative action available to the company?

2. How can the firm improve its operations to make future repair/recall programs more efficient?

3. How can the firm increase the proportion of consumers who fill out warranty information?

4. How can the firm increase the percentage of consumers who agree to have their appliances repaired when they are contacted?

23-3.   Many homeowners, in an effort to have the most lush lawn in their neighborhoods, overapply fertilizers, weed killers, and pesticides. These chemicals can pollute groundwater and air. Overapplication of lawn chemicals by homeowners is not subject to government regulation. What are the responsibilities of consumers and chemical manufacturers regarding the use of lawn chemicals? Should there be government regulation? Explain your answer.

23-4.   Interview ten parents of young children about their views on advertising to children. What do you conclude?

ANSWERS

True/False

1. T, p. 676	11. F, p. 689
2. F, p. 676	12. T, p. 691
3. T, p. 677	13. F, p. 691
4. T, p. 677	14. T, p. 691
5. T, p. 680	15. F, p. 692
6. F, pp. 680-681	16. T, p. 693
7. F, p. 682	17. F, p. 695
8. F, p. 682	18. T, p. 695
9. F, pp. 685, 687	19. F, pp. 700-701
10. F, p. 689	20. T, p. 702

Multiple Choice

1. c, p. 680	11. d, p. 692
2. a, p. 682	12. c, p. 693
3. d, pp. 681-682	13. a, p. 695
4. c, p. 682	14. d, p. 695
5. a, p. 688	15. d, p. 695
6. b, p. 689	16. a, p. 695
7. c, p. 689	17. b, p. 696
8. b, p. 691	18. a, pp. 700-701
9. c, p. 691	19. b, p. 702
10. b, p. 691	20. c, p. 703

Definitions

1. g	7. e
2. h	8. k
3. l	9. j
4. a	10. c
5. n	11. b
6. i	12. f

Discussion Questions

1. p. 677
2. pp. 675-676, 678
3. pp. 689-690
4. pp. 690-691
5. p. 691
6. pp. 691-696
7. pp. 695-696

Part Seven Review Quiz

DEFINITIONS

Define the following terms and concepts in your own words and then check your answers with the Key Terms and Concepts sections of the Study Guide, Chapters 21-23.

standard of living
straight-extension strategy
exporting
industrialization of services
social marketing
ethical behavior
Consumer Product Safety Commission

SEQUENCE

For the following question, arrange the events in chronological order by writing the numbers in the blanks provided, indicating the first in the series by 1.

1. Eras of Consumerism
    _____ increased consumer dissatisfaction, sophistication, skepticism
    _____ business protection against unfair practices
    _____ important issues initiated but seldom resolved

SENTENCES

In each sentence, circle the word or phrase that is most appropriate.

1. The dollar's [high/low] value makes U.S. exports more costly overseas.

2. Because American trade deficits have been so [high/low], many American companies have called for [looser/tighter] controls on imports.

3. [Developing/Less-developed] countries have about 20 per cent of the world's population and almost one third of its income.

4. The devaluation of the Mexican peso meant that Mexican goods became much [cheaper/more expensive] for consumers in other countries.

5. An embargo is an example of a [tariff/trade quota].

6. Direct ownership is the [riskiest/safest] form of international organization.

7. [Backward/Forward] invention appeals to developing countries by making products that are less complex than those sold in its domestic market.

8. Services are usually [separable/inseparable] from the service provider.

9. Labor intensity [increases/decreases] when highly skilled personnel are involved.

10. Data on services are usually [overestimated/underestimated].

11. [Hard/Soft] technologies substitute machinery for people.

12. Nonprofit organizations tend to be [more/less] accountable for their financing, and their benefits are usually distributed [evenly/unevenly].

13. Private nonprofit organizations have [more/fewer] legal advantages than their profit-oriented counterparts.

14. [Donors/Clients] are concerned about efficiency and success rates.

15. Today the use of fluorocarbon propellants in spray cans is [common/prohibited].

16. In [style/functional] planned obsolescence, the manufacturer introduces new product features or improvements.

17. According to a 1983 *Wall Street Journal* survey, most respondents believe that the overall level of ethics has [risen/declined] over the previous decade.

18. In comparison to warranties, guarantees are offered [more/less] frequently in promotion efforts.

19.   Under [misrepresentation/negligence] laws, the seller is liable for falsities leading to consumer misuse of products.

20.   Today there is [more/less] pressure for consumer groups and government agencies to intervene in business and regulate industry practices.

514 Part Seven Review Quiz

ANSWERS

Sequence

1. 3,1,2, p. 689

Sentences

1. high, p. 619
2. high, tighter, p. 620
3. Developing, p. 624
4. cheaper, p. 625
5. trade quota, p. 626
6. riskiest, p. 631
7. Backward, p. 634
8. inseparable, p. 646
9. increases, pp. 647-648
10. underestimated, p. 649
11. Hard, p. 654
12. less, unevenly, p. 660
13. more, p. 661
14. Donors, pp. 661, 664
15. prohibited, p. 680
16. functional, p. 682
17. declined, p. 685
18. more, p. 691
19. misrepresentation, p. 695
20. less, pp. 702-703

Part
Eight

Marketing
Management

24

Integrating and Analyzing the Marketing Plan

CHAPTER OBJECTIVES

1. To show the importance of integrated marketing plans
2. To study the elements that determine how well a marketing plan is integrated
3. To compare two actual marketing plans in terms of their level of integration
4. To examine marketing cost analysis, sales analysis, and the marketing audit as tools for analyzing a firm's marketing performance

CHAPTER OVERVIEW

An integrated marketing plan is one in which all of the various parts of the plan are unified, consistent, and coordinated. A clear organizational mission outlines a firm's commitment to a type of business and a place in the market. Long-term competitive advantages are company and product/service attributes whose distinctiveness and appeal to consumers can be maintained over an extended period of time. A precisely defined target market identifies the specific consumers a firm addresses in its marketing plan. The long-, moderate-, and short-term marketing subplans of the company need to be compatible with one another. Coordination among SBUs is enhanced when the functions, strategies, and resources of each are described and monitored by top management. The components of the marketing mix need to be coordinated within each SBU. The plan must have a certain degree of stability over time.

Kentucky Fried Chicken has a well-integrated marketing plan and is prospering. Timex has a poorly integrated marketing plan and is facing uncertainty about its future.

Marketing plan analysis involves the comparison of actual performance with planned performance for a specified period of time. If actual performance is unsatisfactory, corrective action may be necessary. Plans may have to be revised because of the impact of uncontrollable variables.

Marketing cost analysis evaluates the cost effectiveness of various marketing factors, such as different product lines, distribution methods, sales territories, channel members, salespersons, advertising media, and customer types. Continuous and accurate accounting data are needed. Marketing cost analysis involves studying natural account expenses, reclassifying natural accounts into functional accounts, and allocating functional accounts by marketing classification.

Sales analysis is the detailed study of sales data for the purpose of appraising the appropriateness of a marketing strategy. Sales analysis enables plans to be set in terms of sales by product, product line, salesperson, region, customer type, time period, price line, or method of sale. It also monitors actual sales against planned sales. More companies use sales analysis than marketing cost analysis. The main source of sales data is the sales invoice; control units must be specified. Sales analysis should take the 80-20 principle and sales exception reporting into account.

The marketing audit is a systematic, critical, and unbiased review and appraisal of the firm's marketing objectives, strategy, implementation, and organization. It contains six steps: determining who does the audit, establishing when and how often the audit is conducted, deciding what the audit covers, developing audit forms, implementing the audit, and presenting the results. A horizontal audit studies the overall marketing performance of a company. A vertical audit is an in-depth analysis of one aspect of marketing strategy.

KEY TERMS AND CONCEPTS

Marketing cost analysis	Evaluates the cost effectiveness of various marketing factors, such as different product lines, distribution methods, sales territories, channel members, salespersons, advertising media, and customer types.
Natural account expenses	Costs which are reported by the names of the expenses and not the expenditures purposes. Examples of natural account expenses are salaries, rent, and advertising.
Functional accounts	Occur when natural account expenses are reclassified by function. These accounts indicate the purpose or activity for which expenditures have been made. Examples of functional accounts are marketing administration, transportation, and marketing research.
Sales analysis	The detailed study of sales data for the purpose of appraising the appropriateness of a marketing strategy.
Sales invoice	The main source of sales analysis data. It contains information on customer name, quantity ordered, price paid, purchase terms, geographic location of purchaser, all different items bought at the same time, order date, shipping arrangements, and salesperson.
Control units	Sales categories for which data are gathered, such as boys', men's, girls', and women's clothing.

80-20 principle	States that in many organizations a large proportion of total sales (profit) comes from a small proportion of customers, products, or territories.
Iceberg principle	States that superficial data are insufficient to make sound marketing evaluations.
Sales exception reporting	Lists situations where sales goals are not met or sales opportunities are present.
Marketing audit	A systematic, critical, and unbiased review and appraisal of the basic objectives of the marketing function and of the organization, methods, procedures, and personnel employed to implement these policies and to achieve these objectives.
Horizontal audit	Studies the overall marketing performance of the company with particular emphasis on the interrelationship of variables and their relative importance.
Vertical audit	An in-depth analysis of one aspect of the firm's marketing strategy.

TRUE/FALSE

Circle the appropriate letter.

T   F   1. Organizational mission is involved each time a company adds or deletes products or services.

T   F   2. Smaller firms usually compete on the basis of low prices.

T   F   3. A firm's competitive advantage can diminish if it expands too broadly.

T   F   4. With multiple segmentation, target markets need not be precisely defined.

T   F   5. Short-term plans should be developed independently of long-term plans.

T   F   6. Acquisitions facilitate the coordination of SBUs.

T   F   7. Basic marketing plans should remain in effect for a number of years.

T   F   8. To turn Kentucky Fried Chicken around, priority was given to new store development and remodeling.

T   F   9. Timex's problems arose when it began to cut back on the production of mechanical watches.

T   F   10. In order for marketing cost analysis to be effective, the firm needs continuous and accurate accounting data.

T   F   11. The first step in marketing cost analysis is to determine which accounts are functional ones.

T   F   12. Elimination of a poorly performing functional cost classification may diminish overall total profit.

T   F   13. The main source of sales analysis data is the control unit.

T F 14. In conducting sales analysis, wide sales categories are preferable to narrow ones.

T F 15. A key principle in sales analysis is that summary data are usually insufficient to diagnose a firm's areas of strength and weakness.

T F 16. The 80-20 principle states that a large proportion of total sales comes from a small proportion of products, customers, or territories.

T F 17. Companies err when they examine only total sales (profit) data.

T F 18. To be effective, a marketing audit must be conducted on a regular basis.

T F 19. The first step in the marketing audit process is developing audit forms.

T F 20. Relatively few firms have adopted a formal marketing-audit procedure.

COMPLETION

Fill in the missing word or words in the blanks provided.

[organizational mission, competitive, target market, SBUs, mix, stability, p. 717]

1. A well-integrated marketing plan incorporates a clear sense of _____ _____ , long-term _____ advantage, a precisely defined _____ _____ , compatible long-, moderate-, and short-term subplans, coordination of _____ , coordination of the marketing _____ , and _____ over time.

[integrated, p. 724]

2. Kentucky Fried Chicken's present marketing plan is well- _____ .

[myopia, p. 728]

3. Timex fell from a leadership position because it practiced marketing _____ and did not plan for the future.

[Marketing cost, p. 729]

4. _____ _____ analysis evaluates the cost effectiveness of various marketing factors.

[natural account, p. 729]

5. The first step in marketing cost analysis is to determine the level of _____ _____ expenses.

[Functional accounts, p. 730]

6. _____ _____ indicate the purpose of an activity for which expenditures have been made.

[order-generating, order-processing, p. 732]

7. As the managers of Munsingwear learned, a company should distinguish between _____ _____ costs and _____ _____ costs before making any strategic changes.

[Sales analysis, p. 732]

8. _____ _____ is the detailed study of sales data for the purpose of appraising the appropriateness of marketing strategy.

[sales invoice, p. 732]

9. The _____ _____ contains information on customers' names, quantities ordered, prices paid, purchase terms, etc.

[Control units, pp. 732-733]

10. _____ _____ are categories for which data are collected.

[80-20, p. 733] 11. The _____ _____ principle states that a large proportion of total sales comes from a small proportion of customers.

[iceberg, p. 733] 12. The _____ principle states that superficial data are insufficient to make sound evaluations.

[Sales exception reporting, p. 733] 13. _____ _____ _____ lists situations where sales goals are not met or where opportunities are present.

[marketing audit, p. 733] 14. The _____ _____ examines a firm in a systematic, critical, and unbiased manner.

[horizontal, vertical, p. 735] 15. A _____ audit studies the overall marketing performance of a firm with particular emphasis on the interrelationship of variables, while the _____ audit is an in-depth analysis of one aspect of a firm's marketing strategy.

DEFINITIONS

Match the terms and concepts with the appropriate definitions. Each term or concept may only be used once; there are more terms and concepts than definitions.

Column A	*Column B*
a. control units	___ 1. The main source of sales analysis data.
b. 80-20 principle	___ 2. Costs which are reported by the names of the expenses and not by the expenditures' purposes.
c. functional accounts	___ 3. States that superficial data are insufficient to make sound marketing evaluations.
d. horizontal audit	
e. iceberg principle	___ 4. A systematic, critical, and unbiased review of the marketing function, organization, methods, procedures, and personnel employed to implement policies and achieve objectives.
f. marketing audit	
g. marketing cost analysis	
h. natural account expenses	___ 5. Sales categories for which data are collected.
i. sales analysis	___ 6. States that in many organizations, a large proportion of total sales comes from a small proportion of customers, products, or territories.
j. sales exception reporting	
k. sales invoice	___ 7. Lists situations where sales goals are not met or sales opportunities are present.
l. vertical audit	
	___ 8. Occur when natural account expenses are reclassified.
	___ 9. An in-depth analysis of one aspect of the firm's marketing strategy.
	___ 10. Evaluates the cost effectiveness of various marketing factors.

MULTIPLE CHOICE

Place the letter of the answer you think best in the blank provided.

C

1. Organizational mission is least likely to be reappraised when
   a. the industry undergoes rapid changes.
   b. the firm's performance is mediocre or worse.
   c. company values suit a changing environment.
   d. new opportunities arise.

C

2. Smaller firms cannot usually compete
   a. through specialization.
   b. by gaining customer loyalty.
   c. by lowering prices.
   d. through enhanced product quality.

C

3. Coordination of SBUs can become more difficult when
   a. the functions of each are described in the firm's plans.
   b. crucial SBUs are singled out for special attention.
   c. the firm has new acquisitions.
   d. components of the marketing mix are coordinated in each SBU.

a

4. For a marketing plan to be implemented and evaluated properly, it must
   a. have stability.
   b. be inflexible.
   c. be narrow.
   d. concern the short-run.

d

5. In its worst days, Kentucky Fried Chicken lacked
   a. strong distribution.
   b. a sizable market share.
   c. high potential customer loyalty.
   d. an appetizing product.

b

6. Which of the following was *not* one of Timex's difficulties?
   a. Slow reaction to market trends
   b. Excessive demand
   c. Production reductions
   d. Lack of an organizational mission

7. Which of the following is *not* a function of marketing cost analysis?
   a. Evaluation of sales revenues and costs for various marketing factors
   b. Examination of the firm's marketing organization
   c. Allocation of resources when tactics are developed
   d. Provision of information to substantiate compliance with the Robinson-Patman Act

a

8. An example of a natural account expense is
   a. rent.
   b. marketing research.
   c. general administration.
   d. transportation.

C   9. Which of the following is *not* an example of a functional account?
   a. Marketing administration
   b. Personal selling
   c. Salaries
   d. Warehousing

C   10. The final step in marketing cost analysis is
   a. monitoring results of marketing costs through natural accounts.
   b. assigning natural accounts to functional accounts.
   c. allocating functional accounts by marketing classification.
   d. determining natural account expenses.

b   11. The main source of sales analysis data is the
   a. control unit.
   b. sales invoice.
   c. functional account.
   d. horizontal audit.

b   12. Sales categories for which data are gathered are known as
   a. order-processing costs.
   b. control units.
   c. functional accounts.
   d. SBUs.

c   13. In sales analysis,
   a. wide sales categories are preferable to narrow ones.
   b. the main source of data is the control unit.
   c. it is helpful to select control units consistent with those of other companies.
   d. summary data are sufficient to analyze strengths and weaknesses.

d   14. According to the 80-20 principle,
   a. firms should allocate revenues according to how items relate to sales forecasts.
   b. companies should place equal effort into every sale.
   c. firms should use total sales data to diagnose strengths and weaknesses.
   d. companies should allocate effort by customer, product, and territory.

c   15. The iceberg principle holds that
   a. a large proportion of total sales come from a small proportion of customers.
   b. people purchase fewer items in cold weather.
   c. superficial data are insufficient to make sound evaluations.
   d. companies should develop a clear sense of organizational mission.

d   16. Situations where sales goals are *not* met are listed in
   a. natural account expenses.
   b. sales invoices.
   c. functional accounts.
   d. sales exception reports.

17. The first step in a marketing audit is
    a. developing audit forms.
    b. determining areas to be audited.
    c. deciding who does the audit.
    d. determining when the audit is done.

18. A vertical audit involves
    a. in-depth analysis of one aspect of marketing strategy.
    b. the relative importance of variables or their interrelationship.
    c. an assessment of overall company performance.
    d. an examination of the marketing mix in relation to the overall plan.

19. An audit is complete after
    a. it is conducted.
    b. management responds.
    c. the final report is prepared.
    d. management receives the results.

20. Which of the following is *not* a reason why formal marketing audits have been adopted by relatively few firms?
    a. It is easy to conduct.
    b. Success or failure is difficult to determine.
    c. Company personnel do not have time for audits.
    d. Many companies do not label their analyses as audits.

DISCUSSION QUESTIONS

1 Explain the importance of a clear organizational mission to a well-integrated marketing plan.

2. What competitive advantages do small firms have? Lack?

3. Why must a marketing plan have a certain degree of stability over time?

4. How did Kentucky Fried Chicken's marketing plan help it to become stronger, more profitable, and fast-growing?

5. Outline the steps taken in marketing cost analysis.

6. Why are the 80-20 principle and sales expectation reporting necessary to supplement sales analysis?

7. Why are firms reluctant to adopt formal marketing audits?

EXERCISES

24-1.   As the star marketing analyst for a leading business magazine, your current assignment is to evaluate how well integrated the marketing strategy of Warner Communications is. You are using Figure 1 (Figure 24-1 in the text) as a guide.

Figure 1
Elements Leading to a Well-Integrated Marketing Plan

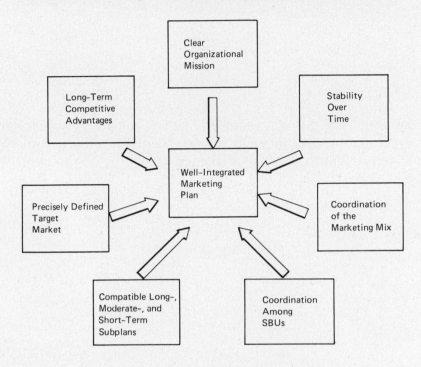

Questions

1.   Develop a questionnaire to assess Warner's marketing plan based on Figure 1.

2.   What sources of information would you use to examine Warner? Why?

3.   Read as much as you can about Warner and complete the questionnaire developed in Question 1. Fully footnote your response and offer overall conclusions about how well integrated Warner's marketing strategy is.

4.   What should Warner do next? Explain your answer.

24-2.   For the first time, your sporting-goods manufacturing company is using marketing cost analysis to better evaluate performance. The procedure for applying marketing cost analysis consists of (1) studying natural account expenses, (2) reclassifying natural accounts into functional accounts, and (3) allocating functional accounts by marketing classification. Tables 1, 2, and 3 show the relevant data for the sporting-goods firm.

Table 1
A Natural Account Expense Classification

Net Sales	$600,000	
Less: Cost of goods sold	200,000	
Gross profit		$400,000
Less: Operating expenses (natural account expenses)		
Salaries and fringe benefits	200,000	
Rent	60,000	
Advertising	30,000	
Supplies	20,000	
Insurance	5,000	
Interest expense	2,000	
Total operating expenses		317,000
Net profit before taxes		$ 83,000

Table 2
Reclassifying Natural Accounts into Functional Accounts

Natural Accounts	Total	Marketing Administration	Personal Selling	Advertising	Transportation	Warehousing	Marketing Research	General Administration
					Functional Accounts			
Salaries and fringe benefits	$200,000	$30,000	$75,000	$15,000	$10,000	$20,000	$20,000	$30,000
Rent	60,000	10,000	10,000	5,000	2,000	20,000	5,000	8,000
Advertising	30,000	-	-	30,000	-	-	-	-
Supplies	20,000	4,000	6,000	3,000	500	500	2,000	4,000
Insurance	5,000	-	2,000	-	1,000	2,000	-	-
Interest expense	2,000	-	-	-	-	-	-	2,000
Total	$317,000	$44,000	$93,000	$53,000	$13,500	$42,500	$27,000	$44,000

Table 3
Allocating Functional Expenses by Product

	Total	Product A	Product B	Product C
Net Sales	$600,000	$300,000	$200,000	$100,000
Less: Cost of goods sold	200,000	100,000	60,000	40,000
Gross profit	$400,000	$200,000	$140,000	$60,000
Less: Operating (functional) expenses				
Marketing administration	44,000	22,000	16,000	6,000
Personal selling	93,000	50,000	30,000	13,000
Advertising	53,000	30,000	15,000	8,000
Transportation	13,500	6,750	4,500	2,250
Warehousing	42,500	20,000	14,000	8,500
Marketing research	27,000	20,000	7,000	-
General administration	44,000	22,000	16,000	6,000
Total operating expenses	317,000	170,750	102,500	43,750
Net profit before taxes	$ 83,000	$ 29,250	$ 37,500	$16,250
Profit as per cent of sales	13.8	9.8	18.8	16.3

Questions

1. Why would a firm go to the trouble of preparing functional accounts by marketing classification?

2. What is learned by studying Tables 1 and 2?

3. What is learned by studying Table 3? How could this information be used to improve the firm's marketing performance?

4. List ten questions you would raise in a marketing audit to acquire further information by which to appraise the firm.

24-3.　　　In a speech at the 1982 marketing meeting of the Conference Board, the president of Del Monte (a subsidiary of R. J. Reynolds) outlined the eight key strategy concepts followed by the firm:

- Establish clear objectives, but do not base them on absolute growth in volume or earnings.
- Take advantage of existing strengths as a mature company in a mature industry.
- Identify and exploit growth segments that exist within every mature market.
- Be prepared to invest heavily in all phases of research and development.
- Emphasize quality.
- Get rid of the dead wood—the products performing poorly.
- Pay increased attention to cost reductions, not just in marketing, but in every aspect of the company.
- Develop effective management in every area of the corporation.

Comment on each of these concepts.

24-4.   Develop a horizontal marketing audit form for your college bookstore. Complete the parts of the form you feel you can accurately judge on the basis of your experiences as a consumer in the bookstore. What recommendations would you make to the manager?

ANSWERS

True/False

1. T, p. 717	11. F, p. 729
2. F, p. 719	12. T, p. 732
3. T, p. 719	13. F, p. 732
4. F, p. 720	14. F, pp. 732-733
5. F, p. 721	15. T, p. 733
6. F, p. 722	16. T, p. 733
7. T, pp. 722-723	17. T, p. 733
8. T, pp. 724-725	18. T, p. 735
9. F, pp. 726-727	19. F, p. 734
10. T, p. 729	20. T, p. 737

Multiple Choice

1. c, p. 718	11. b, p. 732
2. c, p. 719	12. b, pp. 732-733
3. c, p. 722	13. c, p. 733
4. a, p. 722	14. d, p. 733
5. d, p. 724	15. c, p. 733
6. b, pp. 726-727	16. d, pp. 733-734
7. b, p. 729	17. c, p. 734
8. a, p. 729	18. a, p. 735
9. c, pp. 730-731	19. b, p. 737
10. c, pp. 731-732	20. a, p. 737

Definitions

1. k	6. b
2. h	7. j
3. e	8. c
4. f	9. l
5. a	10. g

Discussion Questions

1. pp. 717-721
2. p. 719
3. pp. 721-722
4. pp. 724-725, 728
5. pp. 729-732
6. pp. 733-734
7. p. 737

25

Marketing in the Future

CHAPTER OBJECTIVES

1. To demonstrate the importance of anticipating and planning for the future
2. To study consumer trends and their marketing implications
3. To examine environmental trends and their marketing implications
4. To consider marketing strategies with emphasis on marketing planning and research, and product, distribution, promotion, and price planning over the next decade

CHAPTER OVERVIEW

The next ten years promise to be significant ones for U.S. marketers as they try to anticipate trends and plan long-run strategies. During the coming decade, there will be consumer affluence, technological advances, worldwide markets, and deregulation, as well as energy and material shortages, foreign competition, a stable U.S. market, and an uncertain economy.

There will be many demographic trends, including low population growth, an older society, movement to southeast and southwest regions, continued home ownership, regional mobility, higher real income, more working women, and increases in education, white-collar jobs, and single-person households. Two thirds of adults will be married.

Four newer life-style trends will continue. Voluntary simplicity is a life-style in which people seek material simplicity, have ecological awareness, strive for self-determination, and purchase do-it-yourself products. The me generation stresses being good to oneself. There is less emphasis on obligations and conformity. Blurring gender roles occurs when husbands work in the house, share the tasks of managing a household, and feed the family. The poverty-of-time concept states that for some consumers greater affluence will result in less free time because the alternatives competing for time will expand.

During the decade, a number of environmental factors will affect marketing. The future competitive environment may be analyzed from domestic/foreign, small firm/large firm, generic, and channel perspectives. Government actions will be involved with deregulation, less antitrust involvement, and a lower level of consumer protection than in the 1960s and 1970s. The economy will be difficult to predict and will be influenced by outside factors. The major technological breakthroughs will center on computerization and the resulting changes in consumer behavior and company strategies. Resource shortages may hamper marketing and lead to research efforts aimed at finding acceptable substitutes. The media will offer a variety of positive and restrictive trends. Global events will strongly influence company opportunities and risks.

In order to succeed, marketers must develop strategies that are responsive to consumer trends and the changes in the surrounding environment. The level of marketing planning and research will continue to improve as newer tools, such as portfolio planning, are used more frequently. Formal, systematic product and service strategies will be enacted with greater emphasis on comprehensive analysis. Companies need to identify growing and mature products and react accordingly. Distribution strategy will take into account rising costs, advances in technology, and the evolving nature of retailing. Advertising strategy will be influenced by new video tools and higher television rates. Personal selling strategy will be affected by rising costs and computerization. Price planning will carefully consider costs and offer consumers more alternatives, with greater interest in price bundling.

KEY TERMS AND CONCEPTS

Voluntary simplicity

A consumer life-style in which people seek material simplicity, have an ecological awareness, strive for self-determination, and purchase do-it-yourself products.

Me generation

A consumer life-style that stresses "being good to myself," "improving myself," and "my way of life."

Blurring gender roles

A consumer life-style in which husbands (wives) assume a greater share of the traditional role of their wives (husbands).

Poverty of time

A consumer life-style where greater affluence results in less free time because the alternatives competing for time expand.

Video-shopping services

Can take one of three forms: electronic catalog shown on a video player, cable television system with telephone ordering, or cable television system with ordering through a personal computer.

Electronic banking

Provides centralized record keeping and enables customers to conduct transactions twenty-four hours a day, seven days a week (at many bank and nonbank locations) through the use of automatic teller machines and instant processing of retail purchases.

Electronic mail

Enables letters to be transmitted by computers and telephone lines.

Discount mall

A shopping location in which a variety of low-price retailers are situated together.

Narrowcast

The presentation of specialized programming to a specific audience.

Multiunit advertising

The practice of including two or more products in a single ad to reduce media costs.

Bundled pricing

An offering of a basic product, option, and service for one total price.

Unbundled pricing

A strategy that breaks down prices by individual components. This allows customers to purchase services on an optional basis.

TRUE/FALSE

Circle the appropriate letter.

T   F   1. Consumers who adopt voluntary simplicity as a life-style are more concerned with a product's appearance than with its durability.

T   F   2. Consumers who adopt a me-generation life-style are attracted to no-frills retailing.

T   F   3. The blurring of gender roles will encourage greater supermarket shopping by women.

T   F   4. The poverty of time concept maintains that less affluence results in less free time.

T   F   5. Domestic competition is expected to remain at approximately the same level during the 1980s in mature industries.

T   F   6. To regain their competitive advantage, more U.S. firms will become innovators.

T   F   7. In the future, large firms that dominate many markets will try to concentrate their marketing efforts in one industry.

T   F   8. The growth in generic competition will force firms to define their competitors more narrowly.

T   F   9. Many channel members are expected to engage in vertical integration in order to gain greater control and become more efficient.

T   F   10. Overall, success and failure will come to be determined more by marketing skills than by government supports and restraints.

T   F   11. It can be expected that government will remain less active in consumer protection.

T   F   12. The debit-only transfer system will permit delayed billing without an interest charge.

T   F   13. Newspapers, magazines, and other print media are expected to rely more on the publication of national editions at the expense of regional and local ones.

T   F   14. Firms are expected to become less reliant on systematic planning in the 1980s.

T	F	15. The sales of televisions are expected to remain strong.
T	F	16. Consumers are becoming more willing to pay more for improved product quality.
T	F	17. Nonstore selling is expected to decline, as will scrambled merchandising.
T	F	18. Advertising strategy will shift to greater reliance on cable television.
T	F	19. High commercial television rates in the 1980s will discourage multiunit advertising.
T	F	20. Companies will probably allow consumers a slight discount for items through unbundled pricing.

COMPLETION

Fill in the missing word or words in the blanks provided.

[Voluntary simplicity, p. 748] 1. _____ _____ is a life-style characterized by no-frills shopping, product durability, rational appeals, and ecological concerns.

[me generation, p. 748] 2. The _____ _____ is a life-style involving greater acceptance of diversity, self-improvement, product appearance, and expensive purchases.

[blurred, p. 749] 3. When more women are in the labor force and more men are assuming household responsibilities, gender roles can be said to be _____ .

[poverty-of-time, p. 749] 4. The _____ _____ _____ concept states that greater affluence results in less free time.

[deregulation, pp. 753-754] 5. Overall, government _____ will induce greater price competition and offer consumers further choices.

[video-shopping, p. 754] 6. Three categories of _____ _____ services are catalogs on video recorders and telephone-oriented and computer-oriented cable television ordering systems.

[Electronic mail, p. 756] 7. _____ _____ enables a letter to be transmitted by telephone lines or by computers.

[Electronic banking, p. 756] 8. _____ _____ involves the use of automatic teller machines and instant processing of retail purchases.

[market-share, competitive advantage, p. 761] 9. Firms will place less emphasis on _____ _____ madness and direct their efforts toward profitable _____ _____ .

[Computers, p. 762] 10. _____ will ease the comprehensive analysis that companies will use to better position their offerings, maintain a balanced product mix, and develop long-range plans.

[mature, p. 762] 11. Many _____ products, such as the telephone, will have extended life cycles because of new technology.

[discount mall, p. 764]   12. The _____ _____ is a newer development, locating a variety of low-price retailers together.

[narrowcast, p. 765]   13. The presentation of specialized programming to specific audiences over television is termed a _____.

[Multiunit advertising, p. 766]   14. _____ _____ includes two or more products in a single presentation.

[unbundle prices, p. 767]   15. When manufacturers _____ _____, they break them down by individual components and allow customers to purchase services on an optional basis.

DEFINITIONS

Match the terms and concepts with the appropriate definitions. Each term or concept may only be used once; there are more terms and concepts than definitions.

Column A	Column B
a. blurring gender roles	___ 1. A consumer life-style where greater affluence results in less free time because the alternatives competing for time expand.
b. bundled pricing	
c. discount mall	___ 2. An offering of a basic product, option, and service for one total price.
d. electronic banking	
e. electronic mail	___ 3. Enables letters to be transmitted by computers and telephone lines.
f. me generation	___ 4. A shopping location in which a variety of low-price retailers are situated together.
g. multiunit advertising	
h. narrowcast	___ 5. The presentation of specialized programming to a specific audience.
i. poverty of time	___ 6. The practice of including two or more products in a single ad to reduce media costs.
j. unbundled pricing	
k. video-shopping services	___ 7. A consumer life-style in which people seek material simplicity, have an ecological awareness, strive for self-determination, and purchase do-it-yourself products.
l. voluntary simplicity	
	___ 8. A strategy that breaks down prices by individual components.
	___ 9. A consumer life-style that stresses "being good to myself," "improving myself," and "my way of life."
	___ 10. Provides centralized record keeping and enables customers to conduct transactions twenty-four hours a day, seven days a week through the use of automatic teller machines and instant processing of retail purchases.

MULTIPLE CHOICE

Place the letter of the answer you think best in the blank provided.

 1. Which of the following is *not* a projected marketing trend for the 1980s?
   a. Increased consumer affluence
   b. Greater regulation by government
   c. Technological improvements
   d. Expanding worldwide markets

2. U.S. demographers project that
   a. the proportion of college-educated adults in the population will decline.
   b. real income will increase as rapidly as it did in the past.
   c. the number of two-income families in the population will rise substantially.
   d. the proportion of middle-aged and retired persons in the population will decrease.

3. The life-style of voluntary simplicity is characterized by
   a. an emphasis on product durability.
   b. the pressure to conform.
   c. self-improvement.
   d. a preference for full-service retailing.

4. The blurring of gender roles encourages
   a. using time-saving merchandise.
   b. shopping at convenience stores.
   c. sharing household tasks.
   d. buying more do-it-yourself products.

5. Foreign competitors have almost 100 per cent of the U.S. market in
   a. videocassette recorders.
   b. automobiles.
   c. sporting goods.
   d. computer technology.

6. Channel competition should result in
   a. more horizontal integration.
   b. expansion of private labeling.
   c. greater willingness to carry new items.
   d. less generic competition.

7. Overall, deregulation will
   a. encourage more firms to enter the marketplace.
   b. narrow consumer choices.
   c. reduce price competition.
   d. make firms less dependent on marketing skills.

8. In the 1980s, consumer protection will probably depend more on
   a. local consumer affairs agencies.
   b. the Federal Trade Commission.
   c. business self-regulation.
   d. new congressional laws.

9. To achieve the strongest possible U.S. economy, industry should
   a. separate wages from productivity.
   b. avoid nationalistic practices and slogans.
   c. ignore the successes of foreign competitors.
   d. develop their own credit facilities.

10. Video-shopping services
    a. are in widespread use.
    b. are expensive.
    c. effectively replace seeing products in person.
    d. are error-proof.

11. Comp-U-Card is evidence of the
    a. growth of nonstore retailing.
    b. widening gap between high-end and low-end strategies.
    c. popularity of discounting.
    d. increasing use of retail sales by industrial goods manufacturers.

12. Debit-only transfer systems will
    a. expand the time that consumers have to pay bills without interest charges.
    b. resemble current credit card policies.
    c. send end-of-the-month bills for remittance.
    d. substitute for personal checks.

13. Regarding the media,
    a. technological improvements will lower advertising costs.
    b. national editions will replace local and regional ones.
    c. editorials will be less critical of business practices.
    d. companies will have greater flexibility placing messages.

14. Which of the following is *not* among the products (services) forecast for significant growth?
    a. Electric ranges
    b. Health food
    c. Household appliances
    d. Television sets

15. Which of the following is *not* forecast as a major trend in retailing?
    a. Increases in discounting
    b. Narrower gaps between high-end and low-end strategies
    c. Perpetuation of scrambled merchandising
    d. Rises in nonstore selling

16. The newest development in discounting is the
    a. flea market.
    b. factory outlet store.
    c. off-price chain.
    d. discount mall.

17. The largest shift in advertising strategy will be the result of
    a. higher television rates.
    b. greater reliance on cable television.
    c. shifting consumer preferences.
    d. increased product shortages.

18. The narrowcast will prove beneficial to
    a. network television.
    b. national magazines.
    c. mass marketers.
    d. cable television.

19. Higher television commercial rates will encourage commercial television to increase its use of the
    a. narrowcast approach.
    b. multiunit approach.
    c. unbundling technique.
    d. interactive system.

20. Unbundling
    a. discounts prices.
    b. breaks down prices.
    c. deregulates prices.
    d. computerizes prices.

DISCUSSION QUESTIONS

1. How might a traditional department store respond to the demographic and life-style trends of the 1980s and 1990s?

2. "A woman's place is in the home." Discuss this statement with reference to current demographic trends.

3. Given the competitive environment of the 1980s, explain what U.S. firms can do to improve their position at home and abroad.

4. Project the effects of government deregulation on FM radio stations and banks.

5. How will computerization affect marketing techniques and marketing research?

6. Outline three major trends in retailing and discuss their possible impact on consumers.

7. How should the advertising industry respond to the new video tools?

EXERCISES

25-1.   In his 1982 book *Megatrends* (Warner Books), John Naisbitt identified ten important trends occuring in the U.S.:

- The U.S. is shifting from an industrial to an information-based society.
- New technology will succeed only when people are ready for it.
- The U.S. is becoming more a part of a global structure and less of a dominant force.
- U.S. managers are beginning to plan for longer periods.
- Decentralization is increasing.
- Self-reliance is becoming more important to people.
- Citizens, workers, and consumers want a greater voice in government, business, and the marketplace.
- Hierarchal pyramids are disappearing in organizations.
- The Northeast is declining, as the West and Southwest are rising.
- People are demanding and receiving a greater variety of goods, services, life-styles, etc.

These trends will have a strong impact on marketing strategies in the late 1980s. Therefore, it is imperative that marketers understand their markets, seek out appropriate market niches (differential advantages), clearly position their offerings, implement an appropriate marketing mix, and improve financial analysis.[1]

_____

[1] David W. Cravens, "Strategic Marketing's New Challenge," *Business Horizons*, Vol. 26 (March-April 1983), pp. 18-24.

Questions

1.   Evaluate the megatrends occurring in the U.S. from a marketing perspective.

2. How will the impacts of these trends upon supermarkets and department stores differ?

3. The conclusions in *Megatrends* are based on content analysis (information acquired by reading daily newspapers in all U.S. cities with a 100,000+ population). Comment on the pros and cons of content analysis in planning for the future.

4. What other methods are there for anticipating the future?

25-2.　　　　Marketing inertia, much like marketing myopia, is a concept that has gripped many marketers.[1] Under marketing inertia, management fails "to react appropriately or at all to changed market conditions" because it is "frequently reluctant to tamper with marketing strategies that have been successful in the past." For example, Ford did not downsize its cars until two to four years after General Motors. Texaco, unlike its six major competitors, continued to emphasize refining and distribution rather than exploration and diversification for five years after the 1973 oil embargo.

The effects of marketing inertia will be greatest when "market drift" is high. In this situation, customer preferences, competitive behavior, and/or government actions change rapidly (as with the telecommunications market). Marketing inertia can be reduced by monitoring the environment, collecting quantitative data on productivity, encouraging greater contacts between customers and management, maintaining a differential advantage, implementing product modifications, employing value-based pricing, and reexamining distribution channels.

A survey of attitudes of chief executive and operating officers of thirty major U.S. companies identified a number of issues for marketers to consider in the 1980s:[2]

- Marketing management is not adequately innovative and entrepreneurial in thinking and decision making.
- Marketing productivity appears to be declining as costs are rising.
- Marketing management has a poor understanding of financial dimensions.
- Product management systems may inhibit innovative thinking.
- Marketers with MBAs think alike, avoid risk, want to advance quickly, and are not interested in sales and sales management.
- Acceptance of the marketing concept is incomplete, particularly in small or industrial firms.
- Marketing is the most important management function, becoming even more essential in the future.

---

[1] Thomas V. Bonoma, "Market Success Can Breed 'Marketing Inertia'," *Harvard Business Review*, Vol. 59 (September-October 1981), pp. 115-121.

[2] Frederick E. Webster, Jr., "Top Management's Concerns About Marketing: Issues for the 1980's," *Journal of Marketing*, Vol. 45 (Summer 1981), pp. 9-16.

Questions

1. Differentiate between marketing inertia and marketing myopia. Why are both so difficult to overcome?

2.   In contrast to marketing inertia, can a firm overmarket?

3.   Comment on the attitudes expressed by marketing executives.

4.   How can marketers improve their performance in the 1980s?

25-3.   Evaluate the population and commecial trends in the city nearest your university and describe their impact for marketing decision makers.

25-4.   Develop a checklist of factors that should be considered when planning for the future. Apply this checklist to your own career planning.

ANSWERS

True/False

1. F, p. 748	11. T, pp. 753-754
2. F, p. 748	12. F, p. 756
3. F, p. 749	13. F, p. 759
4. F, p. 749	14. F, p. 761
5. T, p. 751	15. T, p. 762
6. T, p. 751	16. T, p. 763
7. F, pp. 752-753	17. F, p. 764
8. F, p. 753	18. T, p. 765
9. T, p. 753	19. F, p. 766
10. T, pp. 753-754	20. F, p. 767

Multiple Choice

1. b, pp. 753-754	11. a, p. 755
2. c, p. 747	12. d, p. 756
3. a, p. 748	13. d, p. 759
4. c, p. 749	14. a, p. 762
5. a, p. 751	15. b, pp. 763-764
6. b, p. 753	16. d, p. 764
7. a, p. 753	17. b, p. 765
8. c, pp. 753-754	18. d, p. 765
9. d, p. 754	19. b, p. 766
10. b, p. 754	20. b, p. 767

Definitions

1. i	6. g
2. b	7. l
3. e	8. j
4. c	9. f
5. h	10. d

Discussion Questions

1. pp. 746-750
2. pp. 747, 749
3. pp. 751-753
4. p. 753
5. p. 761
6. p. 764
7. p. 765

Part Eight Review Quiz

DEFINITIONS

Define the following terms and concepts in your own words and then check your answers with the Key Terms and Concepts sections of the Study Guide, Chapters 24-25.

sales analysis
80-20 principle
horizontal audit
blurring gender roles
video shopping services
multiunit advertising
unbundled pricing

SEQUENCES

For each of the following questions, arrange the events in chronological order by writing the numbers in the blanks provided, indicating the first in each series by 1.

1.   Procedure in Marketing Cost Analysis
      _____ allocating functional accounts by marketing classification
      _____ studying natural account expenses
      _____ reclassifying natural accounts into functional accounts

2.   Steps Taken in a Marketing Audit
      _____ developing audit forms
      _____ determining when and how often the audit it to be conducted
      _____ conducting the audit
      _____ determining who does the audit
      _____ determining the areas to be audited
      _____ presenting the results to management

SENTENCES

In each sentence, circle the word or phrase that is most appropriate.

1.   Many experts believe that organizational mission should be [maintained/reappraised] when a company is changing size.

2.   The more crucial the performance of a product is to satisfying customer needs, the [more/less] concerned they will be with pricing.

3.   If it expands very broadly, a company's competitive advantage will probably [increase/decrease].

4.   Acquisitions make the coordination of SBUs [easier/harder].

5.   A basic marketing plan should remain in effect for [one/several] year(s).

6.   In contrast to Timex's marketing plan, Kentucky Fried Chicken's plan was [well-integrated/disjointed].

7.   When allocating functional accounts by market classification, the company should recognize that [separable/common] expenses can be eliminated if a category is discontinued.

8.   More companies engage in [marketing cost/sales] analysis.

9.   In setting up control units, a [narrow/wide] category is preferable.

10.   A [vertical/horizontal] marketing audit focuses on overall marketing performance.

11.   In the 1980s and 1990s, families are expected to be [larger/smaller] and the number of college-educated adults is expected to [rise/fall].

12.   The me generation is concerned with self-[determination/expression].

13.   In the future, competition for overseas markets will be [more/less] intense for U.S. firms.

14.   Over the last several decades, there has been a trend toward [larger/smaller] firms, and this trend should continue.

15.   Generic competition is expected to [increase/decrease].

16.   From a manufacturer's or retailer's viewpoint, video-shopping services are [cheap/expensive], reach a [wide/limited] audience, and require advanced technology.

17.   Because of new technology, many mature products will have [shortened/extended] life cycles.

18.   A major retailing trend is the [cessation/perpetuation] of scrambled merchandising.

19.   Advertising costs are expected to [rise/fall], necessitating multiunit advertising.

20.   Bundled pricing makes the purchase of individual items and services [optional/mandatory].

ANSWERS

Sequences

1. 3,1,2, pp. 729-732
2. 4,2,5,1,3,6, p. 736

Sentences

1. reappraised, p. 718
2. less, p. 718
3. decrease, p. 719
4. harder, p. 722
5. several, p. 722
6. well-integrated, p. 724
7. separable, p. 732
8. sales, p. 732
9. narrow, p. 733
10. horizontal, p. 734
11. smaller, rise, p. 747
12. expression, p. 748
13. more, p. 751
14. larger, p. 752
15. increase, p. 753
16. expensive, limited, pp. 754-755
17. extended, p. 762
18. perpetuation, p. 764
19. rise, p. 766
20. mandatory, p. 767